THE INTREPID NONPROFIT

STRATEGIES FOR SUCCESS IN TURBULENT TIMES

TIM PLUMPTRE

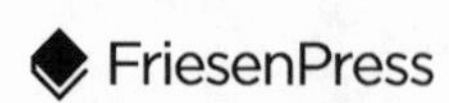

Suite 300 - 990 Fort St
Victoria, BC, V8V 3K2
Canada

www.friesenpress.com

First Edition — 2019

Attention: quantity discounts are available for your nonprofit organization, for charities, foundations, universities, colleges, governments or other institutions for purposes such as board orientation, courses and other educational programs, incentives, gifts, subscription incentives, fund-raiser campaigns, re-selling or similar uses. Please call 613-518-2370 or contact the author: info@meta4consulting.ca

ISBN
978-1-5255-0542-3 (Hardcover)
978-1-5255-0543-0 (Paperback)
978-1-5255-0544-7 (eBook)

1. *Business & Economics, Nonprofit Organizations & Charities*

Distributed to the trade by The Ingram Book Company

TABLE OF CONTENTS

To Barbara,

Bora, and Genny

Je suis, parce que vous êtes.

NAVIGATING TURBULENCE...

A few years ago, some friends and I were on a canoe trip down a spectacular northern river. We'd been told it featured a series of white-water rapids—challenging, but manageable and fun to run. And so they were.

But we'd been warned: beware the Graveyard rapids. They're dangerous. Few people get through them safely. Don't get drawn into them by accident—advice that would've been easier to follow if we hadn't lost our map.

This day was perfect—bright and sunny. But the river swung around a sharp bend. Suddenly, the current was faster and far more powerful. The river was now strewn with large rocks, foaming waves, and waterfalls. Downstream, a tangle of fallen trees trapped the skeleton of a wrecked canoe. We were in the grip of the Graveyards.

We made it through. Several factors sustained us: the alertness of the bowman scanning the river ahead; the crew's ability to respond quickly to emerging obstacles; skilful steering that kept us on course as we were buffeted in many directions; the determination to persist when the going got tough.

Recently, I've come to see parallels between the measures that worked for us on that river and the strategies today's nonprofit leaders will need to survive in coming years. That's the subject of this book.

Over three decades, I've worked in the nonprofit sector in many roles: as a CEO, a director, a board chair, a consultant to many organizations, a community volunteer, a funder, and the founder of the nonprofit Institute on Governance. My work has carried me to every province and territory of Canada, to indigenous communities in the high north, and to over thirty-five countries.

Today, I see many organizations being pulled into much faster and riskier waters, confronting a range of difficult issues such as these:

Financial survival: Classic revenue sources are drying up. Competition is increasing. Pressures on executives are mounting to "run it like a business." But as many have declared, this is not what I signed up for! What does the future hold—for leaders or for the mission and culture of nonprofits?

Harnessing disruptive technologies: Big data, the Internet, social media, artificial intelligence . . . the pace of change will be dizzying in coming years. How can organizations and leaders keep up? What does this imply for issues like leadership style, marketing, recruitment, or stakeholder relations?

Attracting, managing, and retaining people: How can the right people be engaged—on the board, on staff—in light of changing needs and demographics? What does diversity imply for recruitment or programming? How can millennials be engaged, in light of their different values or work styles? What can be done about falling membership or constantly changing HR legislation?

Bringing your board up to speed: What does the increasing professionalization of governance imply for boards? What can be done about a lacklustre board? What can an executive leader do to strengthen it? What else can be done?

In the future, nonprofits will be increasingly called upon to help with issues like homelessness, overburdened health care systems, technologically induced unemployment, or falling personal incomes. We need these organizations to not only stay afloat but to flourish.

Some nonprofits have managed to excel despite challenges similar to those your organization may be encountering. In this book you'll learn about some intrepid leaders and the measures that have helped to sustain them. You'll find out about other strategies that might work for you if more conventional ones aren't meeting your needs.

The Intrepid Nonprofit is a playbook for navigating the new financial, technological, and human challenges confronting today's nonprofit leaders. I invite you to turn the page for help in mapping your course through the turbulent waters ahead.

INTRODUCTION

What Gave Rise to This Book?

In my professional life over the last two or three decades, I have been working much of the time either in or with nonprofit organizations, sometimes as executive director or CEO, sometimes as coach or adviser, and sometimes as a board member or board chair. My work has engaged me on issues of strategy, governance, and organization in public organizations across Canada and in several other countries. A few years ago, as I reflected on this experience, several ideas struck me.

First, it became apparent how demanding the task of nonprofit leadership had become, and how the environment in which that task is carried out in had become complex, turbulent, and unpredictable.

Second, I saw a big gap between the theory and the practical reality of nonprofit leadership. Theory says that responsibility for strategy and oversight rests with the board of directors of an organization. The practical reality I observed, however, was that most boards have great difficulty carrying out this responsibility.

As the idea of a book that looked at the future of the nonprofit sector began to take shape, I thought it important to test my perceptions and ideas against those of individuals with experience elsewhere. So I decided to interview a cross section of people with knowledge of this sector from across North America, and I read quite widely in relevant literature. The experience of others mirrored my own. Public-spirited women and men of good will, volunteering their time to help provide leadership to nonprofit organizations, were finding it very difficult to do the board's job well. Why? I wondered. What might be done to help?

Meanwhile, expectations of boards were going up and up, but board performance, while gradually improving in some quarters, did not seem to be keeping pace with these expectations. This quotation from a 2013 study on leadership in Ontario's nonprofit sector summarizes how leaders in that sector saw board performance:

> Focus groups stressed the challenges of the voluntary board structure, including high turnover, lack of training and support for board members, lack of expertise and awareness board members have about their role, and how these challenges impact their capacity as leaders. Boards hold responsibility for succession planning and hiring the executive director/CEO. However, they were seen sometimes to have limited scope and experience to effectively determine the experience, competencies and skills that are needed in the executive director/CEO role, both to lead and to move the organization forward to the next level.[1]

A third insight emerged as I saw how executive directors and CEOs, cognizant of their board's shortcomings, were struggling to do two interconnected, complex jobs at the same time. On the one hand, faced with an unpredictable environment, they were striving to develop and implement a corporate strategy to sustain their organization over the longer term. On the other hand, recognizing the important role the board was expected to play and its potential to complement the capabilities and experience of staff, many were seeking to reinforce the board and help build it into a more effective leadership vehicle. When it came to strategy, was the board part of the solution or part of the problem? It was not always clear. What might be done to help executive directors cope with this challenge?

In short, it was apparent to me that there were some difficulties facing individual nonprofit organizations that needed to be addressed. I saw this book as a way to harvest insights about these kinds of organizations, to provide perspective for their hard-pressed leaders, and to help them make difficult decisions about the kinds of strategies likely to help them cope with an increasingly difficult environment.

Why the Sector Matters

Beyond the level of individual organizations, it also became apparent to me that at a policy level, in light of social, technological, and economic trends, there was a need for governments and other public-purpose organizations such as foundations to revisit the role of the nonprofit sector as a key institutional player and to determine what measures they might take to sustain and promote it.

My understanding of the importance of the sector was amplified by my experience as president of a nonprofit think tank called the Institute on Governance, which I founded in 1990. I led the Institute for seventeen years, and during that period I had the privilege of engaging in discussions on governance with senior government officials in countries ranging from Lebanon, Dubai, and Egypt in the Middle East, to others on the other side of the world such as Malaysia, the Philippines, Vietnam, Thailand, and Singapore. This experience provided perspective on the institutional building blocks of societies, on the roles of different actors in governance, and on the importance of civil society organizations in a country's national fabric. I became more aware of how they can contribute to a country's well-being, helping to provide services, strengthen communities, forge bonds across jurisdictions, and enhance employment.

Societies deal with the challenges facing them by relying on three kinds of organizations: businesses, governments, and nonprofits (including charities). Businesses promote economic growth and technological innovation; they reward shareholders and provide employment, but most have no mandate or capacity to deal with social problems or to serve common interests. Governments have a very wide span of interests, and they exist, in principle, to serve the public. But today, many citizens regard government with uncertainty or even distrust. Rightly or not, many feel that governments are controlled by self-serving elites, that they are remote from citizens' interests or uninterested in their views, or that they are too top-heavy and bureaucratic to be efficient. Recent elections or referendums in the US, Britain, Canada, and elsewhere suggest that many citizens are looking for a change of some kind. Some are seeking alternatives to conventional political parties and their policies.

Meanwhile, the pace of scientific and technological change is constantly increasing. Governments cannot keep up with these developments: institutional change is slow at the best of times, and if technology is a hare, governments are tortoises. Government structures and decision-making processes lag further and further behind technology as it sprints into the future.

Nonprofit organizations often fill many needs that governments and businesses are unable—or unwilling—to address. They employ thousands of people and are able to call on thousands more as volunteers. In troubled times, they are often nimbler than governments and closer to citizens. They are used to addressing difficult problems and providing opportunities in a wide range of areas: education, health, social services, culture, recreation, and others.

At the turn of the last century, the Canadian government paid tribute to these attributes of the sector as it signed an agreement with sector leaders called the Voluntary Sector Accord.[2] There was a lot of noble language in the Accord about how valuable the sector was, about how it touched "virtually all aspects of our society," about how it embodied "the Canadian way" giving voice to the voiceless, engaging citizens to serve the public good, and enlivening communities.

The idea behind this Accord was that the federal government would work hand in hand with the sector to capitalize on its strengths and revitalize its relationship with it. Unfortunately, as so often happens with high-minded agreements of this kind, very few tangible results were achieved. The Accord did not provide for specific actions by either party. Despite the thousands of hours that volunteers—unpaid, unlike their government counterparts—had invested in developing the Accord with government officials, within a few years of its signing, interest had withered. When a change of government occurred, the Accord was forgotten, leaving many leaders in the sector cynical and disheartened.

But while the Accord itself was a major disappointment, the value of the nonprofit sector, as recognized in the text of the Accord, remains.[3] For reasons that I explore in this book, particularly in the concluding chapter, I believe we need to reassess and reaffirm the value of the sector. We need to consider what measures need to be taken to sustain it and to allow it to play a more effective role in addressing the challenges facing our society.

About the Book

This book draws on three main sources of information. First, the literature on the sector. This is large and growing. I would not pretend to have reviewed it all, a task that would be Herculean, but I was able to review a reasonable range of relevant books and articles; the ones I found more interesting are cited in a bibliography at the end of the book.

Second, I sought to draw upon the experience and expertise of others. Thanks to the generosity of many people, I conducted over fifty interviews with a cross section of individuals. Some were nonprofit executive directors or CEOs; some were professional consultants in both Canada and the US with practices in the nonprofit sector; some were individuals involved in research or educational activities related to the sector; and some were in funding organizations such as foundations. I am most grateful to these individuals, who provided a rich seam of helpful information. A list of respondents appears in the Acknowledgements at the end of the book. Several are cited (with permission) in the text.

Finally, I drew on my own experiences as a board member, an executive head, and a consultant, as one inevitably does in writing a book like this.

As a research methodology, this is imperfect, but it's how a great many books on subjects like management or governance get written. Despite the limitations of the research approach, I hope that this book will have a ring of truth in its observations and conclusions, and in addition, that it will provide insights that readers find informative and helpful.

This book aspires to perform several functions. First, for the benefit of nonprofit leaders, it seeks to shine a light ahead into a future that often appears murky, illuminating issues that many organizations will need to address.

Second, I hope it will provide perspective. Many leaders are under so much pressure that they have little time to lift their heads to examine the larger context within which their organization is functioning. This book examines important features of the contemporary nonprofit landscape and the challenges it poses. It suggests various strategies that may be helpful in confronting those challenges, including ideas about governance that may be useful both at the level of individual organizations and at the societal level.

Finally, this book hopes to encourage fresh thinking on a range of topics. It explores alternative strategies for coping when conventional ones don't seem to be working (such as "working sideways"). It also divulges new responsibilities that a board may need to take on to remain relevant and in tune with contemporary demands.

Why the "Intrepid" Nonprofit?

In musing, as authors do, about what to call this book, the idea of The Intrepid Nonprofit came to me. I felt this really captured the essence of the temperament required of nonprofit leaders, who must aspire to not only survive but to also prosper in a highly uncertain environment. There is no simple formula for achieving these goals, though there are, very often, lessons to be derived from the experience of others. Each nonprofit will need to determine its own course, depending on its mission, history, and context.

There are tough times ahead for nonprofits. What will be required are leaders who are courageous, resolute, persistent, and undaunted by whatever circumstances are thrown at them. Leaders and organizations that are, in short, intrepid.

---

1. Elizabeth McIsaac, Stella Park, and Lynne Toupin, *Shaping the Future: Leadership in Ontario's Nonprofit Labour Force* (Ontario Nonprofit Network, 2013), 31.

2. *An Accord Between the Government of Canada and the Voluntary Sector* (Ottawa: Voluntary Sector Task Force, December 2001), accessed August 7, 2018. http://publications.gc.ca/collections/Collection/CP32-75-2001E.pdf

3. For a parallel assessment of the importance of the voluntary sector in the US, see Lester M. Salamon, *The Resilient Sector Revisited* (Washington: Project Muse, Brookings Institution Press, 2015), 17. "[T]hese organizations deliver critical services, provide outlets for political expression, enrich the country's social and cultural life, promote norms of reciprocity, and contribute to the quality of national life in countless other ways. . ."

CHAPTER 1
GOVERNANCE AND THE NONPROFIT SECTOR: AN OVERVIEW

What Is the Nonprofit Sector?

This book is focused on Canada's nonprofit sector, including charities—a sector also often referred to as the "voluntary sector," and sometimes as the "third sector." It's much bigger and more economically important than many people may realize. It's also a very large and diverse universe, encompassing somewhere around 170,000–180,000 organizations. Estimates vary somewhat, but it is generally agreed that it accounts for over seven percent of Canada's GNP.

Nonprofit organizations have been around in North America for a long time. From the perspective of the twenty-first century, they seem commonplace. But this was not always so. Almost two centuries ago, the French politician and writer Alexis de Tocqueville travelled extensively in the US, and then, in 1831, he published *Democracy in America*, now a political science classic. De Tocqueville was greatly impressed with an important institutional innovation that he discovered on his trip: volunteer-led organizations. He enthusiastically described the role of these associations in the life of the US republic, contrasting them with how things were done in France or England.

> Wherever at the head of some new undertaking you see the government in France, or a man of rank in England, in the United States you will be sure to find an association. . . . Thus the most democratic country on the face of the earth is that in which men have, in our time, carried to the highest perfection the art of pursuing in common the object of their common desires and have applied this new science to the greatest number of purposes.[1]

De Tocqueville predicted that life would become more complex, and thus there would be an ever-increasing need for organizations other than governments to get things done in the common interest. "It is easy to foresee that the time is drawing near when man will be less and less able to produce, by himself alone, the commonest necessaries of life." He was doubtful, even suspicious, of the state's ability to address these needs: "No sooner does the government attempt to go beyond its political sphere and to enter upon this new track than it exercises, even unintentionally, an insupportable tyranny; for a government can only dictate strict rules . . . and it is never easy to discriminate between its advice and its commands."

De Tocqueville concluded that associations were the solution. "Nothing, in my opinion, is more deserving of our attention than the intellectual and moral associations of America. . . . If men are to remain civilized or to become so, the art of associating together must grow and improve. . ."

The nonprofit sector in Canada has two main components. The largest, in terms of its proportion of GNP, is composed of hospitals, universities, and colleges. By value, they account for two-thirds of the sector's revenues (equal to 4.7 percent of GNP) even though, numerically, they represent only one percent of the number of organizations in the sector.

The second component is often referred to as the "core nonprofit sector." By value, it accounts for the remaining one-third of the sector's revenues, but it contains ninety-nine percent of the organizations. These vary hugely in size and character: they "run the gamut from very large organizations, with annual revenues in the billions and tens of thousands of paid employees, to very small organizations that are entirely dependent on volunteers and have annual revenues of less than a thousand dollars."[2]

Canada is reported to have one of the largest and most vibrant nonprofit and voluntary sectors in the world. Even setting aside the big institutions in the sector (hospitals, universities, colleges), it still employs over two million people, which represents nine percent of the country's economically active population—as much as Canada's entire manufacturing industry. Its economic contribution is very substantial: with the value of volunteer work included, the sector's total contribution to GDP is estimated at 8.5 percent.[3]

Yet leaders in the sector are mostly unaware of its scope. It includes organizations with activities and programs in so many areas: arts, sports, education, health, culture, social or medical services, environmental protection, housing, civil rights, international development, heritage, community development, regulation, religion, and others. This list is not comprehensive, but it provides a sense of the breadth of nonprofits' social and economic contributions.

An important distinction within the sector is the different status of charitable and non-charitable organizations. Of the approximately 180,000 organizations in the sector, somewhere around 80,000 are recognized as "charities" by the Canada Revenue Agency (CRA). Charitable status imposes certain accounting restrictions on the organization, and it also limits its ability to undertake certain kinds of activities, notably advocacy. However, the big advantages of being a charity are that this enables the organization to apply for grants from governments and foundations, as well as to receive and issue tax receipts for donations. As one might expect, not all nonprofits can expect to be accorded this status: only those whose principal focus is on relief of poverty, advancement of education or religion, or on other purposes that benefit the community.

With respect to the size and economic importance of the sector, the situation in the US is similar to that in Canada. Comparisons are somewhat crude, as the two countries categorize their nonprofit sectors differently. However, broadly speaking, in comparison to the approximately 180,000 incorporated nonprofits in Canada, there are roughly 1.6 million tax-exempt organizations in America. Economically, the sector is vast. According to the National Center for Charitable Statistics, in 2010 "nonprofits accounted for 9.2 percent of all wages and salaries in the United States." These organizations represented 5.3 percent of GDP in 2014. In the previous year, nonprofit revenues were in excess of US$1.7 trillion dollars. As in Canada, there is a great variety of organizations in the sector, ranging from small neighbourhood groups that meet only occasionally and have no assets, to large universities and hospitals and foundations with millions of dollars in assets. [4]

Governance: Origins & Evolution

In 1990, I founded a nonprofit organization called the Institute on Governance. When told the name of my new enterprise, people regularly asked me, *What's governance?*

Why this uncertainty about what governance meant? Prior to 1990, the English word was virtually unknown. What got people talking about governance was a series of scandals in both the nonprofit and corporate worlds. Some had to do with outright fraud—for example, William Aramony, the high-profile president of the United Way of America, was jailed for six years in 1995 after being convicted on twenty-three counts of felony. His actions blotted the reputation of the charitable sector,[5] as did those of other prominent fraudsters whose stories have been collected in the CharityWatch "Hall of Shame."[6] These scandals led scores of charities to review their business practices.

In Canada, the most high-profile example of incompetence in the nonprofit sector was the tainted-blood scandal, in which thousands of Canadians were infected with HIV or hepatitis C, principally due to the actions or omissions of the Canadian Red Cross, which had been administering the blood system. Justice Horace Krever documented this mismanagement in a landmark report in 1997,[7] and as a consequence, control of the system was removed from the Red Cross and allocated to a new agency, Canadian Blood Services. Governments, the Red Cross, and insurance companies paid out billions of dollars in compensation.

Nonprofit organizations, in general, did not escape accusations of corruption. They too were subject to more public scrutiny and sometimes cast in a negative light in the media.

To respond to concerns about oversight and direction in the sector, a group of nonprofit leaders recruited a panel of high-profile Canadians under the leadership of Ed Broadbent, the well-respected former head of the New Democratic Party and, at the time, founding president of the International Centre for Human Rights and Democracy, to conduct a wide-ranging review. In 1999, the panel produced a document that became known as the "Broadbent Report." It contained forty-one recommendations for changes in governance and accountability, both within voluntary sector organizations and in the sector's relations with government.

In the corporate sector, in the last part of the last century and in the early years of this one, there was a plague of scandals in the US, Britain, South Africa, Italy, Australia, Canada, and elsewhere. Pressures for more accountability increased in many countries. In Canada, a 1994 study commissioned by the Toronto Stock Exchange raised serious doubts about the effectiveness of corporate boards and the diligence of directors.[8]

The most prominent corporate scandal during this period was the collapse of Enron. It was the largest seller of natural gas and other energy products in the US in the 1990s. By the end of 2000, its market capitalization exceeded $60 billion. A *Fortune* survey approvingly cited it as "the most innovative large company in America."

Innovative it was. Through unethical practices, bewildering business deals, and accounting sleight of hand, Enron obscured its business performance, misrepresented its earnings, hid its debt, and falsified its balance sheet. Yet throughout all this, it had a model board of directors rated by some as one of the best in the US. Its auditor was an internationally reputed accounting firm, Arthur Andersen. Nevertheless, in 2001, the Enron house of cards began to collapse, and in November, the company filed for bankruptcy. Several top executives wound up in jail. The Arthur Andersen firm imploded and eighty-five thousand employees lost their jobs, as did several thousand at Enron.[9]

As these instances of dishonesty, corruption, and mismanagement accumulated, more and more people began to ask, *where were the boards of directors?* What were they doing? It became apparent that there was something seriously amiss with these boards. In the private sector, the directors were often cronies of senior management who would be unlikely to ask embarrassing questions. And in the nonprofit sector, serving on a board was frequently perceived as a kind of civic duty devoid of specific responsibilities. Community members were encouraged to take their turn serving on a board, without there being any queries raised as to the capability of the person in question to do the job.

Moreover, the job itself was extremely unclear, in both the private sector and the nonprofit sector. Boards had often been treated as a sort of icing on the cake—as social clubs or places to reward people for past services—rather than as entities with a substantive role to play. The scandals made it apparent that serious thinking was needed about the role of boards of directors and society's expectations of them. A range of questions needed to be addressed—for example:

- Who should serve on boards? What criteria should be used in selecting directors?
- What were their responsibilities, individually and collectively?
- How should directors be appointed? To whom were they accountable?
- How long should they remain in office?

- What was the relationship between the board and the staff of organizations?
- Who should lead the board, and how should that individual be appointed?
- Should boards be evaluated, and if so, by whom?
- Did the legislative framework in which boards were required to operate need to be amended, and if so, how?

The word *governance* turned out to be a kind of missing piece of vocabulary, ideally suited to encompass all this. And so governments, academics, and management experts began the process of investing this little-understood concept of governance with substantive content to answer the foregoing questions and related ones—a process that continues to this day.

How Ideas About Governance Developed

The concept of governance, as it applies to corporations and nonprofits, is a recent phenomenon. Most initial writing on this subject related to the corporate sector. One reason it took time for the idea of governance to gain traction was that in the US, up to around 1975, directors were more or less seen as extensions of management. In a speech in 2004, the then head of the US Security and Exchange Commission (SEC), Cynthia Glassman, stated that historically, boards had tended to be involved in corporate decision making on a whole range of managerial issues.[10] Thus, it was not uncommon for a board to be controlled by insiders who had the necessary knowledge and experience to make informed decisions on these kinds of matters.

Neither state nor federal law imposed structural constraints on boards or their committees. There was a strong culture of voluntary governance, with companies creating and following their own codes based on those of other companies, or the codes of business, legal, and investor groups. The idea that the board had a persona and a role separate from management, and that it had responsibilities in respect of something called "governance," was not widely appreciated, nor was it always welcomed.

Things began to change in the last quarter of the twentieth century. In the wake of the scandals, academics, consultants, lawyers, and others began to explore what the concept of corporate governance might entail. This exploration was accelerated in 2002 with the passing of a piece of US legislation called the Sarbanes-Oxley Act. The Act made public companies secure an independent audit of their finances, and it required top management to certify the accuracy of financial statements. It outlined the responsibilities of corporate boards and introduced criminal penalties for some types of misconduct.

Some critics thought the legislation was too restrictive and that it damaged the competitive position of American companies. But others welcomed the greater confidence in the integrity of corporate practices that it provided for investors. In the wake of Sarbanes-Oxley, many other countries, including Canada, passed regulations with objectives along the lines of the US model. Because of concerns in the business community and among the public at large with respect to accountability, much early literature about governance focused on the structures, roles, and relationships that would give it effect.

In the corporate sector, a tradition had evolved in many big corporations whereby the individual who was the chair of the board was also the CEO of the company. In the view of many commentators, this established a too-cozy relationship between the board and management. However, because this practice was so entrenched in powerful corporations, and because many who served as both chair and CEO disliked the idea that they would be accountable to another party, there was much debate about the pros and cons of separating these positions. This, in turn, led to debate about the role of the board chair. If chairs were no longer to be CEOs, then what was their role, and how did it differ from that of a CEO?

Other debates focused on the role of the board of directors itself. It became generally accepted that the board's job was to safeguard shareholder value and to exercise financial oversight, so that fraud and deception of the kind that had occurred at Enron would no longer be possible. Words like *accountability, control,* and *monitoring* were prevalent in the literature.

Thus, over the period from roughly 1995 to the present, there has been an explosion of interest in governance, and an ongoing quest to define what it means and what it may imply for the individuals who sit on boards of directors. Membership on a board is no longer seen as a social obligation or a reward for past services; instead, it is increasingly understood to be a substantive role involving important responsibilities. In short, governance has become professionalized. This is the subject of the following chapter.

---

1. Cited in James Dalton and Monica Dignam, Decision to Join: How Individuals Determine Value and Why They Choose to Belong (Washington, DC: Association Management Press, 2007),18.

2. David Lasby and Cathy Barr, "Giving in Canada: Strong Philanthropic Traditions Supporting a Large Nonprofit Sector," in *The Palgrave Handbook of Global Philanthropy,* edited by Pamala Wiepking and Femida Handy (London: Palgrave, Macmillan, 2015), 27.

3. Michael Hall, et. al., *The Canadian Nonprofit and Voluntary Sector in Comparative Perspective* (Toronto: Imagine Canada, 2005), IV. http://sectorsource.ca/sites/default/files/resources/files/jhu_report_en.pdf

4. Source of nonprofit data: "Quick Facts About Nonprofits," *National Center for Charitable Statistics* (NCCS, 2016). http://nccs.urban.org/data-statistics/quick-facts-about-nonprofits

5. T. Rees Shapiro, "United Way Leader's Fraud Scandal Marred Charitable Legacy Historica Canada," *The Washington Post,* November 14, 2011. https://www.washingtonpost.com/local/obituaries/united-way-leaders-fraud-scandal-marred-charitable-legacy/2011/11/14/gIQALnwbMN_story.html

6. "CharityWatch Hall of Shame," *CharityWatch,* accessed August 7, 2018, https://www.charitywatch.org/charitywatch-articles/charitywatch-hall-of-shame/63

7. "Krever Inquiry," *The Canadian Encyclopedia* (Ottawa: Historica Canada, 2014). https://www.thecanadianencyclopedia.ca/en/article/krever-inquiry/

8. Gordon Floyd, "The Broadbent Report: An Overview," *The Philanthropist* 15, no. 3.

9. The federal government in Canada was also caught up in the turmoil around corruption. A rightward drift in political discourse in the 1990s had featured demands for reductions in the role of government and more transparency and accountability. When, in 2004, the Auditor General of Canada published a critical report on federal government finances, it fell upon fertile ground. This politically incendiary document drew attention to irregularities in the management of what become known as the "sponsorship program" of the then-Liberal government. A subsequent inquiry, commissioned by Prime Minister Paul Martin, treated Canadians to a long series of public hearings where the themes of political sleaze and mismanagement were constantly aired, a development that played a major role in the victory of the Conservative Party in the next election.

10. Cynthia A. Glassman, "Speech by SEC Commissioner: Board Independence and the Evolving Role of Directors," at the 26th Annual Conference on Securities Regulation and Business Law Problems, February 20, 2004. https://www.sec.gov/news/speech/spch022004cag.htm

CHAPTER 2
THE PROFESSIONALIZATION OF GOVERNANCE

The central concern in the evolving literature about governance was to determine what kinds of rules and practices would foster an effective governance regime, and whether there was a correlation between good governance and organizational performance. It became evident that there was no single, or simple, answer to such questions. At the heart of the discussion was the question of the board's role and how it differed from that of staff.

Fundamentals of the Board's Role

Fiduciary Responsibilities

A fundamental building block of governance is the concept of fiduciary responsibility, set out in a variety of publications. Most jurisprudence related to this concept has evolved with respect to the corporate sector, but the same ideas are generally understood to apply to nonprofit corporations as well. For Canada, a good, succinct statement may be found in the *Directors' Responsibilities in Canada.*

> Directors are fiduciaries of the corporation they serve. This long-standing common law principle governs all aspects of the directors' relationship to the corporation and is codified in the corporate statutes by the requirement that directors act "honestly and in good faith with a view to the best interests of the corporation" in exercising their powers and discharging their duties. . . .
>
> [The Supreme Court of Canada has stated that directors] must respect the trust and confidence that have been reposed in them to manage the assets of the corporation in pursuit of the realization of the objects of the corporation. They must avoid conflicts of interest with the corporation. They must avoid abusing their position to gain personal benefit. They must maintain the confidentiality of information they acquire by virtue of their position. Directors and officers must serve the corporation selflessly, honestly and loyally.

Closely related to the concept of fiduciary duty, and sometimes combined with it, is the duty of care.

> In discharging their duties, directors must "exercise the care, diligence and skill that a reasonably prudent person would exercise in comparable circumstances." This standard of care can be achieved by any director who devotes reasonable time and attention to the affairs of the corporation and exercises informed business judgment. The standard of care is measured against the objective standard of what a reasonably prudent person would do

> in comparable circumstances. This requires directors to devote the necessary time and attention to bring their own judgment to bear on the matter and make an informed decision. . . .[1]

To exercise their fiduciary responsibilities effectively, it's essential that board members have a clear understanding of their role and what the concept of such responsibilities may imply. The following story, derived from an actual case study, illustrates the complexity of these issues.

* * * * *

Sam had not expected this. He had recently joined the board of a local social service agency, thinking that he should do something to support his community. He had some experience in management but had never sat on a board until now.

Sue, one of the longer-standing board members, had come up to him after a board meeting. "Sam," she said, "we had thought that Patrick would carry on as board chair through this year, but he's got a new job and will be moving out of town shortly. So we need a new chair. Some of us got together to discuss this, and with your background in management, we all felt you'd be the best person to take over the role."

Sam protested. "But I've never done this before, and I'm pretty new to the organization."

"Don't worry," said Sue. "It's not a very demanding job. As chair, you just have to run the meetings and make sure people have a chance to have their say."

Sam quite liked the idea of using his management experience in a new way, so after some reflection, he agreed to try out the role.

A little later, Ellen, the agency CEO, happened to mention to Sam that she was planning to appoint a new Deputy CEO, accountable to her, to help run the agency. "Shouldn't this be discussed by the board?" asked Sam.

"Absolutely not," said Ellen. "It's up to the board to set broad strategy for the organization, but staffing matters and organizational issues are my responsibility as CEO. It would be entirely improper for the board to get involved in this kind of matter." Not long after, Ellen arranged for Sam to attend a workshop by a prominent consultant who reiterated her view. The consultant stated that boards needed to focus their deliberations on their organizations' ends, not their means. In effect, the only role of the board in this area was to appoint and evaluate the CEO.

This all sounded plausible to Sam, and anyhow, he was very busy at his job. Moreover, as a newly minted board chair, he wasn't about to get into a confrontation with the CEO, a forceful individual who had been running the organization for years. The board was generally deferential to Ellen in view of her long experience and somewhat combative nature. So there was no further discussion, and the CEO went ahead with her appointment.

However, in the weeks that followed, Sam wondered whether it had been right to keep the board out of a discussion of a key new senior position in the organization. There were cost implications—deputy CEOs were not cheap—and there were questions the board might have asked with regard to the need for this new position and the appropriateness of a one-on-one reporting relationship.

It was some months later that a major confrontation erupted between the CEO and the union representing agency workers. The murder of an agency client had led to much unfavourable publicity and media speculation about the agency's effectiveness. In due course, there was a coroner's inquest, at the end of which, in a media interview, the CEO voiced a scathing criticism of her own staff. The union responded by requesting that a workplace review be undertaken, which the board then endorsed.

The resulting report described an organization in serious disarray—a "toxic" workplace. The CEO had been dominating the organization using bullying tactics to get her way. Workers feared to apply for vacant supervisory positions because they did not want to lose the protection of the collective agreement. The senior management team was fragmented and its members mutually distrustful.

Sam was appalled by these findings. He felt that, as chair, he should have known what was going on; yet he recalled how both the CEO and the consultant she had introduced him to had told him that organizational and personnel matters were outside the board's purview.

But he also recalled the words of a lawyer he had consulted when he took on the chair's role. The lawyer told him that, as a director, he had taken on a fiduciary responsibility. "A fiduciary," said the lawyer, "is a person who has a legal duty to exercise a high standard of care in managing another's property. Fiduciary duties are imposed by law to protect those who are vulnerable from those who have power over them." The lawyer had gone on to explain that directors had a duty to be informed and to act with diligence in the organization's best interests.

I don't think our board did a very good job in discharging its fiduciary responsibilities, thought Sam. He felt undermined by the consultant's advice and realized that the CEO had managed to build a barrier that insulated him and the rest of the board from issues that had a direct impact on organizational performance. Sam pondered, *We should never have allowed this kind of organizational climate to prevail on our watch—but we did. Everyone seems to agree that the board's responsibility is sound governance. But what does that imply with respect to our role on personnel and organizational issues, and our relationship to the CEO and to the rest of the staff?*

* * * * *

Differentiating the Board's Role from That of Staff

A very common complaint about boards is that they try to micromanage the organization. When board members start poking into operational matters, all kinds of problems are created. The authority of the executive director may be undermined. Directors may not fully understand the issues facing the organization or the nature of its business, with the result that they provide direction that is ill-advised or even damaging. Different directors may provide inconsistent instructions to staff, leading to internal conflict. But the most fundamental problem is that accountability is confused. Staff become unclear as to who is in charge. If things go off the rails, it becomes difficult, if not impossible, to determine who was responsible.

One reason boards micromanage is that many directors are temperamentally more comfortable dealing with down-to-earth operational matters[2] than with abstract issues like strategic planning.[3] A more profound reason is that, at a basic conceptual level, there is an overlap between the board's role and that of staff in important spheres, notably strategic planning.

There is no "bright line" that can unambiguously demarcate their areas of mutual responsibility.

Some writers try to assert that this bright line does exist, and they put forward three arguments in that regard. For example, they may assert that the board is responsible for policy while the staff looks after implementation. Others say the board looks after strategy while the role of staff is operations. Another explanation is that the board looks after governance while staff is responsible for management. These observations are correct, in a general sense, but if one examines them more closely, it turns out that the distinction or dividing line that they propose is blurry and open to interpretation.

Governance and Management Overlap

Consider the argument about policy and implementation. In practice, these two concepts blend into each other. The transition from policy to implementation can be gradual. It often involves a process that can unfold over a period of time—weeks, months, or even longer in some cases. The same holds true for strategy and operations. There's often no clear way to determine just when the "strategy" phase has been left behind and "operations" are now under way.

Moreover, how a policy or strategy is carried out can in some cases be just as important as the what—the objectives to be achieved. Furthermore, as a decision moves from policy or strategy into implementation, problems may arise that make it necessary to return to discussions about policy. So to suggest that the board should only deal with policy—or strategy—and not implementation could preclude it from guiding the process of implementation, or from having important discussions about its potential impact on staff or external stakeholders.

Similarly, there is no clear dividing line between governance and management. Conceptually, they overlap. A look at how ideas about management have evolved will make this clearer.

In early writings about management, almost a century ago, the manager was seen as the central player in achieving results. The prevalent view, derived to some degree from military concepts of leadership, was that effective organizational performance depended on the all-seeing manager. His job (managers were always understood to be men) was to plan, organize, direct, and control. Employees were there simply to carry out the manager's instructions. In the language of economists, they were factors of production just like land or capital.

This top-down, authoritative view of management began to crumble towards the mid-twentieth century. A significant contribution to new ideas was provided in the 1960s by American academic Douglas McGregor, who published a book entitled *The Human Side of Enterprise* that was later chosen by an academy of scholars as one of the most influential management books of the last century.

McGregor criticized the view that effective leadership required a dominant style of direction. He called this "Theory X." He argued that in many cases, a different approach to motivation would produce better results. This approach, "Theory Y," was grounded in alternative assumptions about human nature. It proposed that employees could be ambitious, self-motivated, and self-controlled, and that their abilities were under-utilized in most organizations. Theory Y managers were more likely to develop a climate of trust with staff and give them opportunities to provide input to decision making.

The Human Side of Enterprise and related books ushered in a major transition in management thought. This change in thinking gathered momentum with the publication of another book, cited by one enthusiastic critic as the "greatest business book of all time." Published in 1982, *In Search of Excellence: Lessons from America's Best-Run Companies* was written by two management consultants, Tom Peters and Robert Waterman, Jr. It was based on research on the management practices of forty-three corporations that, in the opinion of the authors, had demonstrated top performance in the years leading up to the book's publication.

A central objective of the book was to establish how important people were to business success. It introduced the idea that organizational culture had a significant impact on productivity.

> Without exception, the dominance and coherence of culture proved to be an essential quality of the excellent companies. Moreover, the stronger the culture and the more it was directed toward the marketplace, the less need there was for policy manuals, organization charts, or detailed procedures and rules.[4]

The stress on culture in this book was a significant new insight; thanks to Peters and Waterman, as well as other authors discussed elsewhere in this book, culture is now recognized as an important determinant of both organizational performance and the effectiveness of boards of directors.[5]

This literature had the effect of widening the scope of the discipline of management, as they began to embrace questions of worker motivation and organizational culture. Moreover, in the latter part of the last century, another body of literature was also beginning to emerge on the subject of strategic planning. These writings argued that in addition to focusing on the efficiency of day-to-day operations, management needed to be concerned with the longer-term strategy of the organization. It might be said that as a consequence of these writings, the discipline of management graduated from the shop floor to the executive suite. What this meant for CEOs and executive directors in the nonprofit world was that as managers, they were expected to help define the strategic direction of their organization as well as implement its strategic goals.

Because financial scandals and corruption were the main factors that gave rise to the evolution of ideas about governance, there was a tendency in early writings about governance to see the board's fiduciary duty primarily as a financial responsibility. The board was a steward and an overseer. Its main job was to keep track of the money, to prevent fraud, and to protect shareholders' interests.

However, as thinking about fiduciary responsibilities and the board's role has evolved, it has become apparent that the board's role needs to be seen in much broader terms. The contemporary view is that a board should be concerned with the overall health of the enterprise and its strategic direction, a responsibility shared with the senior staff of the organization.

> Notwithstanding the delegation to senior executives of very broad powers over a corporation's affairs, the board of directors must reserve to itself the ability to intervene in management's decisions and to exercise final judgment on any matter that is material to the corporation. . . . [T]he overriding principle governing delegation is that directors must retain ultimate control over the corporation. Directors must be sufficiently familiar with the business and affairs

> of the corporation to know that it is being managed in an appropriate fashion. They must exercise sufficient leadership to ensure that the corporation is following a course that they have approved.[6]

Thus, when it comes to matters of strategy and overall organizational performance, there is an inherent overlap between the concerns of the board and the role of senior staff. It takes sound judgement on the part of the board to recognize that this overlap exists, to work in partnership with staff in these areas, and to avoid any temptation to get too deeply involved in areas of management that are within the staff's purview.

What Contemporary Directors Need to Know

In addition to understanding the fundamentals of the board's role and its relationship to staff, there are other intellectual challenges facing contemporary nonprofit directors. Ideally, directors should have read and understood the organization's bylaws. They should also know something about board composition and culture, about the roles of different committees and why they are necessary, and about what is appropriate conduct for a board member (as set out in codes of conduct and conflict of interest policies), as well as their own liabilities as directors.

Furthermore, governance is concerned with decision making on issues that are most important to an organization. Thus, it will certainly improve discourse around a board table if directors have an understanding of the following subjects:

- strategic planning
- financial management, including how to read financial statements

- risk management
- performance measurement and evaluation
- the role of social media in supporting organizational performance
- fundraising
- marketing
- human resource management.

As discussed in the following section, there are many opportunities for existing or would-be executive directors or CEOs of nonprofit organizations to deepen their knowledge of governance-related subjects and sharpen their skills. A review of the educational attainments of a sample of nonprofit leaders in Ontario[7] shows they are very well-educated individuals. Almost 90 percent of them have at least a diploma from a community college. Three-quarters have a BA or more advanced levels of education, while almost one-third have an MA or PhD. The majority of them (70 percent) followed a career path within the nonprofit sector, which suggests that they would have a fairly deep knowledge of the nonprofit landscape.

I am not aware of any detailed statistics on the level of education of nonprofit board members, but there is no educational requirement for individuals to serve as such. If the executive director or CEO of a nonprofit is knowledgeable about many aspects of governance and management, whereas board members have little insight into these areas, this can give rise to serious difficulties in board–staff relations. As nonprofit governance becomes increasingly professionalized, more attention will need to be paid to the selection of well-qualified board members and to the provision of educational opportunities to others whose knowledge may need to be enhanced. Indeed, more and more nonprofits, particularly the larger ones, appear to be providing training opportunities of this kind.

Sources of Governance-Related Knowledge

The professionalization of governance has been fostered by the publication of a great deal of literature. Thirty or forty years ago, bookshelves on governance in the nonprofit sector were virtually non-existent. But since then, reams of literature have emerged both from academic institutions and from consultants seeking to share their insights and differentiate themselves from others. The Internet now provides easy access to countless books, articles, and blogs dealing with every dimension of governance.

The Ontario Nonprofit Network report revealed that the majority of leaders in the nonprofit sector tend to rely on workshops, conferences, and seminars to supplement their knowledge, complemented by peer networks or membership in a professional association. Attending a business management or nonprofit certificate program was a much less common practice. Perhaps this is because of the general lack of funding for such courses in many nonprofit organizations (as compared to private sector organizations) and/or the difficulty many nonprofit employees face in trying to find enough time to absent themselves from their workplace to pursue such programs.

A number of organizations offer education for nonprofit staff or for board members interested in becoming more knowledgeable about governance and related disciplines. Several umbrella organizations provide courses, conferences, and webinars, as well as a continuing flow of their own publications. For example, BoardSource is a US-based organization whose mission is "to inspire and support excellence in nonprofit governance and board and staff leadership." Also in the US, the American Society of Association Executives (ASAE), strives "to advance, improve, promote and protect the profession of association management . . . [and likewise] to develop and encourage high standards of professional conduct among nonprofit organization management professionals," as does its sister organization, the Canadian Society of Association Executives (CSAE).

The Canadian accountancy profession has joined the "better governance" parade—its association, Chartered Professional Accountants Canada, offers, as its website proclaims, "a wealth of education, information and resources related to not-for-profit governance," much of which is excellent and is available free of charge. The Canadian Society of Corporate Secretaries, renamed Governance Professionals of Canada in 2016, asserts that it "offers a distinct, unified voice and proven toolbox for best practices in corporate governance."[8]

Universities and other educational organizations provide further options. The Institute of Corporate Directors (ICD), in collaboration with the Rotman School at the University of Toronto, modestly proclaims that its "innovative program is the only national program offered across the country [that] . . . provides learning that can be immediately applied." (The total ICD program cost, at time of writing, was $18,000 plus tax.)

The Conference Board of Canada, in association with McMaster University, runs The Directors College, which "offers Canada's first accredited corporate director development program," featuring "a forward-thinking governance agenda" and promising to help develop "the change-enabling behaviors [*sic*] needed to put what is learned in the classroom, into practice, in the boardroom." (Its Chartered Director program, with five modules, cost $4,370 per module—$21,850 plus tax for the full program.)

Universities and colleges across Canada, from Dalhousie University in Halifax to Simon Fraser in Vancouver, now offer a wide range of other programs and courses, as do scores of similar institutions in the US.[9]

A related factor that has helped to propel nonprofits down the road towards professionalism has been the emergence of standards and various forms of accreditation or certification. Some standards are intended for individuals. Doctors, lawyer, nurses, accountants, and others who are members of a profession are well aware of the importance of certification. There are professional standards to which they must adhere, and there are usually requirements for continued learning and/or for training from year to year to make sure that their service to clients or patients is up to date.

Individuals who are prepared to make the investment of time and money can achieve certification of one kind or another with respect to their knowledge of governance. For example, successful ICD graduates can place the initials *ICD* after their names. Graduates of The Directors College may use *C.Dir.* Graduates of the CSAE program may use *CAE.* Similar individual certification programs are offered at a number of US institutions.

Certification for Organizations

For organizations interested in improving their governance performance, there are other standards or types of accreditation available. The field of health care is understandably very attentive to standards. Accreditation Canada offers standards and accreditation services for hospitals, clinics, labs, long-term care homes, and other kinds of facilities, and it provides coverage in a range of areas, including governance and leadership. There are several other organizations that offer accreditation, mostly for organizations working in the fields of health and community service.[10]

However, for many organizations in the nonprofit sector that have an interest in strengthening their governance (whether they are involved in health or not), the most interesting program may be the Trustmark initiative run by Imagine Canada. Their Standards Program seeks to "strengthen public confidence in individual charitable and nonprofit organizations and the sector as a whole." The program reviews organizational performance in five areas, including board governance, financial accountability and transparency, fundraising, staff management, and volunteer involvement.

There are three levels of standards, tailored to the size and budget of the applicant. Nonprofits that meet the standards appropriate to their level become qualified (for five years, after which they have to re-qualify) to use the Standards Program Trustmark on their website and elsewhere. (Program costs at the time of writing included an application fee plus an annual licence fee that ranged from $500 to $6,000, depending on the organization's budget.[11])

In summary, there are resources available for those individuals and organizations that wish to rise to the challenge of professionalization. And some progress is being made. Don McCreesh is an experienced executive who has had a long experience with the sector, through years of involvement with the YMCA, through Imagine Canada (where he has chaired both their board and their Standards Council), and as a consultant and trainer. In an interview in 2016, he told me:

> There is an increasing realization across a wide cross section of organizations in the sector—in arts, social services, and elsewhere—that there needs to be a level of professionalization, a level of know-how that goes beyond having well-meaning volunteers and good people

> on boards. And there is growing agreement on what best practices look like, and an increasing awareness of the importance of things like transparency and full disclosure and risk management.
>
> It will be harder for smaller organizations to keep up with all this, but they still have to try to observe the principles and be aware of a checklist of things that at least they have to pay attention to. We have to find the people who are willing to make the investment of time and make sure they have the ways and means to learn. Perhaps we can build a cadre of "serial volunteer directors" who are well qualified and who see, as I did, the value in having a kind of side career as a volunteer, perhaps moving from board to board. There's a particular need for this in smaller communities.

Let's bear in mind that the people who sit on the boards of nonprofit organizations, no matter what their size, are unpaid. In the corporate sector, directors are generally paid, so there is an incentive for them and for would-be directors to invest in learning. Not so in the nonprofit sector; nevertheless, the growing sophistication of governance continues to increase demands on directors. Are we asking too much of volunteer board members? Is there an alternative? I return to these questions later in this book.

Meanwhile, let's take a look at the contemporary environment in which nonprofit organizations function, and the challenges it presents to their leaders. These issues are the subject of the next two chapters.

---

1. Osler, Hoskin & Harcourt LLP, *Directors' Responsibilities in Canada,* 6th ed. (Osler, Hoskin & Harcourt LLP / Institute of Corporate Directors, October 2014), 7–10.

2. In developing this book, I interviewed a cross section of individuals who see lots of boards in action. One observed, "We maintain that boards are supposed to deal with strategy as one of their main responsibilities. But the fact is that strategy requires a certain kind of mindset or way of thinking, and a lot of people are not gifted in this area. Many directors are in fact not well suited to deal with strategy."

3. Readers interested in the evolution of strategic planning may enjoy the classic review of this subject in *Strategy Safari – A Guided Tour Through the Wilds of Strategic Management,* by Henry Mintzberg, Bruce Ahlstrand, and Joseph Lampel (New York: The Free Press, 1998).

4. Tom Peters and Robert Waterman, Jr., *In Search of Excellence* (New York: Warner Books, 1982), 75.

5. The book identified eight themes as determinants of performance. One of their findings was that truly effective managers did not sit in their offices developing organization charts and devising strategies. Rather, they spent a lot of time out on the shop floor interacting with people—talking to workers and learning what was on their minds. This led to a maxim, which has become widely cited, that "management by walking around" was a practice that all managers should emulate.

6. Osler, et al., *Directors' Responsibilities,* 5–6.

7. Elizabeth McIsaac, Stella Park, and Lynne Toupin, *Shaping the Future — Leadership in Ontario's Nonprofit Labour Force* (Ontario Nonprofit Network, 2013), 43. It's not clear to what extent these statistics would be applicable in other jurisdictions.

8. *Governance Professionals of Canada* (2016), accessed August 7, 2018. http://www.cscs.org/

9. CharityVillage has compiled a list of post-secondary nonprofit programs: "Post-Secondary Nonprofit Programs," *CharityVillage* (2018), accessed August 7, 2018. https://charityvillage.com/cms/active-learning/related-links/post-secondary-nonprofit-programs

10. For a list, see Lee Anderson, "Accreditation: Is It Right for Your Organization?" *CharityVillage* (2015), accessed August 7, 2018. https://charityvillage.com/Content.aspx?topic=Accreditation_Is_it_right_for_your_organization#.V3rXrZMrJTZ

11. "Standards Program Fee Schedule," *Imagine Canada* (2018), accessed August 7, 2018. http://www.imaginecanada.ca/our-programs/standards-program/how-it-works/standards-program-fee-schedule.

CHAPTER 3
THE NONPROFIT ENVIRONMENT: FINANCIAL PROSPECTS

Without a doubt, the environment surrounding all organizations today, whether commercial or nonprofit, is turbulent and unpredictable. Change has characterized the economic and social environment for many years. However, today the turbulence is increasing to the point where some recent writers adopt an almost apocalyptic tone in discussing the prospects of nonprofit organizations. For example, the co-authors of *Race for Relevance*, a contemporary American book about associations, argue that the business climate has changed dramatically over the past twenty years, whereas most associations and nonprofit organizations have not.[1] If organizations are to survive, what's required is "radical change."

Others have suggested that the nonprofit sector is entering "a new reality":

> The nonprofit sector . . . is being tested as generational and other demographic shifts change the face of its client base and workforce, technology affords and demands greater responsiveness and transparency, and the blending of the public, private and nonprofit sectors creates new competitive and collaborative opportunities while simultaneously calling into question just what it means to be a nonprofit organization. . . . Although change is nothing new, the

> highly accelerated pace at which social, technological and economic shifts are now occurring . . . demands increasingly adaptive responses. The traditional approaches of nonprofits, funders and capacity builders will fall short, and the old rules will no longer apply.
>
> Five key trends [are] converging to reshape the social sector. While each dynamic has profound implications for how nonprofits will do business in the future, it is their convergence that will transform the sector.[2]

The figure below, conceived by Lapiana Consulting, illustrates the five trends.

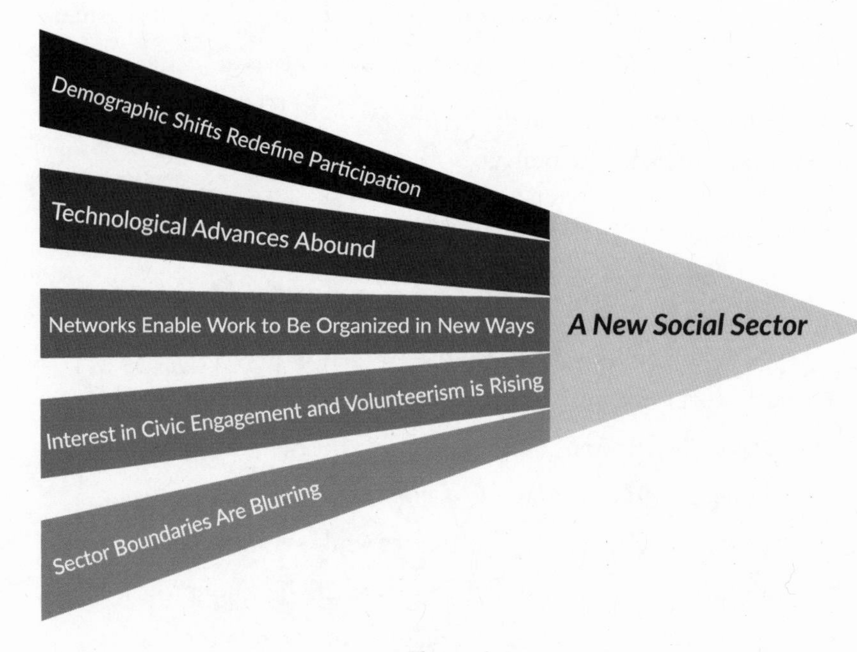

Figure 3.1

Working in the nonprofit sector is demanding and has been so for many years. The most common challenges involve money. Perhaps in previous decades this was a less general problem, but certainly today, maintaining revenues and achieving the elusive goal of sustainability has become a never-ending preoccupation of most organizations in the sector.

There are many reasons for this: It has been partially driven by a steady growth in the *number* of organizations, which reflects a growing public awareness of many social, economic, and environmental problems facing our societies. Another contributing factor appears to have been a decline in public confidence in governments' abilities to deal with these problems. And the situation is aggravated further by the tendency of many governments, beset by their own financial difficulties, to cut programs and delegate functions to nonprofit organizations, without providing the funding that would allow these organizations to sustain those functions.

More and more organizations in the sector began to explore what they could do to improve and diversify their revenues. This, in turn, increased competition among organizations that might have previously enjoyed somewhat fraternal relationships. And, as it's often said, when the watering hole begins to dry up, the animals start to look at each other differently.

Sources of Nonprofit Revenue

Most nonprofits that are contemplating their strategies for the future will almost certainly be considering their financial options. Setting aside the possibility of making more use of volunteers, a unique and very important dimension of the sector,[3] most nonprofits that want to improve their financial picture have these sources to consider:

Earned income, such as:

- fees for services, including consulting and other contract work
- sales of performances and events, such as galas, auctions, etc.
- publication sales
- membership fees
- related businesses, including social enterprises that drive funds back to the nonprofit

Contributed income, including:

- government grants and transfers

Donations and philanthropy (generally only accessible to organizations with charitable status):

- grants from foundations
- grants from other public charities, including federated funds such as the United Way or community foundations
- charitable contributions from individual and corporate donors, including bequests and interest from endowments
- corporate philanthropy, including sponsorships, cause-related marketing, employee volunteer programs, and matching employee contributions

Nonprofit leaders need to ascertain which of these sources of income offer the best potential for their organization, and then consider which strategy or strategies might permit them to realize that potential.

According to a Statistics Canada survey covering the period 1997–2007 (the most recent data available at the time of writing), core nonprofits in Canada get by far the greatest portion of their revenues from the sale of goods and services (including government contracts).[4] Government transfers or grants account for just under 20 percent of their annual revenues, membership fees account for 16 percent, and donations (private business) account for about 14 percent. (Grants from foundations to the core nonprofit sector don't appear explicitly in these Statistics Canada survey results.)

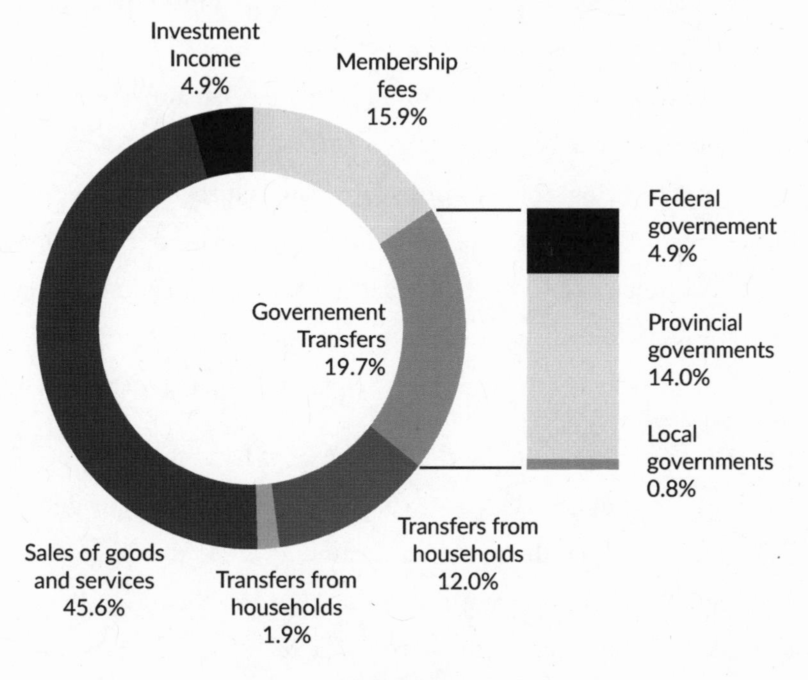

Figure 3.2

Let's look at what the future may hold in each of these areas.

Government

Some nonprofit leaders may have liked to think of government grants as a kind of strong wind at the back of their organizations, sustaining them from year to year, driving them forward. Government transfers are certainly very important for the big players in the nonprofit sector—hospitals and educational institutions—accounting for roughly 75 percent of their funding. However, these days, governments' role in relation to the core nonprofit sector—organizations other than hospitals and universities—is much less important.

Broadly speaking, the amounts that nonprofits received from the different sources listed above remained the same over the ten-year period covered by the Statistics Canada survey; in fact, during that time, government transfers (as a percentage of revenues) declined slightly. Looking ahead, there is disappointingly little cause to anticipate that governments' support for core nonprofits will increase much. The Canadian federal government's revenues declined substantially early in the twenty-first century when the Conservative government (then in power) eliminated 2 percent of the goods and services tax that had been helping to sustain federal revenues.

At the time of writing, this level of government had moved significantly into deficit territory, and it was moving deeper. There are many questions about how or whether the federal government will be able to meet a very wide range of electoral commitments unrelated to the nonprofit sector. In addition, the election of the unpredictable Trump administration in the US has raised many other questions and uncertainties for the federal government there.

Provincial budgets have been under great pressure for years, as successive federal governments have reduced transfer payments while off-loading more and more program responsibilities to the provinces and territories. Meanwhile, municipal governments complain of being perpetually under-resourced, given their dependence on property taxes for the majority of their funding. Yet the demands on this level of government constantly escalate, as more and more citizens are drawn to cities, imposing pressure on aging urban infrastructure and increasing the range of social problems associated with big-city life.

Governments at all levels are typically allergic to raising taxes—cutting them is always a more popular theme at election time—yet they are very often reluctant to reduce their responsibilities. As a result, they are chronically short of funds. There is very little to suggest that the nonprofit sector should anticipate a significant influx of new money from this source. The competition for those grants that are available is likely to become more intense. So, while governments should still be kept on the list as a potential source of funds for some organizations, most will have to look to other sources of financing to help them meet their responsibilities.

Fundraising and Donations

What about donations? Will fundraising help to fill the sails of nonprofits if government can't or won't?

In 2013, Jeanne Bell, then CEO of a nonprofit consulting and coaching firm called Compass Point, and her colleague Marla Cornelius published a study on the state of nonprofit fundraising in the US.[5] The study included "a great diversity of organizations" with a wide range of budget and staff sizes and many mission types, but each had "a senior level development staff person on their organizational chart." The study focused on the contributions of these individuals and executive directors, as well as boards, to fundraising.

The study found—no surprises here—that nonprofit organizations tend to be stuck in a vicious cycle where their needs outrun their resources. Various avenues are available to the nonprofit that wishes to enhance its revenues through fundraising. One option is to hire an individual to focus on this challenge—a development director.

However, the study documented a number of problems associated with efforts to engage an effective development director. One was an insufficiency of qualified candidates; another was a shortage of resources to hire candidates. A related difficulty was a serious lack of board support for fundraising activities ("three out of four executive directors . . . [called] board member engagement insufficient").

Some nonprofit executives might think that fundraising success has eluded them because they have not yet been able to recruit the right development director. But that's a doubtful assumption. In January 2013, Ruth McCambridge, editor of the US *Nonprofit Quarterly*, wrote an article entitled, "Firing Your Development Director? Join the Club." In it, she stated, "many smaller nonprofit organizations and boards have spent . . . 20-plus years chasing the dream of the magically effective development director only to be disappointed by the results . . . "

In their responses to the Compass Point study, executive directors often voiced concerns about the abilities of their development directors (a problem particularly prevalent in the case of smaller organizations with budgets under US$1 million). But reciprocally, development directors complained about an insufficiently robust relationship with the executive director and the lack of broad-based support for fundraising activities in their organization. There was a widespread view among these individuals that their organizations had an inadequate appreciation of the fundamentals of fund development. It seems that hiring a development director may help—but this step, on its own, is very unlikely to yield a dramatic increase in funding from donations.

Another avenue for fundraising that has opened up is the online world. Writing in 2007, Reynold Levy, then-president of the Lincoln Centre for the Performing Arts and a former executive director of the famous 92nd Street Y in Manhattan, pointed out how potent online fundraising was becoming in the world of politics. However, "when it comes to nonprofits, online giving is still in its infancy. . . . Plenty of experimentation is in order."[6]

Three years later, Beth Kanter, a reputed author on social media and nonprofits, and her colleague Allison Fine wrote, "[O]nline fundraising is growing quickly."[7] Organizations, she said, had two channels they could pursue: one was linking to a donor portal (such as CanadaHelps) using a "donate" button on their website. The other was turning "friends into funders" by expanding the network of friends and followers on social media sites such as Facebook and Twitter, and by using those vehicles to build support for the cause. The latter approach, they said, was "at an even earlier stage of development than general online giving."

Not surprisingly, the "friends into funders" strategy is developing. In 2014, a small team of UK academics examined what led to success when online platforms were used for fundraising. In general, they found that online donations were still "a relatively small part of overall giving"—only about 7 percent in both the US and UK, a finding echoed by Kanter—but they found online and text giving were growing faster than total donations, suggesting that this share would continue to grow. The study focused on individuals participating in an event such as a marathon and soliciting donations via social media. It examined the types of fundraising pages used by different individuals and assessed the results. Its conclusions were interesting.

Among its conclusions was the idea that "[online fundraising] can be highly cost-effective compared to alternatives such as professional face-to-face fundraising.... [I]ndividuals can be highly effective fundraisers." The amount raised in any particular situation depended on several factors, some of which were much more important than others. The more successful individual fundraisers had typically mastered what the authors called "the perfect ask,"[8] and the difference in results could be striking: for instance, the top 10 percent of "pages" examined in the study generated £1,343 or more in donations (about CAN$2,700 at the then-current exchange rate). The bottom 10 percent garnered less than £38 (CAN$76).

Clearly, online fundraising is growing in importance in the nonprofit sector, but as Kanter and Fine caution, "[O]rganizations must raise money from a variety of different sources, and that mix now includes social media." A related vehicle that seems to be acquiring increasing popularity is crowdfunding, using websites such as Kickstarter or Indiegogo. However, these methods are better suited to one-off events or requirements than to filling an organization's ongoing operational needs. In general, fundraising online or using social media is not seen as a panacea. Most experts agree that fundraising continues to require building relationships, telling your story, and taking potential donors through the process of cultivation, stewardship, and solicitation.

A factor often overlooked with respect to fundraising is how much work is involved. As noted earlier, the prospective recipient organization has to have charitable status. Securing grants is almost a kind of mini-industry now, and there are consultants who specialize in grant writing. Every granting organization has its own procedures, its own calendar, and usually its own forms that have to be completed. Even different departments within the same government will very frequently have different criteria to which the applicant must conform. Organizations hoping to benefit from grants have to be on high alert for application and reporting deadlines and the particular requirements of different granting bodies.

Moreover, most government granting programs require that organizations generate revenues of their own, whether through foundations, sponsorships, fundraising, or other sources. They may penalize applicants if they appear to rely too heavily on government, yet they are more and more allergic to providing core (operational) funding that would enable the recipient organization to hire the staff needed to do the careful development work. Many programs will only provide targeted funds or seed money to support special projects or programs. These by their nature do not build organizational capacity, and they run the risk of raising expectations that cannot be met when the project money runs out.

What may we conclude about fundraising as a sustaining source of support for nonprofits in coming years? Is it likely to provide the financial stability so widely sought? I'm not optimistic. There are interesting developments in the field, but the situation described in the Compass Point study seems to be very similar to the one facing Canadian nonprofits. In both countries, the majority of nonprofits have a difficult job ahead of them if they hope to make fundraising a reliable source of financial support over the longer term.

Effective fundraising is a multi-dimensional challenge that needs to be seen as a component of a broader financial strategy. The Compass Point study argues that the reason so many nonprofits have been unable to break out of the "vicious cycle" of insufficient funding is because they "lack the fundamental conditions for fund-development success—basic tools such as a fundraising plan and database, essential board and executive leadership and development skills, and a shared culture of philanthropy across the organization." The study asserts that what's needed is a systemic, organization-wide approach.

Organizations and their leaders need to build the capacity, the systems, and the culture to support fundraising success. Among the signs that an organization is up to the task:

- It invests in its fundraising capacity and in the technologies and other fund-development systems it needs;
- The staff, the executive director, and the board are deeply engaged in fundraising as ambassadors and, in many cases, as solicitors;
- Fund development and philanthropy are understood and valued across the organization; and
- The development director is viewed as a key leader and partner in the organization and is integrally involved in organizational planning and strategy.

Here's what's meant by a "culture of philanthropy," according to the study:

- Most people in the organization (across positions) act as ambassadors and engage in relationship building.
- Everyone promotes philanthropy and can articulate a case for support.
- Fund development is viewed and valued as a mission-aligned program of the organization.
- Organizational systems are established to support donors.
- The executive director is committed and personally involved in fundraising.

There will no doubt be instances where an organization manages to achieve a significant advance in fundraising without adopting this kind of systemic approach. I recall a nonprofit I used to chair where we had the good fortune of recruiting a woman to the board who proved to be an extraordinarily effective financial leader. Within a year, this woman—I'll call her Susan (not her real name)—had taken on the fundraising role, energized the staff, and instituted a new approach. Susan's strategy generated around twenty times as much as had been achieved by a previous well-intentioned—but lacklustre—fundraising committee.

Unfortunately, Susans are few and far between. Those of us in charge of nonprofit organizations cannot count on being able to recruit such an individual. Moreover, relying on one exceptional leader is not a sustainable strategy. A durable approach to fundraising that holds the promise of a more or less continuous stream of meaningful financial support requires sustained effort and inspired leadership over a period of years, not months.

Individuals with experience tend to agree: "Fundraising is a marathon, not a sprint."[9]

What can—or will—the board of directors do? When board members turn over frequently, as is so often the case, it can be difficult if not impossible to mount a sustained fundraising program dependent on board participation. Even in the short run, executive directors or CEOs who try to engage their board members in fundraising typically face an uphill battle. This may be truer in Canada, where the tradition of board members contributing to their organization or helping it to raise money may not be as well established as in the US. But even in the US, it's typically arduous.

Nell Edgington is a Texas-based consultant who has published a range of thoughtful articles and booklets on nonprofit issues. Her experience conforms with my own. In many nonprofits, she finds that the board's role as a financial leader is either lacking or nonexistent. "I would like to see boards opening doors, connecting to key decision makers, thinking strategically about what is next for the organization." Too often, this is not occurring, a difficulty she attributes in many cases to a lack of effective leadership. Edgington has developed a practical list of ways boards can help with fundraising; many of them don't involve buttonholing friends for donations.[10]

Jim Schwartz is a very experienced nonprofit consultant based in Florida who has chaired several boards and sat on others, both in Florida and New England. His view:

> Getting boards into fundraising is like pulling teeth. Most people will tell you flat out, "I don't like asking for money." What I hear about people who are good at this, they say

> that they realize that if they ask their friends for a big gift, they will come right back and ask for a big donation in return. If you have a really good ED or good development people, they can use the board strategically . . . for introductions or a fundraising event, but not to do asks. Fundraising is not impossible, but it takes a good ED and a good staff member who knows how to use board members well.[11]

Most nonprofits, beset by the many operational challenges that dominate the daily agenda of the executive head, and, in many cases, unable to rely on the support of a committed board of directors, will have trouble building a strong development initiative. Furthermore, to be successful, organizations normally have to fundraise on, or at least consider, multiple platforms: grants, foundations, online, in-kind, direct mail, events, planned giving, bequests, etc. It's a complex field, typically difficult for a group of volunteers to take on, especially when, as is very often the case, they have no expertise in the area. The problem is compounded in smaller organizations when there are few staff and no one with specific responsibility for this function.

Hence my conclusion that for nonprofits struggling to reach the elusive goal of sustainability, fundraising is likely to be, at best, a partial answer. All too often, fundraising absorbs much time and energy but yields disappointing results.

If fundraising is problematic and government support cannot be expected to increase, what other options are available to nonprofits?

Members and Memberships

Another potential source of revenue for organizations that are member-based may be members themselves. On average, according to Statistics Canada data cited earlier, membership revenues represent about 16 percent of the total in Canada's core nonprofit sector.

Perhaps in the past, membership revenues represented one of the more reliable sources of income for these types of organizations. This is no longer the case today and, except in certain cases, it will probably be even less so in the future. Experience indicates that extracting resources from members, whether in the form of fees or volunteer time, is becoming more and more difficult. This is linked to another troublesome challenge, namely, how to reinforce connections and enhance the engagement of members when everyone seems to be busier and to have less free time to devote to activities outside of daily work and family responsibilities.

A 2013 study of Canadian trade associations illustrates this point. The study involved interviews with the presidents of fourteen major industry associations, all of which had global connections. It highlighted the increasing frustrations that presidents were facing with regard to their relationships with member organizations. Even getting attention from members was problematic in a world of communication overload. "Many associations complain about the disappointing results achieved from member communications initiatives, even when more contemporary media such as social media are used. It's tough to communicate value when no-one is listening."[12]

The associations represented in the study were all in the business of government relations. Their presidents found it challenging to communicate the value of their work to member organizations who persistently asked what they were getting for their money. "Communicating value for money is inherently difficult to do, since the value is often intangible, may consist of small or longer-term gains and cannot easily be quantified." These difficulties seem likely to augment in the future in light of the difficult economic environment.

Sarah Sladek paints the issue of membership on a broader canvas. While the study cited above was focused on industry associations whose members were all organizations, Sladek has cast her eye over a wide panorama of nonprofit organizations and associations where membership was more typically an individual, rather than an organizational, relationship. She portrays membership decline as a kind of cancer or process of erosion gradually pervading many facets of American society: traditional civic organizations, service clubs, churches, veterans' associations, trade unions, fraternal organizations, and others.

> As Generation X came of age (1965 – 1981), it became increasingly obvious that engagement was changing and a member shift was underway. . . . While declining engagement among younger generations has been a recognized and researched trend for the past 10 years and even longer, the severity of the situation is gaining momentum as the largest generation in history moves into adulthood.[13]

Briefly surveying the situation in other countries, Sladek asserts that outside the United States, "red flags [are] popping up all over the world"—for example, in the UK, in Canada where associations "have consistently identified growth and retention as top priorities," in Holland, and in Australia.

The phenomenon of membership decline is certainly not confined to the US. In Canada, membership has been falling away in many kinds of civic and voluntary organizations. In the case of churches, many are now being de-consecrated and adapted to other uses, as they can no longer maintain a viable congregation.

Not all associations are losing members, though. Ondina Love is the CEO of the Canadian Dental Hygienists Association (CDHA). In an interview, she told me that her association had been progressively gaining members every year, in contrast to a number of national associations in her city that had been losing staff and were facing declining membership. "There is a disturbing trend in the nonprofit sector," she said, "too many associations are continuing as if it's 'business as usual' and they are suffering from the lack of a well-articulated value proposition that resonates with their evolving membership base. They need to focus on the question that potential members always ask: *What's in it for me?*"

To do this, she suggested, they need to conduct market research, similar to businesses, so that they understand their market and are able to develop programs or offerings for specific membership segments. She attributes the success of the CDHA to the fact that they have been conducting this research and have responded by launching many new programs and forming new partnerships. In addition, they make extensive use of both traditional and social media to communicate with members. "It's amazing what you can do with social media—it has the potential to save a huge amount of time and energy."

In addition to traditional member benefits, such as advocacy, magazines, a journal, and professional development opportunities, members get access to both personal and professional discount programs that save them money.

The response to these programs has apparently been excellent. "Millennials, in particular, are looking for a strong value proposition—what will it cost me to join, and what do I get out of it?"

In general, it seems probable that membership fees, specifically, are unlikely to provide much relief for hard-strapped member-based organizations unless they are able to adapt to changing demographics and social values. What may provide some financial relief, however, are non-dues revenues derived from the sale of various benefits and services to members—revenues of the kind that helped to sustain Ondina Love's organization while others were losing members. Non-dues revenues take us into the domain of sales or "earned income," which, according to Statistics Canada, was responsible for almost half the revenues of nonprofits in their survey of the sector.

Earned Income

According to the cited Statistics Canada survey, "sales of goods and services are, by far, the most important source of revenue for the core nonprofit group in 2007, accounting for 45.6 percent of the total income."[14] According to the head of the US National Council of Nonprofits, the situation is similar in America, where most nonprofits secure around half their revenues from earned income of various kinds.[15]

Unfortunately, the Statistics Canada survey provided no breakdown of the types of revenue earned by nonprofits, but experience and other sources suggest that sales of goods and services probably break down into three broad categories: non-dues revenues, revenues from contracts, and funds garnered from related businesses and social enterprises. While more up-to-date data on this subject is currently not available, it is unlikely that this situation has changed in the decade or so since that survey was conducted; in fact, it is probable that, if anything, the proportion of nonprofit revenues attributable to sales of goods and services has increased since 2007.

Non-Dues Revenues

In member-based organizations, non-dues revenues embrace a wide range of services, events, and activities that will be familiar to many individuals working in the nonprofit sector. Typically, these services and activities are designed to appeal to members; they serve the dual purpose of promoting adherence to the organization while enhancing its finances. Nonprofits have become imaginative in pursuing this kind of income in recent years. Here are examples:

- conferences
- sponsorships
- training
- trade shows
- publications
- research
- member directories
- benefits programs
- bulk purchasing
- sporting events such as golf tournaments

- affinity programs (discounted products and services such as insurance, credit cards, travel, etc.)
- credentials, accreditation.

Websites have amplified the ability of organizations to pursue revenues of this kind—for example, by providing search capabilities that make it easy for members to find content on the site or to locate other members, job boards for members, or vendor listings for businesses that give discounts to members. Sponsor ads or logos on the website can provide another source of income.

Contract Work

A second category of earned income comprises contract work undertaken by a nonprofit on behalf of a client. Both in Canada and the US, governments appear to be the main sources of work of this kind. Faced with financial pressures of their own, government departments have been increasingly looking to nonprofits to help them relate to certain sectors of society, understand policy issues, or assist in the delivery of programs.

More and more, governments seem to expect nonprofits to compete for this work. Thus, nonprofits find themselves lining up against other organizations in the sector, and often against better-financed organizations in the corporate sector as well. Contracts can be for many kinds of services, such as research, program delivery, facilitation, or evaluation. This is one of several areas where the border between nonprofits and commercial enterprises is becoming increasingly blurred.

In Canada, the trend towards competition has been particularly apparent in the field of international development. In the past, many NGOs (non-governmental organizations that do international development work) saw themselves as working in partnership with the federal government. There used to be a unit in the now-defunct Canadian International Development Agency (CIDA) called Partnership Branch, to which NGOs could relate. In the past, many could anticipate grants from year to year, as long as their programs were seen to be consonant with government priorities; this allowed them to concentrate their activities on program delivery.

More recently, however, governments seem to have abandoned the concept of partnership in favour of a more commercial relationship with nonprofits. (In Canada, both CIDA and Partnership Branch have been disbanded.) This change in government–nonprofit relations, visible across all levels of government, has been driven in large measure by the zeal at both the political and bureaucratic levels for "more accountability." The consequence for nonprofits has been the need to behave increasingly like commercial firms, writing proposals for contract work and preparing multiple reports to governments documenting how funds are being spent and what results are being achieved.

A recent study in the US examined how the relationship between government and human service nonprofits[16] evolved in light of an economic slowdown.

> The current deep recession has produced serious strain on the relationship between state governments and their nonprofit social service providers. . . . At a time when demand for many necessary services—such as vocational training, mental health counseling, afterschool programs, and domestic abuse assistance—has peaked and production of many human services has moved from the public

> to the nonprofit and private sectors, the public fiscal resources previously used to support these services have reached a low point not seen for decades. Governments at all levels, stressed by budget shortfalls, have instituted cuts to programs that enlist nonprofits for service delivery.
>
> Traditionally human service nonprofit organizations have prized government contracts and grants for their abilities to legitimize the work of organizations and to stabilize revenue over a long period of time. [Today, however, there is] an increased focus on human service organizations as suppliers, as opposed to partners. The result is a system that has increasingly moved from relationships to transactions, with the implication that service recipients are more likely to see great fluctuations in the continuity of their care due to nonprofit contractors being unable to meet the terms of government contracts. . . . [H]uman service nonprofits are more likely to have to draw down financial reserves, reduce salaries, or lay off staff as their dependence on government contracts increases. . . . [G]overnment funding can potentially serve to weaken the ability of nonprofit organizations to serve their clients.[17]

While this study focused on the US, anecdotal evidence suggests that its conclusions would be valid in Canada as well. Many Canadian nonprofits seem to feel deeply ambivalent about their relationship with governments. On the one hand, they recognize that governments are an important source of revenue, one that cannot be overlooked in times of economic stress. And government dollars can enhance their ability to pursue key aspects of their mission.

On the other hand, the transition from "partner" to "supplier" status has introduced new stresses and uncertainties into their relationship with government. Moreover, this transition has been accompanied by government demands for multiple reports, evaluations, and other types of documentation. Executive directors complain that a disproportionate amount of their time is now taken up with filling out these reports, time that, in their view, could more usefully be spent providing services to clients. Different agencies, even ones from the same level of government, often require similar kinds of information, but in a different format and at different times. It can be difficult or (more likely) impossible to persuade agencies to coordinate their requests so as to diminish the burden on respondents. At the extreme, the CEO of one nonprofit told me he had cancelled a multimillion-dollar contract with a government organization in mid-term because he believed the endless requests for reports had become unconscionable, undermining the very objectives that the contract was supposed to be serving.

For the nonprofit seeking avenues to shore up its finances in times of uncertainty, governments represent both an opportunity and a challenge. The trend towards continued devolution of public services from governments to the nonprofit sector seems likely to continue. Contracts will continue to be available, though most likely offered on a competitive basis. On the other hand, the transformation of the government–nonprofit relationship from "partner" to "supplier" appears to be well established now, as is the trend towards increasing demands for accountability and its consequences. As a result of the latter trend, some nonprofits, and some commercial firms as well, now shy away entirely from contracting with governments because of the baggage that so often accompanies such contracts.

Social Enterprise

In 2002, an article in the *Nonprofit Quarterly* by Yale professors Cynthia Massarsky and Samantha Beinhacker stated, "[T]he movement toward income generation continues to build as an increasing number of nonprofits investigate and initiate business ventures."[18] This article, based on a survey of over 500 American nonprofits, reported that enterprises were being established in many fields, including "at-home eldercare services and educational classes . . . product related enterprises [that] sell merchandise such as a catering or bakery business, thrift shops and museum stores . . . real estate properties that throw off income like parking garages and leasing buildings . . . and cause-related marketing such as licensing their logo for use in a joint marketing campaign."

A decade later, in 2013, a report by the UJA Federation of New York described the emergence of for-profit organizations owned by nonprofits[19] as a growing trend in the sector.

> We understand the pressures of fundraising, and the challenges of nonprofit service delivery. We are challenged by the continued rise of operating costs and depleted reserves. We see diminished governmental support and private giving, growing competition among nonprofit organizations, and increasing demand for service. We are expected to do more with less, while producing better results and greater accountability. . . .
>
> [T]here are some practices that might be pursued to help organizations become more self-reliant. Social enterprise is one such practice. It offers a way for . . . agencies to achieve a double bottom line—to pursue their social objectives

> while generating earned revenue to reduce dependency on charitable contributions and public sector funding.

As someone who has founded both a for-profit and two nonprofit organizations, I see the transition by a nonprofit into the for-profit world as a venture into a new kind of territory. This territory may initially seem to be quite similar to the nonprofit world, but experience is likely to reveal that in some important regards, it is significantly different—for example, in terms of both the mindset and values required, as well as the business skills.

The phrase "social enterprise" is sometimes used to describe the kind of business that a nonprofit may launch. (Although, reflecting the trend towards convergence of the nonprofit and the for-profit sectors, this term is also used to refer to commercial organizations that aspire to produce social benefit as well as shareholder returns.) There are four kinds of enterprises a nonprofit may contemplate launching, as illustrated in the chart below.

C **"Internally social or affirmative"**	**D** **"Dual agenda"**
A **Commercial, no social agenda**	**B** **"Externally social"**

Different types of social enterprise

The simplest kind would be one whose objective is just to make money for the nonprofit (quadrant A)—a strictly for-profit venture that in itself has no social goal, and which may, in addition, bear no relationship to the mission of the nonprofit—for example, a parking lot. A second kind of enterprise would be an "externally social" one, intended both to provide benefits to a community while also furnishing a financial return to the nonprofit (quadrant B). A third type (C), in addition to the usual goal of financing the nonprofit, pursues "internal" affirmative action objectives; for example, by providing employment inside the enterprise or ownership opportunities for employees who are mentally, physically, economically, or otherwise disadvantaged. Finally, the "dual agenda" organization (D) seeks to achieve both internal and external benefits while also providing revenues to the nonprofit (such as, for example, a bistro serving a community that might provide jobs and training for homeless people, while channelling profits to the owner of the enterprise: a nonprofit shelter.)

Venturing into the for-profit world means respecting the principles of sound business management; a nonprofit does not get a pass on these just because it has a social mission. In practical terms, this entails developing a business plan, typically including some or all of the following:

- *Overall business description*: type of business (retail, wholesale, manufacturing, or service); target market; management team; projected sales and net income; and any unique characteristics.
- *Industry and market analysis*: substantiation of demand based on industry size and trends; growth potential of the market; typical consumers and their buying habits.

- *Marketing plan*: product or service attributes; geographic area served; production and delivery processes; pricing strategy, selling, advertising, public relations issues; competitive analysis.
- *Governance and management plan*: organizational structure; the role of the board of directors; staff roles and expertise; training; compensation.
- *Operations plan*: processes required to provide the product or service; facility; requirements for fixtures, furniture, and equipment; purchasing of inventory and supplies; cost and quality control.
- *Financial plan*: projected income statements and balance sheets (three years); cash-flow projections; capital requirements including anticipated sources of funds (such as grants or debt); fund-development strategy and timetable.
- *Risk assessment and contingency plan*: major risks and plans to mitigate them.
- *Supporting documents*: such as market data; list of product or service offerings; floor plan; capital equipment list; rent, lease, and purchase agreements; bios of key management; letters indicating line of credit or loan; or letters.

Many enterprises established by nonprofits fail because they don't develop a proper business plan.[20]

In addition to addressing conventional business-related questions, nonprofits need to confront other issues that arise precisely because, as nonprofits, they are entering new territory:

- Does the proposed enterprise bear any relationship to the nonprofit's mission and values? Will it be a distraction from the nonprofit's purpose?
- What if the nonprofit is also a charity? Would the establishment of this enterprise entail any risks to the nonprofit's tax-exempt status?
- Will board, staff, or members support it?
- What legal issues may have to be addressed with regard to incorporation?
- Is there a credible champion who will take responsibility for moving the venture forward—and is there a successor in case that individual decides to leave?
- What will be its impact on relationships with existing funders?
- What happens if both the nonprofit and the enterprise simultaneously run into an urgent need for capital: whose interests would prevail?

There are also governance considerations to address,[21] among them:

- What kind of board should be established for the enterprise, with what kinds of directors?
- What criteria should be used for the recruitment of directors?
- Should there be cross-representation between the nonprofit board and the enterprise board?
- Who should appoint the enterprise chair and other board officers?

- Should the nonprofit (as the owner) have any role in the appointment of the CEO?

- Who should be mandated to speak for the parent nonprofit in its relationship with the enterprise?

If dealing with these questions sounds like a lot of work, it is.[22]

Nonprofits are sometimes a bit naïve when it comes to the establishment of a social enterprise. They may not appreciate how a commercial enterprise, or even a quasi-commercial enterprise with a social overlay, differs from a nonprofit. They may be carried away by their hopes instead of confronting hard facts, or because pressing financial needs cloud their perspective as they press for the establishment of a hoped-for new source of income. Experts agree: the desperate need not apply.

Despite the challenges associated with the establishment of a social enterprise, the idea may remain an intriguing possibility. In a world where revenue enhancement is increasingly important, it may be an option worth exploring. However, it is best done with "eyes wide open." The following observation from Massarsky and Beinhacker is worth bearing in mind:

> [N]onprofit enterprise is a serious endeavor that requires a significant amount of research and planning. It usually requires a change or shift in attitude among board and staff, as well; many nonprofit managers lack the business skills required to launch or otherwise grow successful ventures. . . . Nonprofit enterprise is not for everybody. . . .

Conclusion

In this chapter, I have looked at the territory that lies ahead for nonprofits seeking to improve their financial picture. The analysis does not paint a very rosy picture. Each area presents its own challenges.

Many nonprofits have found that among the various sources of revenue discussed in this chapter, earned income seems to offer the greatest promise of improved financial returns in the future. However, more emphasis on this source of revenue may raise some important questions about mission and leadership, and about the sector generally. I return to this issue in the final chapter.

---

1. Harrison Coerver and Mary Byers, *Race for Relevance: 5 Radical Changes for Associations* (Washington, DC: ASAE, 2011). Other authors have echoed these kinds of sentiments—see for example Mario Morino, *Leap of Reason, Managing to Outcomes in an Era of Scarcity* (Washington, DC: Venture Philanthropy Partners, 2011), 37, 42. "[W] e are now in the midst of a profound structural shift. . . .The magnitude of the combined hit—greatly reduced funding and increased need—will require organizations to literally reinvent themselves. Incremental responses will be insufficient."

2. Heather Gowdy, et. al., *Convergence: How Five Trends Will Reshape the Social Sector* (San Francisco: The James Irvine Foundation, 2009). http://lapiana.org/Portals/0/Convergence_Report_2009.pdf

3. The importance of volunteering should not be underestimated. According to Imagine Canada, 12.5 million Canadians volunteered in 2010, almost half the population aged 15 years and over. These volunteers contributed 2.1 billion volunteer hours, translating to 1.1 million full-time jobs. See "Volunteering in Canada," *Imagine Canada* (2012), accessed August 7, 2018. http://sectorsource.ca/sites/default/files/resources/ic-research/imagine_volunteering_infographic_en_2012.pdf.

4. Statistics Canada, *Satellite Account of Nonprofit Institutions and Volunteering* (2007), Catalogue no. 13-015-X, Figure 11. Readers may wonder why more recent statistics are not available. Following this survey, the Conservative government of the day refused to authorize any further research into nonprofit revenues.

5. Jeanne Bell and Maria Cornelius, *Underdeveloped: a National Study of Challenges Facing Nonprofit Fundraising* (San Francisco: Compass Point Nonprofit Services and the Evelyn and Walter Haas, Jr. Fund, 2013).

6. Reynold Levy, *Yours for the Asking* (New Jersey: Wiley, 2008), 159.

7. Beth Kanter and Allison H. Fine, *The Networked Nonprofit* (San Francisco: Jossey-Bass, 2010), 138.

8. Abigail Payne, Kimberley Scharf, and Sarah Smith, "Online fundraising - the perfect ask?" *CAGE Online Working Paper Series* 194. https://ideas.repec.org/p/cge/wacage/194.html

9. See, for example, Levy, *Yours for the Asking.*

10. Nell Edgington, "Nine Ways Board Members Can Raise Money without Fundraising," *Social Velocity* (2012), accessed August 7, 2018. https://www.socialvelocity.net/2012/01/27/9-ways-board-members-can-raise-money-without-fundraising/

11. Author's interview.

12. Ron Knowles, George Toner, and Richard Paton, *Report on the Study of Strategic Issues In the Canadian Trade Association Study* (Toronto: Western Management Consultants, 2013).

13. Sarah L Sladek, *Knowing Y: Engage the Next Generation Now* (Washington, DC: ASAE, 2014), 5, 8.

14. Statistics Canada, Satellite Account of Nonprofit Institutions and Volunteering (2007), Catalogue no. 13-015-X.

15. Remarks by Tim Delaney, President and CEO, US National Council of Nonprofits at the annual conference of the Ontario Nonprofit Network, Toronto, November 9, 2017.

16. Human service nonprofits in the US work in these areas: crime- and legal-related, employment, food and nutrition, housing and shelter, public safety, youth development, multipurpose human service, and community and economic development.

17. Never, Brent; De Leon, Erwin, "The Effect of Government Contracting on Nonprofit Human Service Organizations," *Human Service Organizations: Management, Leadership & Governance* 38, no. 3 (2014): 258-270.

18. Cynthia Massarsky and Samantha L. Beinhacker, "Nonprofit Enterprise: Right for You?" *Nonprofit Quarterly* (Sept 21, 2002). https://nonprofitquarterly.org/2002/09/21/nonprofit-enterprise-right-for-you/

19. UJA Federation of New York, *Power Your Mission: A Guide to Social Enterprise* (New York: UJA Federation of New York, 2013), 1.

20. A planning tool that nonprofits contemplating the establishment of a social enterprise may find helpful is the "business model canvas," developed by Alexander Osterwalder. Osterwalder's work provides a very clear delineation of the elements of a business model, and raises questions with respect to each that could usefully be addressed in building a business plan. See Alexander Osterwalder and Yves Pigneur, *Business Model Generation: A Handbook For Visionaries, Game Changers, And Challengers* (New Jersey: Wiley, 2010).

21. See Tim Plumptre, Nonprofits As Business Owners: A Strategy for Sustainability? (Ottawa, 2012). Available from author.

22. Another resource that may help nonprofits moving in this direction is a CPA Canada publication, available online: *20 Questions directors of NFPs should ask about social enterprise* (Toronto: CPA Canada, 2018). https://www.cpacanada.ca/en/business-and-accounting-resources/strategy-risk-and-governance/not-for-profit-governance/publications/social-enterprise-questions-for-nfp-directors

CHAPTER 4
PEOPLE, TECHNOLOGY, & OTHER ISSUES

Literature about the nonprofit sector nearly always alludes to the financial difficulties it faces. Less often mentioned—but increasingly onerous—are its people-related challenges.

Leadership and Legislative Issues

The mission of many nonprofit organizations is focused on people and their problems, and most are reliant on people to deliver their programs and carry out their activities. But attracting and retaining individuals to do so, both at the working level and at the managerial level, isn't easy. Nonprofits have to compete with for-profit companies or government agencies that are typically able to pay higher wages and offer benefits far beyond the reach of most nonprofits.

In addition to recruitment and retention issues, the ever-growing forest of government rules and regulations concerning human resources is an added challenge. These bear upon a wide range of subjects, including employment practices, health and safety issues, human rights, privacy, lobbying, labour relations, and accountability. A small nonprofit that cannot even afford to hire a full-time accountant is expected nonetheless to conform. Just keeping up with the changes, let alone implementing each new requirement, is becoming an increasingly taxing responsibility. (With luck, such an organization may be able to attract a volunteer with expertise in HR legislation to its board of directors.)

Keeping up with legislation is an area where board responsibilities are growing: in addition to signing their names to financial statements, directors may be expected to attest periodically to the fact that their organization is operating in compliance with such legislation. Many boards may have difficulty doing this; a study published a few years ago by the HR Council for the Voluntary and Non-profit Sector[1] stated,

> Organizations in the non-profit sector are increasingly challenged by the same HR issues as organizations in other sectors – an aging workforce, falling recruitment levels and rising skills requirements. However many boards and managers in our sector lack the skills, tools and resources to address these challenges.

What draws many individuals to the sector is the inherent value of its work, the ability to address a cause they care about, and perhaps the satisfaction derived from a job where it's often possible to see how the work improves the lives of others. A related appeal of the sector is the ability to collaborate with like-minded colleagues who share similar values. But these sources of attraction may be losing some of their magnetic pull for a variety of reasons, including stress, long hours, instability of part-time work, lack of professional development opportunities, low pay, and lack of benefits.

The impact of some of these factors is visible at the leadership level in the sector. A relatively recent US article stated,

> Nonprofit leaders are leaving the sector. In 2008, a national study, "Ready to Lead?"... found that three out of four executive directors planned to leave their positions within three years. The major reasons cited were lack of adequate compensation, burnout, overwhelming fundraising responsibilities, and a fear that they would not be able to retire properly.[2]

Similarly, a 2013 study of the HR situation in Ontario's nonprofit sector found that for demographic and other reasons, half of the executive directors surveyed expected to retire in the next five years. A focus group participant in this study stated, "I have a lot of colleagues that are ready to retire and [they are] incredibly knowledgeable people and are taking a lot of knowledge with them. I think there's going to be a huge hole, and it's very concerning."

Another participant noted that most executive directors found little time to act as true leaders in their organizations: they were too consumed with managerial or administrative tasks. "We are overwhelmed with the amount of reporting, and on top of that, the funders . . . want money to go directly to the programs, but they are forgetting that we need to have an apparatus to do that. We are constantly reacting and responding . . . we are losing the battle of leadership."[3]

Other HR-related challenges were cited in this study. While the research was limited to Ontario, the issues raised seem very likely to correspond with those facing other nonprofits across both Canada and the US. One of these was the great difficulty faced by many boards of directors in measuring up to the HR leadership responsibilities inherent in their role.

> Focus groups stressed the challenges of the voluntary board structure, including high turnover, lack of training and support for board members, lack of expertise and awareness board members have about their role, and how these challenges impact their capacity as leaders. Boards hold responsibility for succession planning and hiring the executive director/CEO. However, they were seen sometimes to have limited scope and experience to effectively determine the experience, competencies and skills that are needed in the executive director/CEO role, both to lead and to move the organization forward to the next level.[4]

This issue is discussed in more detail in chapter 8, "The Challenge of Imperfect Governance."

Another issue raised in this study was the need for more leadership development for existing executives and also for upcoming executives new to the sector. Leaders surveyed identified a range of competencies that were required for them to be successful in their jobs. The highest priority needs were change management, strategic visioning, and balancing personal life and work. Others were the ability to demonstrate outcomes, social entrepreneurship, and leveraging technology. The latter were all seen as critical capabilities to help nonprofit leaders navigate in the future. With regard to the development of leadership capacity in the sector for the years ahead, the study noted, "Boards of directors are especially important players as they have the task of hiring the future leaders of organizations. Supporting their capacity in this process will be critical."[5]

Diversity

Although at the national level there are undoubtedly differences between Canada and the US on issues related to diversity, within the nonprofit sector in both countries the importance of this subject is increasingly acknowledged. It carries important implications for nonprofit organizations.

In Canada, there are several reasons diversity is an important issue for nonprofits. One is legislative: the Canadian Human Rights Act, the Employment Equity Act, not to mention the Charter of Rights embedded in the constitution all affirm the importance of various aspects of diversity. Legislation in some provinces, such as Ontario's Human Rights Code or its Accessibility for Ontarians with Disabilities Act, provides further direction.

Another reason is the increasingly diverse character of the Canadian population. Most Canadian classrooms today look radically different from those of even twenty-five years ago in terms of the social, racial, cultural, and linguistic profiles of the students. It's these students who will be—and in some cases, already are—taking over the leadership of our institutions. By 2031, visible minorities are expected to comprise almost one-third of Canada's population.

The religious profile of the country is changing rapidly as well: "The number of people having a non-Christian religion would more than double by 2031, reaching between 5.3 million and 6.8 million in 2031 compared to an estimated number of 2.5 million in 2006."[6] The Ontario Nonprofit Network (ONN) study cited above asserts, "Although Ontario is the most diverse and immigrant-rich province in Canada, the nonprofit sector is not effectively leveraging immigrants and diversity in leadership positions."

Diversity can have very practical implications on the ground. Colleen Mooney is the Executive Director of a Boys and Girls Club. At the time of writing, it had a budget of about CAN$5 million, and over 40 full-time and 140 part-time staff. They run programs in seven different locations, as well as a camp for young children. "We have 4,500 members, including many new Canadians, many Muslims and other ethnic groups. Different locations in the city have different ethnic characters." Colleen wonders about the requirement for more representation of such groups on boards like hers in the future if Clubs are to reflect the needs and culture of these diverse populations in their strategic planning. "Other Clubs in other cities face the same issues that we do."

Increasingly, respecting diversity is seen not only as the "right thing to do" but also as a sound business practice. The Royal Bank of Canada (RBC) is a leader in this domain and has been recognized as one of the country's best diversity employers. At this company:

> We define inclusion as a state of being valued, respected and involved. It is how diversity is put into action. It's about recognizing the needs of each individual and having the right conditions so that each person has the opportunity to achieve their full potential. Inclusion is reflected in an organization's culture and practices, in addition to its programs and policies. It results in individuals feeling they can bring their entire selves to work and contribute their ideas, experiences and talents to the fullest.
>
> In simple terms, diversity is the mix, and inclusion is the mix working well together. We believe diversity is a fact and inclusion is a choice we make as individuals and as leaders.[7]

Diversity has become an important value for nonprofits to embrace. A very practical reason is that a growing number of governments and other funding bodies now require grant recipients to show evidence of their commitment to it.

What does a commitment to diversity imply in practice? Some nonprofit leaders see it simply as a need to show more diversity in their staff, or in the membership of their board. However, the concept is much more all-encompassing than that; it is closely linked to two other values, equity and inclusiveness. An organization with an authentic commitment to diversity would likely see the concept permeating almost every aspect of its activities and policies. It would recognize that diversity considerations relate to such issues as gender, sexual identity, nationality, socio-economic status, skin colour, physical ability, educational attainment, age, linguistic capability, and cultural or religious identity. A commitment to diversity would need to take account of its multifaceted character.

At a practical level, when an organization has embraced this principle, diversity would probably be reflected in its strategic plan, its vision statement, and its culture. It might also appear in targets for the composition of boards and committees, in board recruitment practices, and in training programs for both board members and staff. Diversity considerations might also be reflected in communications practices (website, blogs, newsletters, job postings, job descriptions, fundraising materials, social media), in marketing initiatives, and in policies related to employees, volunteers, stakeholders, or the public. In organizations such as museums, galleries, or theatres, a commitment to diversity might affect their programming or collections and could have significant implications for their audience development practices.

In short, diversity is another very significant dimension of the ever-shifting landscape that the intrepid nonprofit and its leaders must address to maintain the relevance and legitimacy of their organization.

HR and the Board's Role

Some who write about the role of the board in people management suggest that its responsibility is limited to the appointment and performance review of the CEO. This point of view is very dated. These days, it is increasingly understood that the board cannot simply wall itself off from the human side of governance. Here are some of the main areas in which boards need to take an interest.

- Undoubtedly the board has the responsibility to select, appraise, and, if necessary, replace the CEO.
- In addition, the board, or one of its members, needs to set annual performance objectives for the executive leader. Many nonprofit boards do not take their responsibilities vis-à-vis performance management as seriously as they should. Such inaction creates a significant flaw in the organization's governance arrangements.
- A contemporary nonprofit with staff should have a set of clear personnel or HR policies. The board needs to approve and periodically update these policies or their main provisions.
- The board needs to be sensitive to important emerging issues such as diversity and ensure that its organization is taking appropriate steps to keep pace with expectations. This is not only because this

may be "the right thing to do" but also because their organization's response may have a bearing upon its ability to attract funding from governments or foundations.

- The board should recognize that issues such as morale and internal culture can have a significant impact on organizational performance. It should have both "hard" and "soft" sources of intelligence about what's going on inside its organization. Hard information would include statistics on such matters as turnover trends, frequency of grievances or complaints, or employees' use of sick leave. Soft information would be derived from directors' observations when they visit the organization's workplace (as they should from time to time) or of informal contact initiated by directors with staff (in the context of field visits or one-on-one discussions in informal settings). If the performance evaluation of the CEO includes a 360-degree assessment (inviting input from above, beside, and below), this may provide other valuable insights.

- In reviewing the annual plan, the board should approve the overall HR budget and the salary ranges for staff (not specific salaries, with the exception of the CEO's), ensuring that the organization is sustainable and comparable to peer organizations in its relevant sector. It may also set the framework for benefits, but it is up to staff to determine what specific benefits are offered.

- These days, more and more laws are being enacted on a widening range of issues dealing with personnel matters. As noted above, the board should ensure that its organization is compliant with relevant legislation.

While boards have a role to play in people management issues, they must tread carefully in this area. It's all too easy for them to tumble into micromanagement. A key player to guard against this is the board chair. I have described this position elsewhere as the fulcrum upon which sound governance pivots.[8] Ideally, the chair should be working in close collaboration with the executive director or CEO; together, it's up to them to ensure the board deals with the issues it is responsible for and, at the same time, to help it resist any temptation to get into micromanagement. As the story related about Sam in chapter 3 illustrates, it can sometimes be difficult to determine where the board's role leaves off and that of staff begins.

Lyn McDonell is an experienced consultant who has served on many boards and who has also acted in the role of executive director. She affirms that boards cannot close their eyes to the human side of governance.

> Human resources is surely a weak spot in many not-for-profit organizations given the sector's precarious temporary and contract work, thin management structures, strong competition for talent, and the retirement of senior staff expected in the next decade. Making sure that our not-for-profit organizations focus on people will help revitalize them.
>
> To be clear, we are not talking about getting involved in choosing or managing staff other than the executive director or CEO. Rather, future-focused directors will be concerned with the overall strength of the management pool—whether there is a leadership development strategy for "high potentials"; the satisfaction of employees and volunteers, since their well-being translates into the

> culture for innovation; and what type of people will be attracted to serve. . . . Good boards foster that culture; bad ones dampen it.[9]

Digital Technology

Every so often, a technology comes along that changes everything—or almost everything. "Transformative" is a word so overused these days that its meaning has been sadly diluted. Nonetheless, there does not seem to be a better word to capture the essence of the revolution ushered in by digital technology.

Historically, there have been other transformative technologies; for example: writing, the printing press, iron, bronze, glass, steam, electricity, and the internal combustion engine. A truly transformative technology displays these characteristics:

- It has a "triple bottom line," in that it has a vast impact on society, the economy, and the environment.
- It brings about profound changes in life at the individual level: it tends to change basic assumptions about what's valued in society, about how people work or live (such things as hours of work and play, modes of entertainment, use of free time, or the layout of cities or worksites).
- It shifts socio-economic relationships (there are winners and losers).

- In due course, it alters socio-political structures and conventions (because it adjusts the distribution of power, and thus, the fabric of governance).

Its effects are unpredictable, and they manifest themselves over long periods: decades, if not generations, or even centuries. They sprout up here and there in sometimes surprising ways that very often could not be anticipated. For example, the invention of writing led to irrigation in the desert in Sumeria. (Why? Because it made taxation possible.) That, in turn, made it possible for small villages to grow into large cities. Printing contributed to the overthrow of the Catholic hegemony over Europe. Electricity led to the disappearance of the domestic economy and the invention of the assembly line.

Clearly, digital technology meets all these criteria. This makes writing about it problematic, since its impacts are so vast and so unpredictable, and also because many of its effects remain to be discovered—the transformation is ongoing. Nonetheless, many impacts are already evident.

Digital technology has profoundly altered workplaces, notably through the advent of remote working and hotelling.[10] It has blurred the line between the home and the office, and it has disrupted conventional ideas about the allocation of time since, with the spread of portable devices such as computers and smart phones, it has become more difficult to define when individuals are at work and when they are not.

It is disrupting many ideas about what constitutes sound management. For example, digital technology renders previous notions of management control limitations (a maximum of eight persons, according to early theories) obsolete. It suggests new ideas about how organizations should be structured (more horizontally), about the role of managers (less hierarchical), and about the concept of authority. It raises questions with respect to accountability, legitimacy, and how control should be exercised. It's also raising many issues regarding the concept of privacy and the control of sensitive personal information, as illustrated by the major controversy in the spring of 2018 over the role of Facebook and its impact on elections and democracy.

Digital technology is altering, and continues to alter, relationships between organizations and their customers, their stakeholders, their members, their employees, and their owners. Particularly through the impact of social media, it is changing the way interpersonal relationships are developed and maintained.

It has helped to foster a rise in public expectations regarding consultation and citizens' right to be heard or to participate in important decisions. Thus, it is changing ideas about democracy and how it should work. But it has a double-edged impact on many aspects of governance. For example: on the one hand, it makes decision making more rapid and more transparent; it makes decision-related information more accessible; it makes the communication of decisions to interested parties much easier; and it lowers the cost of board meetings through the use of online technology.

On the other hand, it facilitates the spread of falsehoods about governance-related issues: why certain decisions were taken, the motivations of decision makers, or the context within which decisions were taken. Some people hide behind the anonymity of the Internet to circulate misinformation to discredit decision makers. And as a former CEO told me, the concept of confidentiality surrounding discussions in the boardroom is now virtually dead. More worrisome are recent developments in facial recognition software and artificial intelligence which are making it possible to create fake videos of individuals (such as political leaders). Such videos can make it appear as though these individuals are making statements that are untrue, offensive, or otherwise unrepresentative of their views. Apparently, it will soon be very difficult to tell a fake video from the real thing.

The digitally based technology that makes Twitter possible played a surprising role in changing the outcome of the election of the US president in 2016, ushering Donald Trump into the White House against the predictions of most political experts. This has led to important changes in American domestic policies on a wide array of subjects and it has reshaped political discourse. I would argue, as have others, that it has significantly eroded America's international stature. Overall, there is little doubt that digital technology is affecting governance in innumerable ways, but its effects are still playing out, and its ultimate impact remains to be fully understood.

Digital technology has vastly increased the speed and reach of communication, with the paradoxical result that a great increase in business productivity has been accompanied by a rise in stress among many employees and a pervasive sense of having insufficient time to cope with business and domestic life. Instead of an increase in leisure time, as was predicted when new technologies were introduced towards the end of the last century, we are witnessing its erosion.

It has made possible the accumulation of enormous private wealth and the establishment of global companies whose net worth and power significantly exceed that of many countries. How trade is conducted and how capital is accumulated and controlled have been greatly altered. It appears that the distribution of wealth in society is undergoing changes as well, the impact of which have yet to be fully understood. Power relationships within society appear to be shifting at the same time.

However, on a more superficial level, some of its effects are evident within nonprofit organizations. For example, it has changed the way in which board elections may be held, and also the way board meetings may be run, with more reliance on distance technology. Board portals—password-protected websites (or parts of websites) for the exclusive use of board members, and for the retention of governance documents, policies, and archival records—have made it possible to make the management of governance-related information both more efficient and more reliable. Possibilities for the engagement of different groups in decision making, including stakeholders and employees, have been enhanced, as have possibilities for the promotion of the organization and its services through social media. As discussed earlier, the concept of membership is changing and may require adaptation by membership-based organizations such as associations.

There is another effect of digital technology that is less than obvious, but nonetheless worrisome, and that is what Lester Salamon has characterized as the "technology challenge."

> Pressures from for-profit competitors have . . . accelerated the demands on nonprofits to incorporate new technology into their operations. . . . But enticing as the opportunities opened by technological change may be . . . they pose at least equally enormous challenges. Most obvious, perhaps, are the financial challenges. As one recent study has noted, "Information technologies are resource intensive. They entail significant purchase costs, require significant

> training and upkeep, and yet become obsolete quickly." Because of the structural disadvantages nonprofits face in raising capital due to their inability to enter the equity markets, however, the massive intrusion of new technological requirements into their work puts them at a distinct disadvantage vis-à-vis their for-profit competitors....
>
> [Technology] also threatens to alter the structure of the nonprofit sector itself, advantaging larger organizations over smaller ones.[11]

In summary, the impact of digital technology on society at large, and on nonprofit organizations in particular, continues to be profound. Much (if not most) of the turbulence referenced throughout this book is attributable to it. Like other organizations in society, nonprofits will need to be attentive to the effects of this technology and prepared to ride the waves it produces. To do this, they will need people on their boards or among their staff who are comfortable with and knowledgeable about how digital technology is changing things. Most of those people are likely to be millennials.

Generational Change: The Advent of Millennials

Millennials, or Generation Y, have grown up swimming in the ocean of digital technology, enjoying the extraordinary access to information and interpersonal communication that it provides. Much of the literature that has developed around millennials describes them in more or less homogeneous terms, a practice that some observers find questionable.

According to this literature, millennials tend to think, interact, and work differently from people who did not have this experience. They are extremely reliant on technology to communicate and are very tech-savvy. They are said to like flexibility in their work life and to favour a collaborative workplace culture. They value and expect transparency and openness. They tend to dislike, or at least to be puzzled by, hierarchy. They like to be inspired by and work in organizations that make a valuable social contribution.

They enjoy workplace socialization. They expect value for money and are very effective comparative shoppers. They will often prefer to share rather than buy and are natural networkers. They are very used to multitasking, easily frustrated if things don't seem to be moving fast and have little patience for bureaucracy. They may tend to feel that their careers should be moving forward more quickly than they are, leading to a sense of dissatisfaction despite positive attributes their current job may have.

Millennials are also said to be mobile and expect to have to change jobs frequently; this is particularly the case for those caught up in the hi-tech world. Jonathan is a millennial who works at one of LinkedIn's offices in an expensive downtown office tower, where one can find the obligatory scooters, ping pong tables, lounges, and foosball games, as well as standing desks and a wide selection of free drinks for workers and visitors. At his office, says Jonathan, they talk about a "tour of duty" rather than an employment contract.[12] The expectation is that most employees will only stay a few years and then move on; the underlying premise is that the organization contributes to the employee just as the employee contributes to the organization. "It's a two-way street," he says. The employer even helps the employee plot his or her next career move, which may not be within the company.

Some authors proclaim that this generation is radically different from previous ones in its values, its behaviours, its patterns of work, and even its cognitive ability. For example, Jeff Howe, author of one of the first books on crowdsourcing, wrote in 2008,

> [T]eens are developing radically new social behaviours and cognitive abilities. These will surely create wholesale changes to the workplace when they enter the labour force in, say, five to ten years. . . . For starters, they'll help accelerate the obsolescence of such standard corporate fixtures as the management hierarchy and the nine-to-five workday . . . [T]hese conventions are artifacts of an earlier age when information was scarce and all decisions, for the sake of efficiency, trickled down from on high.[13]

Don Tapscott, another guru of the information age, maintains that what he calls "Net Geners" share eight norms: freedom, customization, scrutiny, integrity, collaboration, entertainment, speed, and innovation. These define how they interact, work, and socialize.[14] Tapscott argues they are profoundly changing the ways in which our institutions need to function and relate to existing and potential employees. He envisages significant implications in all spheres of life: consumerism, democracy, management, education, and others. The net-gen workplace, says Tapscott, would be democratic, location-insensitive, technologically advanced, transparent, collaborative, non-hierarchical, permissive of telecommuting, open to the conduct of "pet projects" by staff, ethical, fun, and speedy, with minimal "inter-generational firewalls."

These and other authors argue that contemporary organizations need to adapt their approaches to employees, customers, and stakeholders by widely sharing information both internally and externally, by moving away from traditional organizational hierarchy, and by fostering speed in their responses to a changing environment.

It's difficult to know how much weight to accord to all these generalizations. Many have a ring of truth. On the other hand, organizations and people are different. What characterizes LinkedIn will certainly not be true of many other workplaces. It seems facile—if not presumptuous—to assume that all, or nearly all, the members of any cadre of the population will exhibit the same attitudes, values, and behaviours, or that all its members should be dealt with in the same way. Moreover, a great deal of the literature that ascribes certain general characteristics to millennials seems to be based on studies limited to the wealthier cadre of the American population—individuals who, for instance, were students at US colleges.

Millennials themselves don't like to be pigeonholed—as an experienced consultant who has worked with various members of this generation told me in a discussion, "Every time I try to stereotype millennials, one of them smacks me on the head."

Eric Termuende is a millennial and a consultant who assists organizations in understanding the workplace and becoming future-ready. According to him, generational differences are often overemphasized. Most people, no matter what generation they belong to, tend to look for autonomy, complexity, a sense of drive, and purpose in their work. What distinguishes millennials from previous generations is not some kind of shared genetic characteristic, but rather the context: their familiarity with access to information and their ability to integrate technology into their work and their lives.

Emerson Csorba is another millennial who takes an interest in the characteristics of members of his generation and their involvement in contemporary workplaces. He has reflected on the changing socio-economic environment, and how institutions of higher education in particular need to adapt. He told me he is doubtful about much of what he calls the "pop writing" about millennials: "There is little that is nourishing or insightful here."[15]

A straightforward way to get to know members of the upcoming generation and to meet their needs, both writers suggest, is simply to talk to them. Communication can solve all kinds of problems, both within the workplace and in external relationships. It's been suggested that a good start would be to challenge some members of a board to hold a dozen or more conversations with individuals who are in their twenties, asking them what organizations they admire and why, and what they see as their greatest professional challenges.

Termuende shared this thoughtful post on LinkedIn:[16]

> The most cringe-worthy statements I hear on a regular basis are when people talk about hiring Millennials. Often I hear that 'Millennials like X', 'X is how we engage Millennials', or 'Millennials are X'. The truth is Millennials are, and aren't, all of the things we generalize them to be. In Canada alone there are 7.5 million people born between the ages of 1980 and 1995. To suggest that all of them like to be treated in a certain way is a gross misunderstanding of people, as we simply can't generalize them based on year. When it comes to recruiting them, the conversation must shift from recruiting Millennials to recruiting

individuals. The age that people are born is irrelevant, as the desires and qualities we generalize them to have can be displayed in people of any age.

With respect to the impact of digital technology, while much of the future remains foggy and uncertain, several things seem clear.

- First, there is no way anyone can reliably forecast all the ways that digital technology will be changing the global socio-economic landscape, any more than someone might have predicted the impact of printing in 1439, when Gutenberg unveiled his printing press. While we do not know just what changes may occur or where, what we do know is that they will continue to take place, and at an accelerating pace. Like it or not, nonprofit leaders will need to keep their personal radars turned on to monitor how digital technology may be altering things, and to determine which adaptive measures they may need to take.

- Second, it is also clear that millennials will be playing increasingly influential roles in society in the years ahead.

- Third, millennials will comprise an ever-growing percentage of the consumer population. If a nonprofit has items to sell—theatre or museum tickets, memberships, affiliation programs, or whatever—more and more of the buyers will be millennials.

- Finally, one advantage shared by the great majority of millennials—certainly those in North America—is their access to and familiarity with information technology. This is a tech-savvy generation. Therefore, to thrive in the years ahead, nonprofits will want to adapt their strategies for recruitment, management,

> and marketing in ways that reflect this reality. (Kanter and Fine counsel, "If alarm bells aren't ringing inside of nonprofit organizations right now, they should be—loudly."[17])

How to do this will obviously vary by organization, but here are some questions to consider: Are the current leaders in your organization reasonably adept at using information technology? Social media? If not, a good point of departure would be to encourage them to read a book such as *The Networked Nonprofit*. The millennials of greatest interest to your nonprofit are surely the ones closest to your orbit. Who are the ones in your neighbourhood? How could you find out? What about Sarah Sladek's idea of getting each board member to talk to several millennials face-to-face to find out what might cause them to be interested in your organization, or what might motivate them to become a member, an employee, a volunteer, or a donor?

Do you currently have staff members who are proficient in the use of social media? What might they say about the culture of your organization with respect to its probable appeal to other millennials? Do their job descriptions encourage them to deploy their expertise on behalf of your organization? Have you invited them to provide you with suggestions about how to use social media to promote your organization's services, or to assist with recruitment?

As for the board of directors, do you have a nominating committee for your board? Has the committee been challenged to identify tech-savvy individuals, younger or older, who might be interested in serving on your board, or supporting it through committee work? If you can identify a potential board recruit who is knowledgeable about social media but who knows little about what it takes to be an effective board member, do you have an on-boarding program, such as mentoring, that might help this new recruit become a constructive contributor to board deliberations?

Outreach and Engagement

Another development that nonprofit leaders may need to take into account in coming years is the growing expectation that members of the public and organizations be consulted on important decisions that may affect them. This is a relatively recent phenomenon. Up to around the middle of the twentieth century, it seems that there may have been a greater degree of trust in public and private institutions, and perhaps more of a willingness to defer to established authority. People might even have considered it presumptuous on their part to ask for an opportunity to express their views.

The 1960s initiated a sea-change in this passive attitude towards decision making; it was accompanied by a steady decline in trust in institutions over the last half of the twentieth century. David Zussman, an academic who has studied this issue, has written that "[W]estern democracies worldwide watched public trust decline from an all-time high of more than 70 percent in the 1950s to less than 30 percent in some countries by the early years of the 21st century."[18]

Why is there a growing demand for consultation and public participation? A report by the Auditor General of British Columbia provided this explanation:

> [A] growing number of Canadians expect to be involved in . . . decisions that directly affect them. Several trends contribute to this growing expectation. One is that the

> public has easier access to greater amounts of information than ever before. Another trend is rising education levels, combined with a younger retirement age, which means that more people are willing to get involved with the issues of the day. Increasingly, Canadians . . . expect their views will be considered in decision making.[19]

Public Participation and National Governments

In 2008, Catherine MacQuarrie, a senior official in the Canadian government, wrote a thesis exploring why the decline in trust of governments had occurred. She concluded that one of the major contributing factors was a growing gulf between citizens' expectations of government and government behaviour. What we are seeing, she said, is "[a] significant change in citizens' expectations of their governments—expectations for more information, a greater say between elections and higher standards of conduct—to which . . . the present political system and style of government has yet not caught up." Moreover, efforts by the Canadian government to engage citizens more effectively, such as they were, had shown few results.

The disconnect between citizens and government has not been confined to Canada. Carolyn Lukensmeyer was a senior official in the White House when Bill Clinton was President of the United States. As a consultant to the White House Chief of Staff, she had a privileged insider's view of how the federal government's decision-making system actually worked:

> There I sat, at the nexus of our nation's major institutions, where the executive branch, Congress, the media, corporate special interests, and the Washington think tanks

> determine our policy frameworks, and I could see clearly that not one of them had the slightest interest in bringing in the public's views except through opinion polling. Further, it was clear that we were failing to make progress on the major challenges our country was facing in part because the public's voice was not at the table—because people couldn't demonstrate their will about these challenges to our governing institutions.[20]

Despairing of existing institutions' disinterest in connecting more meaningfully with American citizens, and fearful of its implications for US democracy, Lukensmeyer quit the White House. She embarked on a personal mission to use modern technology to provide a platform for dialogue and deliberation among citizens, elected leaders, the private sector, community organizers, the media, and others. Through the methodology that she developed, citizens' voices could find their way back into major issues of public policy. In due course, she founded an organization called AmericaSpeaks, which, over two decades, provided "more than two hundred thousand people in the United States and around the world a voice in decision making on the critical issues that have an impact on their lives."

Among the initiatives led by Lukensmeyer was an extraordinary citizens' forum called "Listening to the City" on the future of the site of the World Trade Centre in New York City, following its destruction by terrorists in September 2001. This brought together over 4,500 people from all communities and income levels in New York for a full day to take part in an intense and highly emotional debate. Despite the enormous commercial and political interests at play, and despite vast differences in participants' background, income level, ethnicity, social position, and age, the forum was successful in fostering constructive discourse among those present. This resulted in the rejection of all the costly proposals previously prepared by architects for the future of the site. It sent them back to the drawing board to prepare new proposals that more accurately reflected the input of citizens.

When citizens don't trust their government, democratic institutions wither. People don't bother to vote; they shrug their shoulders about public policy issues as they see little opportunity to influence them. If leaders perceive disinterest and they have little regard for citizens' views, they may seize opportunities to undermine democracy further. Authoritarian government may not be far off. In conversation, Lukensmeyer told me that a public servant once explained to her that when you lose or violate trust, it evaporates by the ton, yet when you are trying to rebuild that trust, it has to be done one thimbleful at a time. It is much easier to stifle a democracy than to establish one.

What Lukensmeyer and other pioneers like her have revealed is that it is possible in contemporary society to devise ways of giving stakeholders and citizens a chance to have their say in a meaningful way on important decisions. Perhaps, in due course, more of this thinking will find its way into our democratic institutions, leading to significant changes in processes or structures.

The need to provide a more effective voice for members of society is not confined to senior governments in Canada and the US. Examples abound of subordinate governments—provinces, states, cities—and of major business corporations and nonprofits where there is little, or in some cases, no connection, between boards and the members or stakeholders affected by their decisions. Moreover, there is often little interest in fostering such a connection. Although high-minded policies about public engagement may exist, in practice, consultation and engagement are often seen as an inconvenience and an impediment to efficiency.

Consultation by Nonprofit Organizations

Even at the level of a local community, consultation may matter. A few years ago, in the community where my family lives, controversy erupted over the prospective sale of an exceptional heritage residence to a foreign embassy, which wanted to use it for offices. The home was situated in a residential neighbourhood with a heritage designation. The city sought the views of the local nonprofit community association, which responded with a letter supporting the sale.

The letter was not based on the outcome of a forum or consultative process where members of the community might have had an opportunity to discuss the proposed sale. When the association's decision became known, many local residents were affronted. A petition of over 300 names was quickly mounted opposing the association's position. However, the board of directors refused to meet or to modify its stance. In due course, the sale was concluded, and the home was turned into offices. The heritage character of the building was somewhat degraded; local traffic increased.

Many local residents were offended at what they perceived as the high-handedness of the association; some were more upset about the process than they were about the decision itself. They thought their voices should have been heard and that they had been straight-armed by the board. On the other hand, board members thought that they had performed their due diligence and that they had given the issue careful consideration. Some wondered why community members would not simply trust their judgement. Overall, the wounds left in the community were quite deep. Had there been some meaningful prior consultation with residents, much of this might have been avoided.

In the case of membership-based organizations such as associations, there are practical reasons directors and managers may need to work harder in the future at forging strong connections with their members. The old model of association membership, where people paid their dues once a year to access a whole year's worth of benefits, won't appeal to many millennials. Increasingly, associations and similar membership-based organizations will need to listen to their members, to ask what they would like, and to get creative and devise new membership strategies in light of responses.

Is consultation always necessary? Of course not. Decision makers have to exercise judgement as to when they need to reach out and when they don't, which kinds of issues are appropriate for public engagement and which ones may not be, and what strategy for consultation would be most appropriate. Sometimes public consultation on complex issues can be unwise, as David Cameron, the former Prime Minister of Britain, may have concluded in the wake of the referendum he launched on Britain's membership in the European Union. The result, which he had surely not anticipated, was a decision to quit the Union. It cost Cameron his job and led to enormous uncertainty and turmoil, both economically and politically, in Britain.

There's Consultation, and Then There's Consultation...

One of the major concerns of practitioners and experts in consultative techniques is that so much of what passes for consultation is in reality mere window-dressing. This kind of "consultation" is often initiated by governments anxious to be seen reaching out to citizens, but not in a way that might interfere with entrenched interests or decisions already made.

Exhibit 1
The Public Participation Continuum

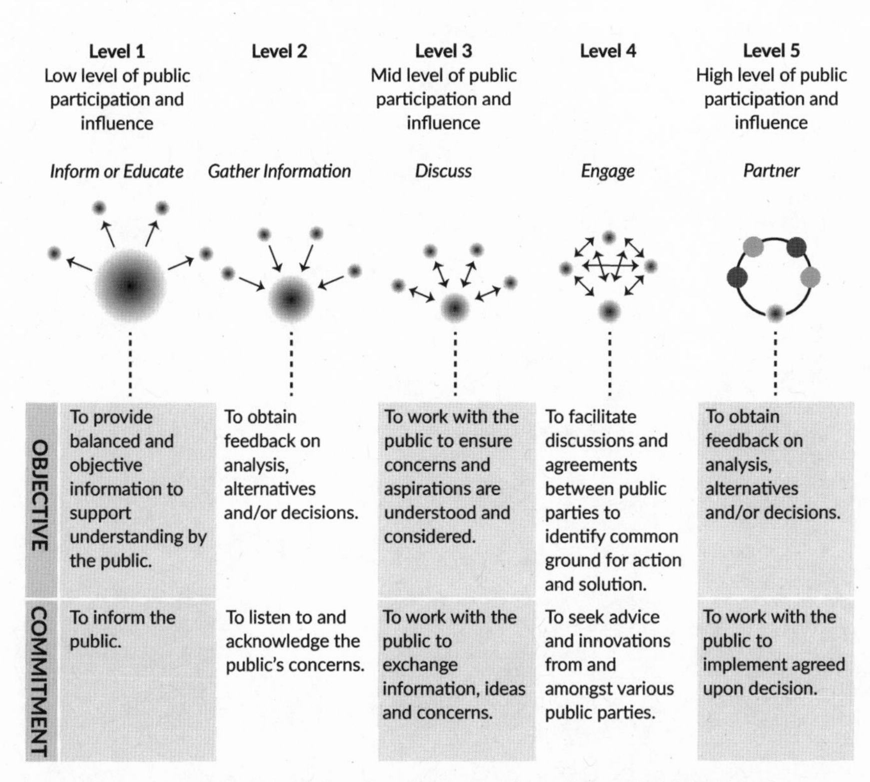

	Level 1 Low level of public participation and influence *Inform or Educate*	Level 2 *Gather Information*	Level 3 Mid level of public participation and influence *Discuss*	Level 4 *Engage*	Level 5 High level of public participation and influence *Partner*
OBJECTIVE	To provide balanced and objective information to support understanding by the public.	To obtain feedback on analysis, alternatives and/or decisions.	To work with the public to ensure concerns and aspirations are understood and considered.	To facilitate discussions and agreements between public parties to identify common ground for action and solution.	To obtain feedback on analysis, alternatives and/or decisions.
COMMITMENT	To inform the public.	To listen to and acknowledge the public's concerns.	To work with the public to exchange information, ideas and concerns.	To seek advice and innovations from and amongst various public parties.	To work with the public to implement agreed upon decision.

Source: Adapted from Health Canada and International Association of Public Participation

If some kind of outreach activity is to be undertaken, the objectives need to be clear both to proponents and to stakeholders to avoid misunderstandings and prevent cynicism among members of the public. In some cases, decision makers may simply wish to convey information to stakeholders or members. Although this kind of activity may be characterized as "consultation," it is generally not seen as genuine public participation. However, in other cases, the opportunity may be provided for the direct involvement of stakeholders in decision making. In fact, there is a continuum of possibilities; the BC Auditor General's report cited above provides one example (among many) of such a continuum.

There are many ways to gather input to a decision, including online surveys, various forms of polling, focus groups, or the engagement of independent parties such as consultants to gather information and report on the results. If there is to be an event where stakeholders are to be brought together to discuss options (as in the case of the Listening to the City event mentioned above), or even for events on a much smaller scale, this requires careful preparation and attention to detail. Many questions need to be considered, such as:

- what issues will be put on the table?
- what undertakings will be made by the organizers with respect to the input received at the consultation?
- who should be invited?
- will provision be made to include a diversity of viewpoints?
- will measures be taken to facilitate access for participants who, because of economic, physical, geographic, linguistic, cultural or other considerations, may have difficulty taking part?
- what role will decision makers play at the event?
- where and when will the event be held?
- how will the space be configured? (Yes, this affects outcomes.)

- who will guide the process? Will steps be taken to ensure that opportunities for input are balanced among different participants?
- what kind of information will be made available before or at the event?
- will any content experts be present to answer questions?
- how will the results be summarized or reported, and how widely will the report be distributed?
- what follow-up is contemplated?

Fundamentally, an authentic engagement process needs to be based on a commitment to openness, a willingness to listen and to give serious consideration to the results of such engagement in subsequent decision making. To help foster this kind of authenticity, in 1990, an organization of practitioners interested in developing and disseminating engagement methodologies was formed. A few years later, the International Association for Public Participation (IAP2) was established to affirm "core values" with regard to public participation and to provide training, certification, and other activities aimed at promoting these values. It now has affiliates in the US, Canada, and a number of other countries.

Implications for Nonprofit Boards

Often, perhaps most of the time, boards of directors may safely set their organization on a kind of cruise control. Absent any burning issues of concern to stakeholders, the organization can go forward on a business-as-usual basis. But effective leaders will know who their stakeholders are and will have their fingers close enough to the pulse of these stakeholders to know whether concerns might exist with respect to an upcoming decision. They would not always presume that no one is interested.

Thus, the trend in public expectations poses new questions with respect to the role of individual directors, of the board as a whole, and the kind of advice that a CEO or executive director might provide to a board. The directors of nonprofit organizations may not always have a very strong connection back to the community from which they are drawn, or to the members or stakeholders who elected them. If issues arise that, in the view of stakeholders, have a significant impact on interests important to them, then some form of outreach or engagement may well be required.

Here are some questions boards might consider.

- Are there sufficiently strong connections between the board and the constituencies that the organization is serving?
- What responsibility do directors have to maintain an ongoing connection to members or stakeholders—is this connection refreshed only once a year at the AGM, or might there be a larger responsibility for directors to keep in touch with stakeholders? If so, how should that be done?
- A fiduciary responsibility of board members is to be loyal to the best interests of the organization. Are these interests always identical to the interests of members or stakeholders? If not, which should prevail?
- What if the interests of stakeholders are conflicted? What process or mechanism could be used to explore areas of conflict, and perhaps reconcile differences of view?

- What values are at play around the board table? Are directors open to seeking input from members or other stakeholders on difficult issues, or is the prevalent view, "We were elected. It's up to us to decide what's in the best interests of the organization and its members"?

In summary, the world of governance is changing and churning with each passing year. Whether it's the influence of digital technology, or growing affluence, or the impact of millennials, or an increasingly competitive environment, or new legislation, there is more interest in, and often demand for, participation in decision making on important issues. As Ruth McCambridge, the Editor of the *Nonprofit Quarterly,* wrote recently:

> [Nonprofits] are living today in a brand new environment with a different set of rules for survival. Some of those rules are bound up in expectations about connectedness and responsiveness. . . . [P]eople do expect to be shown that you are LISTENING to them and at least beginning to understand where your nonprofit's purposes connect with or separate from theirs. This means you must forget all your old notions about what 'active listening' means. . . . [N]ow, you must listen even when the noise is sub rosa, a rumble of energy coming at you or deserting you. It's a whole new frontier.[21]

---

1. *HR Management Standards* (Ottawa: HR Council for the Voluntary & Non-profit Sector, 2009). http://hrcouncil.ca/resource-centre/hr-standards/documents/HRC-HR_Standards_Web.pdf The HR Council no longer exists as it was one of several sector councils wound up by the Government of Stephen Harper.

2. Simon Mont, "The Future of Nonprofit Leadership: Worker Self-directed Organizations," *NonProfit Quarterly* (March 31, 2017). https://nonprofitquarterly.org/2017/03/31/future-nonprofit-leadership/

3. Elizabeth McIsaac, Stella Park, and Lynne Toupin, *Shaping the Future — Leadership in Ontario's Nonprofit Labour Force* (Ontario Nonprofit Network, 2013), 30, 46.

4. McIsaac et. al., *Shaping the Future,* 31.

5. McIsaac, 41.

6. *Strategic Plan* (Toronto: Imagine Canada, 2016), 26. http://www.imaginecanada.ca/sites/default/files/2016_strategic-plan.pdf

7. *RBC Diversity and Inclusion: Blueprint 2020* (Montreal: RBC, 2016), 5. http://www.rbc.com/diversity/pdf/rbc-diversity-blueprint.pdf

8. Tim Plumptre, *Not a Rocking Chair: Providing Effective Leadership to Public Organizations* (Ottawa: Institute on Governance, 2007). http://www.tpaconsulting.ca/app/media/Not%20a%20Rocking%20Chair%20dr%208%20%20May%2017%2007.doc

9. The Conference Board of Canada, "Challenges Ahead in the Governance Zone," *Stewardship Review* (Spring 2016), 16.

10. "hotelling," *Oxford English Dictionary* (British & World English): "The short-term provision of office space to a temporary worker."

11. Lester M. Salamon, *The Resilient Sector Revisited: The New Challenge to Nonprofit America* (Washington: Project Muse, Brookings Institution Press, 2015), 45–46.

12. Author's interview.

13. Jeff Howe, Crowdsourcing: Why the Power of the Crowd is Driving the Future of Business (New York: Crown Business, 2008), 275–76.

14. Don Tapscott, Grown Up Digital: An Exploration of the Impact on Society of Digital Technology (New York: McGraw-Hill, 2009), 34–36, 162–69.

15. Author's interview.

16. Eric Termuende, "5 Things to Consider When Recruiting in 2016," *LinkedIn* (April 14, 2016). https://www.linkedin.com/pulse/5-things-consider-when-recruiting-2016-eric-termuende

17. Beth Kanter and Allison Fine, *The Networked Nonprofit* (San Francisco: Jossey-Bass, 2010).

18. Cited in Catherine MacQuarrie, "Putting the "Demos" Back in Democracy: Declining Citizen Trust in Government and What to do About it," unpublished research paper (Ottawa: August, 2008).

19. *Public Participation: Principles and Best Practices for British Columbia* (Victoria: Office of the Auditor General of British Columbia, November 2008).

20. Carolyn J. Lukensmeyer with Wendy Jacobson, *Bringing Citizen Voices to the Table — A Guide for Public Managers* (San Francisco: Jossey-Bass, 2013), xxxi.

21. Ruth McCambridge, "Active Listening for Nonprofits: 21st Century Edition," Editor's Note, *NonProfit Quarterly* (May 23, 2016).

CHAPTER 5
SURVIVAL STRATEGIES FOR INTREPID NONPROFITS

Today's environment keeps shifting in ways that are difficult or simply impossible to predict. The intrepid nonprofit may survive and even thrive despite this, but to do so will require initiative, imagination, and a willingness to persist when the going gets tough. It is also likely to require a strategy, or a blend of strategies, that holds the promise of success. What are those strategies?

Some contemporary writers posit that the current landscape is so challenging that nothing less than a fundamental and dramatic change to conventional structures and practices is required. Perhaps they are right. However, the executive directors or CEOs of most nonprofits I am familiar with would be very unlikely to welcome "a complete rethinking" of their organization. Reorganizations are always time-consuming and upsetting, and very often they deliver less than they promise. Also, they tend to consume a very large amount of executive time—time that would normally be devoted to running the organization. Many nonprofit boards would have difficulty according their executive director a holiday from day-to-day leadership responsibilities so that the incumbent's energies could be almost entirely devoted to a general reorganization or rethinking of the organization.

In these circumstances, it seems to me that the practical place to start may be with an assessment of the need for change: What's not working? Where are the gaps? What are the threats and challenges facing your particular organization? This initial step is one that most nonprofits would do well to take in the near future if they haven't already. "Business as usual" is unlikely to be an adequate response to a shifting, evolving business context. An assessment may or may not reveal a need for drastic alterations to existing structures or processes, but it would certainly provide the organization with a basis for charting the way forward.

Following this assessment, the organization should ask what it could do to fix problems, address gaps, or meet new challenges that have become apparent—and what approach to change would be feasible given its circumstances and resources. In many instances, a stepwise strategy may make sense, whereby changes are implemented over time and at a pace that can be accommodated while allowing the organization to continue carrying out its mission.

Furthermore, if there is one maxim about both governance and management that bears repeating, it is that there is no such thing as a "one-size-fits-all" approach. Every organization is unique, every organization's circumstances are different, and each nonprofit will need to make its own judgements about what kinds of adjustments or restructuring are necessary to confront the turbulence in its environment.

Because of this, unlike some other authors, in what follows I have resisted the temptation to assert that every organization must do this or that. Rather, I have provided below a kind of menu of approaches or strategies that I hope will be helpful to nonprofits wondering how to move ahead. These are informed by a fairly extensive review of relevant literature, complemented by over fifty interviews with nonprofit leaders, consultants, and executives in foundations or umbrella organizations for the sector, plus my own experience over at least a couple of decades.

A Focused, Clear Mission

Organizations that are coping well with this turbulent environment tend to be lucidly clear with respect to their mission and the results they hope to achieve through their work. Take the example of Pathways to Education Canada, a nonprofit organization with the following mission: "For youth in low-income communities, Pathways to Education provides the resources and network of support to graduate from high school and build the foundation for a successful future." [1] A pathway addresses systemic barriers to education by providing leadership, expertise, and a community-based wraparound program proven to lower dropout rates. Its program has been shown to diminish high school dropout rates by as much as 75 percent. The organization has achieved exceptional growth over the past fifteen years, with an ongoing record of sustaining corporate, foundation, and government support. It is a recipient of the Imagine Canada Trustmark. A study of the Pathways Program by the Boston Consulting Group in 2007 reportedly revealed, "[F]or every one dollar invested in Pathways, a $24 social return on investment was generated for the broader community."

Sue Gillespie was appointed CEO of Pathways in June 2015. One of the factors that has contributed to its success, she says, is its determination to stick to its knitting.

> What is different about Pathways is its singularity of focus. Our objective is graduating kids from high school. In the past I have worked in multi-service agencies. As a CEO I had to be a super generalist and expert at the same time. At Pathways we focus on breaking the cycle of poverty through education.[2]

She notes that it's not always easy to maintain this focus, because of the organization's success:

> Popularity can become a challenge. When you are successful, there is pressure to expand your scope of work. Pathways has been asked about our capacity to establish new initiatives to solve other challenges—for example, to establish a new Pathways initiative for integrating new immigrants or supporting university level students. We have to ask ourselves, how many programs can we support? We cannot be everything to everyone. One of my challenges is to rein in the organization and keep us on track to achieving our strategic plan and ultimately our mission and vision.

Teri Thomas-Vanos was Executive Director of Rebound for five years, an organization based in Sarnia, ON, that was started in 1984 to try to divert at-risk youth from the court system. It has since broadened out to include over twenty different kinds of outreach and engagement services, but all with the same purpose. Every year, they deal with between five hundred to six hundred young people. Thomas-Vanos advised me that over the last thirty years or so, Rebound has received gratifying recognition—they have earned thirteen awards from the Donner Foundation, they've been nominated for business achievement awards through their local Chamber of Commerce, and they've received a Peter Drucker award.[3] Furthermore, on three subsequent years, they won a "Voluntary Sector Reporting Award" from Queens University for the quality of their annual report. And they've received other types of recognition, including Imagine Canada's Trustmark.

Like Gillespie, Thomas-Vanos credits mission clarity and focus as central to the success of Rebound. "Our mission and values are pivotal to the agency. Our mission drives us, and the focus on one thing is important. I love the simplicity of the mission."

The theme of mission clarity and focus is echoed in contemporary literature about nonprofit governance. For example, Jim Collins, author of *Good to Great and Built to Last*, attributes the success of what he calls "great" organizations to several factors, one of which he calls the "Hedgehog Concept."[4] Organizations that observe this principle identify what they are passionate about, what they can do best in the world, and what drives their economic engine. Then they situate their mission in a locus consistent with all these factors. Says Collins, "The essence of the Hedgehog Concept is to attain piercing clarity about how to produce the best long-term results, and then exercising the relentless discipline to say 'No thank you' to opportunities that fail the hedgehog test."

An example of a focused, well-crafted, outcome-oriented mission statement is that of the nonprofit called Charity: Water: "Charity: Water brings clean and safe drinking water to people in developing nations." Other excellent examples are those from Teach for America ("Teach for America finds, trains, and supports individuals who are committed to equality and places them in high-need classrooms across the country."), Girl Scouts of America ("Girl Scouts of America helps young girls grow into proud, self-confident and self-respecting young women."), and the Salvation Army ("The Salvation Army makes citizens out of the rejected.").

Crafting an effective mission statement is no easy task. It can take time to develop the appropriate language. There are a lot of poor mission statements sprinkled through the nonprofit sector that fail to inspire or provide direction. Peter Drucker is one of the most famous writers about management in North America, and his insights into issues of organization and leadership are nearly always wise and thoughtful. He has made these observations about nonprofit mission statements:

> One of our most common mistakes is to make the mission statement into a kind of hero sandwich of good intentions. It has to be simple and clear. [For] a successful mission . . . you need three things: opportunities; competence; and commitment.
>
> [Ask] first, what are the opportunities, the needs? Where can we, with the limited resources we have . . . really make a difference, really set a new standard? . . .
>
> Then, do [the needs] fit us? Are we likely to do a decent job? Are we competent? Do they match our strengths?
>
> [And finally,] what [do] we really believe in. A mission is not, in that sense, impersonal. I have never seen anything being done well unless people were committed.
>
> Every mission statement, believe me, has to reflect all three or it . . . will not mobilize the human resources of the organization for getting the right things done.

> Nonprofit institutions exist for the sake of their mission. They exist to make a difference in society and in the life of the individual . . . and this must never be forgotten.[5]

The Nonprofit Hub is an "online educational community dedicated to giving nonprofits everything they need to better their organizations and communities." The Hub has developed a helpful summary of the attributes of good and bad mission statements.[6]

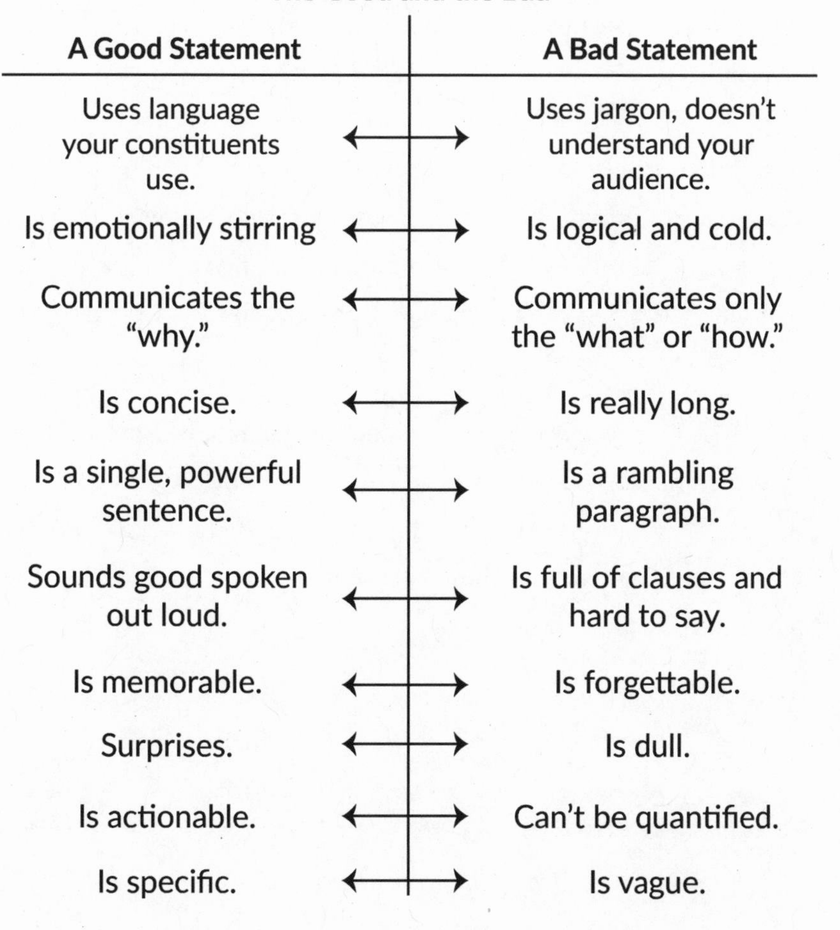

The Good and the Bad

A Good Statement	A Bad Statement
Uses language your constituents use.	Uses jargon, doesn't understand your audience.
Is emotionally stirring	Is logical and cold.
Communicates the "why."	Communicates only the "what" or "how."
Is concise.	Is really long.
Is a single, powerful sentence.	Is a rambling paragraph.
Sounds good spoken out loud.	Is full of clauses and hard to say.
Is memorable.	Is forgettable.
Surprises.	Is dull.
Is actionable.	Can't be quantified.
Is specific.	Is vague.

Being Clear About Desired Results

The nonprofit that wants to make sure its mission is sound needs to clearly identify the results it wants to achieve. To that end, it may be useful to make explicit the "results chain" that underpins its programs or activities.

Much writing about results chains and related concepts may be found in literature on international development and public administration that has been around in one form or another ever since the 1970s. In the field of development, this literature evolved because organizations that were funding projects became concerned about the lack of durable project results and insufficient rigour in project planning and evaluation. The literature to which these concerns gave rise is now very extensive, and a variety of methodologies have developed to help guide managers to become more rigorous in planning initiatives or assessing results. "Theory of change" is one such methodology. It is becoming increasingly well known in the nonprofit world. A similar discipline that has evolved in response to this need is known as logical framework analysis.

A results chain illustrates anticipated causal relationships between resources and activities over time (see graphic below).[7] Increasingly, funding organizations are expecting grant recipients to show evidence that they are familiar with these ideas and that they have incorporated them into their management.

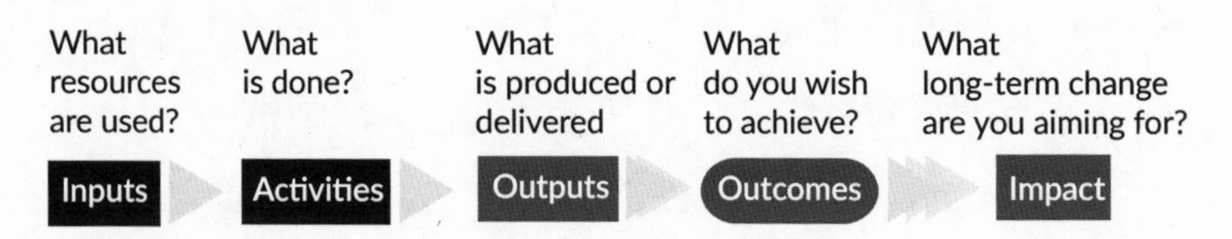

Figure 5.2 – The Results Chain

Working through a results chain or "logic model," as it is sometimes called, for a particular program or activity can be challenging. The process gives rise to questions that may be difficult to answer, such as: What is the problem that the program is supposed to address? What is the rationale underlying program design? What assumptions have been made about the causal relationships between the various steps in the chain? What durable outcomes is the program supposed to achieve? How can results be measured? What means of verification can be used, given limited resources?

The fundamental idea underlying results-based management is that, as both Collins and Drucker have stated, an organization should have "piercing clarity" as to its mission; the mission should be articulated in terms that indicate what societal change the organization aspires to achieve, and why.

The "why" is important. Having reviewed various programs during my career, I found that program architects seldom bothered to articulate the underlying rationale—that is, the assumptions that explained why the program was necessary—or the logic that connected the program's activities to anticipated outcomes. Perhaps they presumed that all this would be obvious; but even if the need for the program was obvious at the time of inception, things change over time. What was a compelling rationale for a program when it started may seem much less so a few years later. The lack of a program logic model may make it difficult to determine what assumptions were made about the relationship between program activities and desired results.

A well-crafted rationale provides a solid platform for a project or program; when one is lacking, the quality of programming may suffer because the rationale was not well thought through. In addition, evaluation becomes more difficult because there is no clear framework or logic model against which to assess results.

Nonprofit boards are sometimes unclear about their role. Here is an area where a board can, and should, make a valuable contribution to the work of a nonprofit. Board members who are serious about their governance responsibilities need to be asking questions about the "why" of their organization. Why is it there? What is, or should be, its value added? What outcomes ought to flow from its work? Questions such as these help to draw out what inspires the work of the organization. The answers will illuminate key decisions about priorities and how to deploy scarce resources most effectively.

Alignment

A second attribute of organizations that cope well, and which may even excel in this turbulent environment, is alignment. The idea of alignment is not new—it has been a theme in literature on organizational design for years. Alignment of programs or activities with one's mission is another key attribute of resilient, well-performing associations.

Alignment within an organization is sometimes expressed as the concept of "fit." Elements of the organization fit together—that is, they are characterized by complementarity and alignment. In other words, the elements are mutually supportive—there is "internal fit" among them, and in addition, they are connected to, or aligned with, the organization's strategy. The fundamental idea is that there must be coherence among all the different elements of an organization: strategy, structure, decision processes, monitoring systems, culture, communications policies, incentives, and technology. And these must, in turn, be connected directly to the organization's mission. The concept rejects the crude notion of an organization as a somewhat mechanistic, simple hierarchy. Rather, it envisages an organization as a more organic entity, in which the parts link together in mutual support.

In this concept, an organization is, in effect, a kind of miniature ecosystem in which the components depend upon and sustain each other. If a serious weakness exists in one part of the system, the system as a whole no longer performs as well as it could. The fit concept could also be seen as analogous to the idea of an orchestra, where each instrument has a separate score to play, but harmony only results when they play in time and in tune with each other.

The fit concept serves to remind executives that an organization won't naturally grow unattended into an efficient productive entity. Just like a garden, it requires planning and nurturing. An organization is a complex web of individuals, relationships, expectations, structures, systems, and beliefs. There should be a plan or vision as to how it should develop that takes account of this complexity. Peter Drucker once observed, "The only things that evolve in an organization are disorder, friction, malperformance. . . . Organization design and structure require thinking, analysis, and a systematic approach."[8]

The idea of alignment asserts that every organization is to some extent unique and cautions against mindless or random efforts to import "best practices" or "exemplary practices" from elsewhere. Just because an approach worked in one organization does not mean that it will be appropriate in another. The concept also stresses the integral nature of organizations. That is, since all elements of the organization are linked, what managers do in one part of the organization should be aligned with what is done in others. The objective, in building and managing an organization, is to get its elements working together in harmony to increase productivity. If they are not integrated, they will either drag the organization off course or dampen (or even nullify) each other's effects. The framework, or "glue," to hold the different components together and align them should be provided by the organization's mission and strategy.

If an organization does not seem to be performing well, the fit idea cautions its board or executive director not to jump to the conclusion that what is required is a reorganization—a structural change. Many managers seem overly impressed with the ability of structural change to improve the way an organization performs, and they are insufficiently heedful of how other factors may be the cause of the organization's problems.

When there is harmony among the different components of an organization, and they are well aligned with each other, the organization becomes a more integrated, efficient entity, and thus better equipped to cope with external turbulence. Think of the hull of a well-designed boat: a sleek design enables it to navigate waves and other types of turbulence more effectively.

Refocusing and Cleaning House

The concept of alignment as well as the ideas about mission discussed above have a corollary. Contrary to what some may believe, a mission should not be static. It should probably not be carved in stone. If a mission is designed to confront real needs, if it is "actionable" and actions are being taken to pursue it, then we might hope that, with the passage of time, the needs will be addressed, or they may evolve. Likewise, new, more effective ways of pursuing the mission may come to light, because of feedback from the field, because of insights gathered from other organizations, because new staff with new capabilities are recruited, because of possibilities offered by technological innovation, or other reasons.

Resources are always tight in the nonprofit world. Given the financial challenges inherent in the current environment, the intrepid nonprofit needs to make sure that scarce dollars are used as efficiently as possible. To maximize impact, a nonprofit needs to be prepared to take stock periodically of existing programs or projects and, if necessary, shed those that are less effective in favour of new ones that promise better results. That is, the nonprofit that is serious about maintaining its focus and achieving results needs to be prepared to do intermittent housecleaning, getting rid of activities or programs that have outlived their usefulness. In addition, as time passes and circumstances change, there may be a need to review and recalibrate the mission itself.

Adaptability

Nonprofits that wish to cope well with turbulence must know how to be adaptive. To be adaptive does not mean that leaders tweak the organization in response to every new trend or fad. That approach would certainly not be consistent with the idea of alignment. However, in today's environment, the mottoes "business as usual" or "we've always done it this way" won't serve as reliable guideposts.

How adaptive is adaptive enough? As noted above, to address environmental challenges, some writers argue that radical change is essential. This kind of assertion may be necessary to seize the attention of organizations that are sleepwalking towards the future. However, not all organizations are the same, and to urge all to adopt the same prescription is in my view too simplistic. The decision as to whether change is necessary for a particular organization, and if so, how much and of what kind, is one that each nonprofit must take for itself in light of its circumstances, history, resources, and capabilities. As is the case for all important decisions, judgement and wisdom are required to determine what course of action is appropriate.

Whatever degree of change is judged to be suitable, the question of timing is of central importance. A couple of decades ago, an executive or a board confronting an important decision might reasonably have thought it prudent to take a certain amount of time for discussion and contemplation. However, in recent years, the time frame for decision making may have shrunk. A lot.

Dominic Barton is the global managing partner and CEO of McKinsey & Company, the international consulting firm. In October 2016, he gave a speech on leadership to a group of senior government officials and others in Ottawa.[9] He shared results of discussions he had conducted over the years with some 2,300 executives. He had asked them how, if given the opportunity, they might advise their younger selves about decision making and leadership now. What might they do differently?

People told him that contemporary leaders have to face the fact that "dealing with crises is now a part of the job. Expect one annually that's life defining." Leaders today have to move faster on their agendas; they have to know how to drive change in an organization, with both speed and versatility. Moreover, they may find that this has to become an ongoing practice, not just a one-time event. Said Barton, "You have to know how to lean into the fire, and it's not always pleasant."

His general thesis was that the leader of tomorrow has to be prepared to be "in the arena." Effective leadership will be demanding and difficult; it will depend increasingly on character, requiring resilience, judgement, patience, persistence, and an ability to absorb blows—the ability to "get up off the ground when you are smacked down" because mistakes are inevitable. Barton also argued that in the volatile environment now facing organizations, "there's no way one person can absorb and deal with all the issues that are coming up … the notion of building a network of leaders . . . is going to be vitally important."

He did not use the term intrepid to describe such leaders, but I believe he might have.

Managing Organizational Change

Organizations that will thrive in the years ahead will be open to adaptation and prepared to actually implement change, not just talk about it—and perhaps to do so more rapidly, as discussed above. A British peer once coined the memorable phrase, "Change is a fine and wonderful thing, but let it proceed elsewhere." In my experience, the prospect of organizational change is seldom greeted with enthusiasm. Boards of directors will be challenged to foster and oversee changes that may be necessary, and they would benefit from having directors with expertise in this area.

People who have explored the literature on change will be familiar with the little bell curve below, which illustrates the dynamic usually at play when change is proposed. A few enthusiasts or leaders perceive a need and are anxious to move ahead; their motto: "Let's go!" The majority are a bit dubious; they hang back and want to be convinced before committing ("Show me!"). Then there's nearly always a rump group, the naysayers, deeply attached to the status quo, who see change as upsetting and counterproductive ("Over my dead body!")

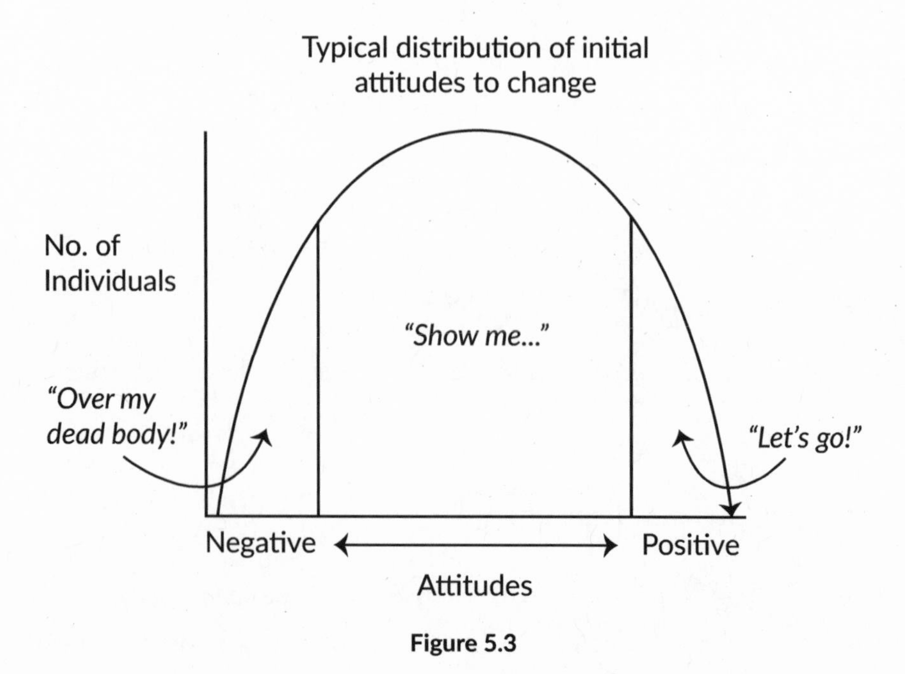

Figure 5.3

Who will lead the process of adaptation, and what elements of the organization will it implicate? Organizational change almost never happens without committed leadership, and the leaders or champions of change, at least initially, are usually very small in number—maybe one, two or three individuals. In a nonprofit, there may be a few board members—perhaps the chair and one other director—who see the need and are prepared to play this role. In other cases, leadership may come from the CEO/ executive director, perhaps supported by one or two staff colleagues.

Or there may be an alliance of staff and board members, an advantageous formula if it works, since it links governance and management. However, board members are often not close enough to the action to understand why change may be required, or they may not be prepared to commit the time necessary to analyze what degree of change is needed and to drive the process forward. In most circumstances, much if not all of the catalytic and leadership functions will fall to senior staff. The CEO who waits for the board to pick up this challenge may wait a long time, for reasons discussed later in this book.

If the organization has a strategic planning process underway, the issues raised here would normally be discussed in that context. An external catalyst such as a well-regarded past board chair or a consultant with appropriate expertise may also be helpful in getting a conversation started and sustaining it. Consideration of these matters is not likely to be a one-time event—the pressures for change will undoubtedly evolve with the passage of time.

Being adaptive may involve more than a readiness to adjust internal governance, management, or program arrangements in response to environmental challenges. The leaders of a truly adaptive nonprofit may need to look beyond their own organization and ask themselves whether, by networking, forming new partnerships, or even merging with another organization, they might amplify their ability to pursue their mission or enhance their chances of survival. These possibilities are discussed in the two subsequent chapters which invite an "outside the box" way to think about strategy in tough times.

Metrics and Managing to Outcomes

In the early years of governance awareness, particularly in the corporate sector, there was much emphasis on the fiduciary role of boards, particularly their financial responsibilities and their need to protect shareholder value. However, in more recent years, there has been a growing realization that the board's fiduciary role goes well beyond financial stewardship to encompass the overall effectiveness of the organization. For the board of a nonprofit, this means that it has to be concerned with the kinds of questions discussed above related to mission, purpose, and impact.

In the future, I believe we are likely to see growing interest in the theory of change methodology, as it directs attention to questions such as these. I also believe that forward-looking nonprofits will devote an increasing amount of attention to the development of organizational metrics that report on these issues.

I have served on several nonprofit boards and chaired a number of them. In every case, the board had difficulty coming to grips with the question: what kind of performance information do we need, and how do we use it? It is not easy to answer this question in most organizations—it takes time and careful reflection, and the circumstances are not always felicitous for dealing with such issues.

I used to chair the board of an organization with a budget of over CAN$100 million. The CEO had invested a considerable sum in the development of a "balanced scorecard." The idea was that this scorecard would report on key indicators and help the board to keep on top of important dimensions of progress. But the board had not been involved in the development of the scorecard and the directors did not understand it, nor did they make much use of it. Moreover, the organization was caught up in a major government-initiated reorganization, the purpose of which was not entirely clear. Significant changes to structure and budget were being initiated outside the control of the organization. In the circumstances, the idea of systematically tracking performance seemed academic.

Another organization whose board I chaired was a palliative care hospice. Board members were very reluctant to intrude into the sensitive and highly personal dimensions of end-of-life care; I doubt if we ever addressed the question of performance indicators as well as we might have, or should have. Perhaps we were all a bit uncomfortable about how to address the issue of metrics and, in addition, uncertain about what kind of "results" or "outcomes" the staff might have been asked to track on our behalf.

A child welfare society was responsible for investigating situations where a child or youth might need protection. When the circumstances called for it, the agency organized foster care or adoptions for young persons. Each case was subject to privacy legislation, and each was sensitive and highly individual. It was difficult to know what kind of outcome-related information board members might appropriately receive.

A choir that had been in existence for several decades was interested in improving its governance and in adopting a new strategic plan. However, the board of the choir had a lot of difficulty deciding what kinds of results it should be focusing on and how to measure them. They asked themselves: should results be assessed in terms of the complexity of the choral repertoire and the choir's ability to deal with it? What about audience size? Audience retention? What about revenue? How about the size of the choir itself and retention of members? What about choir composition and diversity (a big issue for some funding organizations)? Performance quality? How can that be assessed? Did the choir exist principally for the benefit and enjoyment of its audiences, or was its main purpose to provide opportunities for an engaging musical experience for choir members?

There were no obvious answers to these questions. Unlike commercial businesses whose objectives are clearly financial, many nonprofits, like this choir, serve multiple objectives. This increases the difficulty of arriving at a set of performance measures suited to the organization or of determining how to collect the information necessary to inform those measures.

Nevertheless, there are several reasons why, in the turbulent world that lies ahead, nonprofits will need to address the challenge of outcome measurement, despite the difficulties involved. One is that this is the kind of information that is increasingly required by funders and, moreover, that resonates with donors, particularly those from the corporate sector. The CEO of a nonprofit that has enjoyed consistent financial support from a group of major investors told me that when she took over her job, she met one-on-one with thirty key corporate stakeholders and asked them why they supported her organization. "There were really only two reasons," she said.

> One was that they were passionate about the mission of the organization—about trying to help young people. And the second was that we had always tracked the performance of the program. We had researched the ROI—the return on investment. We were able to talk the language that corporate investors understood, and we demonstrated results.[10]

Mario Morino is the co-founder and chair of Venture Philanthropy Partners (VPP), a philanthropic investment organization, and of the Morino Institute, which aspires to stimulate innovation and entrepreneurship and promote "a more effective philanthropy." He is also the principal author of a persuasive book about outcome measurement, *Leap of Reason*. Here, he states,

> Despite all the right intentions, the vast majority of nonprofits do not have the benefit of good information and tools to determine where they're headed, chart a logical course, and course-correct when they're off. They're navigating with little more than intuition and anecdotes. Only a fortunate few have a reliable way to know whether they're doing meaningful, measurable good for those they serve.[11]

Morino points out that US philanthropic organizations are increasingly insisting on performance information from organizations they fund. "The Edna McConnell Clark Foundation, Robin Hood, New Profit, New Schools Ventures Fund, REDF, and other private funders tie their investments to performance criteria." He recognizes that researching program results requires resources and he urges philanthropic organizations to provide financial support to grant recipients for this purpose.

There's another reason outcome measurement matters, says Morino.

> Drug Abuse Resistance Education (D.A.R.E.), a drug-prevention program whose advertising bumper stickers are about as ubiquitous as McDonald's restaurants, is present in more than half of US school districts, all fifty states, and thirteen foreign countries. Created in 1983 by then Los Angeles police chief Daryl Gates, D.A.R.E. is typically delivered in schools by visiting police officers presenting the dangers of drug use. The program

> has gained enthusiastic support among educators, law enforcement agencies, and the media.
>
> But there's a hitch: Numerous studies have shown D.A.R.E. to be without impact. It simply does not measurably affect drug use. There is an enormous social cost to this lack of results—the lost resources that could have been put into prevention programs that actually work, and the lost potential of children and young adults who might have been diverted from drug use by such programs.

If they want to ensure that their organization's resources are effectively deployed, the boards and executives of nonprofits need to know, insofar as is possible, what outcomes their organization is achieving. The ultimate reason for doing so is that it's integral to ensuring tangible and sustainable good for the benefit of those they serve.

In summary, for both practical and conceptual reasons, it can be difficult to engage a board in the kind of in-depth discussion of performance-related metrics that would provide the foundation of a sound reporting system. And because of cost considerations, it will be harder for smaller nonprofits to devote the time and thought to this issue that might, in principle, be desirable. However, if both public and private funders are calling for better metrics, the need for metrics will be difficult to ignore. The demands for this kind of data will almost certainly grow in the years ahead, and intrepid nonprofits will recognize this in their planning.

The logic model described earlier provides a helpful framework to inform a conversation about performance information and the feasibility of collecting and reporting it. The difficulty, and the cost of providing such information, nearly always increases as one works stepwise along the model from "inputs" to "activities" to "operational outputs" to "impacts" or "outcomes." However, the importance of the information also increases as ones moves along this spectrum, since the *raison d'être* of most nonprofits is to achieve socially meaningful results. And even if outcome measurement proves elusive, there is still great value in having information that shows whether the organization is making more efficient use of its resources, or whether its operational outputs are improving year-to-year.

Unquantifiable Information

What if the organization's outcomes seem to be too difficult to measure or quantify in a meaningful way? Collins provides an interesting discussion of this apparent dilemma.[12] He uses the example of performance assessment at the Cleveland Orchestra. "Superior Performance" would be measured by such things as emotional response of the audience, the wide technical range of pieces played, the increased demand for tickets. "Distinctive Impact" would be assessed by whether the Cleveland style of programming is copied elsewhere, or comments of local cab drivers, or how orchestra leaders are increasingly sought for leadership roles and perspectives in elite industry groupings. "Lasting Endurance" would be assessed through excellence being sustained across generations of conductors, through the donations of time and money relative to the long-term success of the orchestra, the growth of the endowment, and the strength of the organization during and after the current conductor's tenure.

I have high regard for Collins' work, but in this case, I believe he may oversimplify the challenges involved in developing metrics, particularly in the case of smaller nonprofits, or ones involved in fields such as the arts. However, he is right in his insistence on the importance of trying to address the challenge of performance measurement:

> [I]t doesn't really matter whether you can quantify your results. What matters is that you rigorously assembled evidence—quantitative or qualitative—to track your progress. If the evidence is primarily qualitative, think like a trial lawyer assembling the combined body of evidence. . . . To throw our hands up and say, 'But we cannot measure performance in the social sectors the way you can in a business' is simply a lack of discipline. All indicators are flawed, whether qualitative or quantitative. . . . What matters is not finding the perfect indicator, but settling upon a consistent and intelligent method of assessing your output results, and then tracking your trajectory with rigour.

Avoiding Overemphasis on Measurement and Accountability

The emphasis on performance metrics is not, however, without its dangers. At times, the stress on metrics has been coupled with an emphasis on accountability that is too often defined in market-driven terms. Einstein is reputed to have had a sign in his office that read, "Not everything that counts can be counted, and not everything that can be counted, counts," but this wisdom is often overlooked. Salamon argues,

> The . . . 'accountability environment' in which nonprofits are having to operate will doubtlessly [*sic*] produce many positive results. But it also increases the pressures

> on hard-pressed nonprofit managers for demonstrations of progress that neither they, nor anyone else, may be able to supply. . . . What is more, accountability expectations often fail to acknowledge the multiple meanings that accountability can have. . . . The risk is great, therefore, that the measures most readily at hand, or those most responsive to the market test, will substitute for those most germane to the problems being addressed. That, at any rate, is the lesson of public sector experience with performance measurement. . .[13]

Whatever the perils of an overemphasis on metrics, leaders in the nonprofit sector are becoming more aware of their importance. In 2013, the ONN published a report on human resource issues in the nonprofit sector. The authors asked sector leaders to identify their priorities for training and skills development. At the top of the list, cited by over 60 percent of respondents, was "measuring and demonstrating outcomes."[14]

Presenting Performance Information to a Board

A related area in which I would not be surprised to see progress in the next few years has to do with the representation of performance-related information. Most boards receive reports on finances and on other dimensions of performance in numeric form—tables and charts. In recognition of the fact that board members are busy, that they may not be very financially literate, and that most are unlikely to devote a lot of time to poring over numbers, some nonprofits have developed "balanced scorecards" or "dashboards." These tools are intended to isolate important information from more routine or run-of-the-mill data, and to do so in an easy-to-understand format. Efforts to improve communication between staff and board on strategic issues can make a valuable contribution to effective governance.

Building a dashboard well suited to a board's needs is not a trivial undertaking. It helps enormously if the board in question is able to articulate what its information requirements are. In my experience, this is often not the case. Many board members would be unlikely to understand the difference between measuring activities and measuring impacts or outcomes. Many do not even know how to read financial statements. Part of the role of the executive director or CEO, therefore, is to coach board members so that they better understand the reports that are given to them and are thus better able to take informed decisions.

Setting this important issue aside, a dashboard should satisfy a number of criteria. An effective dashboard would

- encourage dialogue about progress towards goals;
- facilitate timely identification of successes and challenges;
- ground decisions in concrete evidence; and
- illuminate relationships between different activities.

It would also

- effectively communicate high-level results;
- present data in a user-friendly format;
- create a snapshot of current status as well as trends over time;
- illustrate performance in relation to defined targets;

- highlight any out-of-the-ordinary results; and
- be based on a manageable set of key performance indicators (KPIs).[15]

It has to rest on a sound understanding of the purpose and expected results of an organization. It requires the identification of performance indicators that report on the most important aspects of performance—not just the financial aspects but also programmatic and organizational ones. An effective dashboard will help to focus conversation among both board and staff members on what really matters; it can also be a valuable tool in demonstrating to funders that the organization is progressing and that it is having an impact where it counts.

How to display information in a manner that is both attractive and informative is another question to be addressed in the design of a dashboard. Information can be reported in many different ways, and not just in conventional charts and tables. Edward Tufte, a professor emeritus at Yale University, has been described by the *New York Times* as the "Leonardo da Vinci of data" and by *Business Week* as the "Galileo of graphics." He writes about how the graphical display of information has evolved through history, and argues,

> Modern data graphics can do much more than simply substitute for small statistical tables. At their best, graphics are instruments for reasoning about quantitative information. Often the most effective way to describe, explore, and summarize a set of numbers—even a very large set—is to look at pictures of those numbers. Furthermore, of all methods for analyzing and communicating statistical

> information, well-designed data graphics are usually the simplest and at the same time the most powerful.[16]

Finding effective visual ways of communicating ideas—albeit not with quite the same elegance as Tufte—is a subject also explored in Dan Roam's *The Back of the Napkin*, which provides a business-oriented guide to visual problem-solving.[17] Given the growing recognition of the importance of metrics, it seems to me that it is only a matter of time before the ideas of writers such as these will become more widespread.

Finance: Strategic Leadership Supported by a Robust System

Many nonprofits are weak in the area of finance. A frequent complaint about boards is that the members lack financial literacy and are not able to exercise their fiduciary responsibilities adequately. In an interview, the CEO of the Ontario Trillium Foundation, Andrea Cohen Barrack, told me,

> The financial capacity of boards is often poor. We rejected a number of organizations who wished to register with our foundation because their deficit exceeded our policy. We were surprised to learn that some of these boards could not read their financial statements properly and did not even know they had a deficit. Similarly, often the board members just don't understand that fiduciary obligations also include things like employment standards, record keeping, or legislation they are required to follow.

There seem to be several reasons finances often don't get the attention they should from board members. One is the belief among directors—or the hope—that money should be someone else's business. Especially when it comes to fundraising. No one wants to have to do it. Board members think, *If I stand aside from this, surely some other person on staff or on contract will take it on.*

Another reason is a lack of self-confidence with regard to things financial. Many volunteer board members don't have expertise in reading balance sheets or income statements, in managing risk, or in knowing what kinds of financial control systems their organization should have. They don't know what statements to ask for, and they hesitate to raise questions about financial issues. I recall asking one nonprofit board, while in session, how many board members understood the financial statements distributed to them. Not one director put up a hand. But no one had ever expressed any concerns about financial matters. In this organization, as in many others, financial issues stayed on the back burner. Far back.

A related reason may be that the role of the board in respect of financial matters has never been clearly articulated. This may also be true of the role of the corporate treasurer or the finance committee. I find boards are often uncertain about these important matters; and if roles are unclear, it is unlikely that they will be performed well. This uncertainty may be due, in part, to a failure to understand the distinction between two important, related, but ultimately different functions. One is the need to articulate and implement an effective financial strategy for the organization that is tied to its strategic plan—in other words, a financial strategy that supports the execution of the plan. And the other is the need to support the work of fundraising or fund development to enhance the organization's financial position. These responsibilities are not the same.

Perhaps in the past, it has been possible for many nonprofits to limp along financially, constantly aware of the insufficiency of their resources relative to their mission, but doing their best despite indifferent board leadership, thin staff resources, or insufficient expertise among staff. However, in the turbulent environment now facing nonprofits, leaders may need to reaffirm their understanding that, in a basic sense, a nonprofit is still a type of business. It is accorded different tax treatment from a commercial business, and if classified as a charity it will be able to accept donations and grants. But despite these differences, a nonprofit still has to generate revenue, manage its expenditures responsibly, take action if it is drifting off course financially, and develop a financial strategy for the longer term. Just like a commercial business. A nonprofit does not get a pass on these requirements simply because of its classification in law.

In the uncertain future that lies ahead, the intrepid nonprofit will almost certainly want to ensure that it has a strong financial leadership capacity, supported by a reliable financial management regime. These objectives cannot be achieved through a quick fix; in most organizations, they are likely to require focused attention over a period of years. To realize them, nonprofits that have not already done so will need to move financial issues off the back burner into a high-priority position.

Building a Financial Management System

The responsibility for moving this process forward will nearly always rest with the executive director or CEO.[18] Board members are typically too transient, and it's the fortunate nonprofit that has someone on the board with the expertise, time, and commitment to drive a process that may take several years. Moreover, in the absence of a robust financial management system, strong financial leadership is virtually impossible, and building this system is the responsibility of the executive head. (That said, if there is a director on the board who has the requisite expertise and who is prepared to work hand in hand with the executive director to strengthen finances, this would certainly be a huge asset.)

What is meant by a financial management system or regime? It's useful to think of the finance function as having three components or elements.

> [There are] three functional aspects of the finance function: transactional, operational, and strategic. The transactional are the clerical tasks that support the accounting function, such as copying, filing, and making bank deposits; they require someone with excellent attention to detail and exposure to basic accounting principles. The operational are the range of accounting functions, such as paying bills and producing monthly financial statements; they require someone with strong nonprofit accounting knowledge, including managing grants and contracts. And the strategic are the systems development, financial analysis, planning, and communication about the organization's financial position; they require what we think of as CFO-level knowledge and skills. . . . Every organization needs all three functions, but organizational size and complexity will determine how much time each requires and the optimal staffing approach.[19]

If the operational and strategic functions are being performed adequately, if some basic financial controls are in place, and if the executive director prepares a budget each year that is linked to an operational plan, then much of the basis of a strong financial regime will be in place. Upon this base, it should be possible for the organization to produce the key reports that enable the board to understand the financial situation of the organization from both a static and a dynamic point of view:

- What are its assets and liabilities at any point (balance sheet)?
- Is it meeting its revenue targets and managing its expenditures effectively, and how does this year's (or month's) performance compare with past results (income or operating statements)?
- Will it have the funds it needs to continue to operate in the next few months or quarters (cash-flow projections)?

The latter report is particularly important. In many nonprofits, too much time is spent looking at the rear-view mirror instead of through the front window—that is, focusing too much on how money has been spent, rather than what is likely to happen to revenues, or how to cope with variations from budget.

The organization that hopes to prosper in coming years needs to make sure that it is not falling victim to two misconceptions about nonprofits. One is the notion that nonprofits can't earn a surplus. The phrase "nonprofit" is short for "not-for-profit corporation," which speaks to the mission of the organization: namely, that its central purpose is to achieve some kind of public good, not to maximize profits or enrich investors (as in the case of for-profit companies). Most people who have led a nonprofit know that if there is no surplus (profit) at the end of the fiscal year, the ability of the organization to carry on from one year to the next will be in jeopardy. Nonprofits have operating cash needs, just like commercial organizations. But some government organizations or foundations seem not to understand this requirement. And board members may not understand this either.

The second, related misconception is that nonprofits can't put funds aside into a reserve. Some people believe that accumulating funds in this manner is somehow inconsistent with the social mission of the organization. In fact, the nonprofit that does not have the goal of building up a reserve is likely to be in trouble in the event of a shortfall in *anticipated* revenues, an unexpected crisis, or a requirement for funds for a capital investment. Building a reserve is sound financial management. To accomplish this, the organization needs to generate unrestricted surpluses and designate a portion of any excess cash as a reserve fund, incrementally increased from year to year. This process starts with budgeting that specifically anticipates the development of a surplus; then board and staff together need to ensure that achieving that surplus is a priority.

Strategic Financial Leadership

A well-led nonprofit will look beyond its short-term operational needs to consider its longer-term goals and broader objectives—hence the need for a strategic plan. While in a changing environment, it may be necessary to revisit and perhaps update that plan more often than in the past, this plan should provide a reference point for staff and for the board itself in considering upcoming decisions. A well-crafted strategic plan should be based on a financial strategy that supports both short-term and longer-term objectives, as well as the programs and infrastructure of the organization.

An important element of a nonprofit's financial strategy is its "economic engine." From time to time, it's a good idea to ask, *what is our economic engine, and will it be able to continue powering our organization in future?* The figure below, adapted from author Jim Collins' reflections in his paper "Good to Great and the Social Sectors," illustrates this point. An exploration of this issue would give rise to these kinds of questions:

- What are the organization's current revenue sources?
- Does the current profile make financial sense, or does it simply reflect the fact that "we've always done it this way"?
- How effectively is the organization exploiting each of these sources? Could steps be taken to augment revenues from any of them? Which are most promising?
- What are the prospects for these sources in coming years? Are revenues from each likely to rise or fall?
- Would it be desirable to work towards redesigning the organization's economic engine so that its revenue profile changes?
- From a practical viewpoint, what would be involved in making such a transition?
- What might be the consequences for the organization's mission or values?

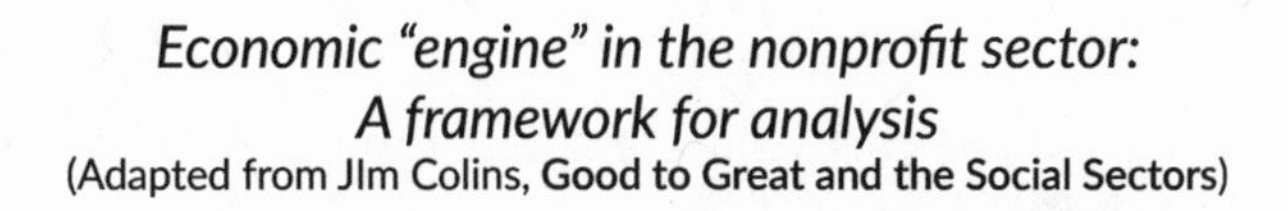

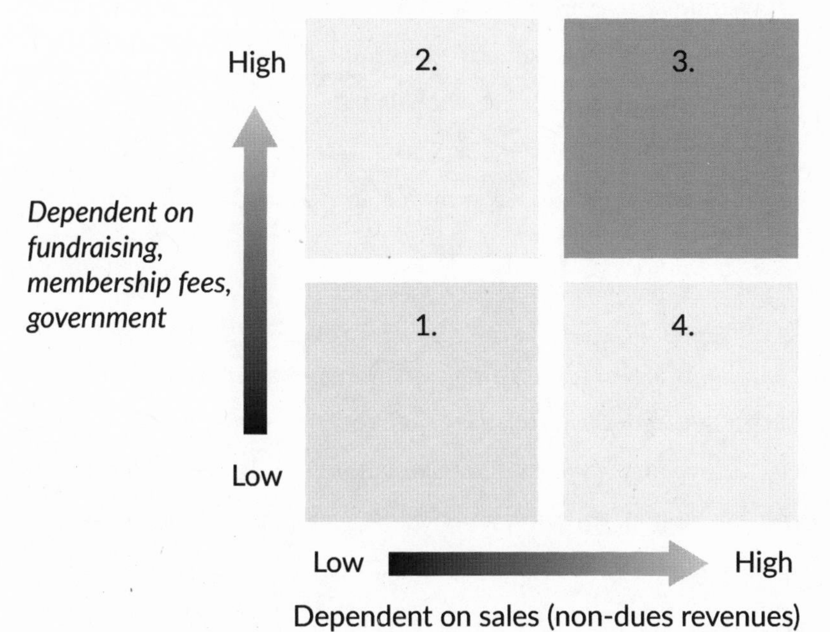

Figure 5.4

A strategic approach to a nonprofit's finances may well call for a discussion of the pros and cons of revenue diversification. Some consultants argue that revenue diversification is an important goal for all organizations, that to have only one main revenue source establishes too great a dependency. Others suggest that the pros and cons of diversification need to be weighed.

> Diversification sometimes means building a much more complex—and potentially fragile—business model. For many organizations, concentrating on one revenue source can help focus, strengthen, and build the business model.

> For example, the skills and capacity to successfully raise funds from foundations and corporations is different from special events, major donors, or government grants. Without sufficient activity in each, the business model may not be able to support the required levels of diverse skill sets. It is somewhat of a balance—a diverse revenue strategy means a diverse skill set and capacity to succeed; often not found in a common staff position or limited organizational infrastructure.[20]

Another question to explore as part of the organization's financial strategy may be its approach to fundraising, and to finances generally. Consultant Nell Edgington argues that too many nonprofits—or at least those engaged in social change that may be reliant upon donors and grants—are wedded to an old-fashioned, tin-cup approach. Some key points in her analysis are as follows:

- Fundraising in its current form just doesn't work anymore. Indeed, traditional fundraising is holding the sector back by keeping nonprofits in the starvation cycle of trying to do more and more with less and less. Really, what the sector needs is a financing strategy, not a fundraising strategy…
- Fundraising messaging moves from an emphasis on the tin-cup mentality and donor benefit to an emphasis on the social impact a nonprofit is creating.
- Money is raised to support not only the direct services that a nonprofit provides but also the infrastructure (staff, technology, systems, evaluation, training) of the organization. Nonprofits

understand that they will only get better at delivering impact if they have an effective organization behind their work.

- Other types of financial vehicles, such as loans and equity, are added into a nonprofit's financing mix.
- Earned income opportunities are evaluated and, if appropriate, launched.
- The net revenue of every moneymaking activity a nonprofit engages in (events, individual fundraising appeals, corporate sponsorships, earned income, etc.) is calculated and evaluated. Low net revenue activities are replaced with higher net endeavours.[21]

An organization's financial strategy may also require attention to the composition of the board of directors. In a turbulent, changeable environment, the need for financial expertise on the board becomes more acute. A nonprofit that may have previously adopted a fairly passive approach to board recruitment may now wish to make more proactive efforts to bring in a new director (or directors) who are better able to oversee the organization's finances.

Risk Management

This is a subject frequently associated with financial management, and it has become much more prevalent in the nonprofit sector, as well as in the corporate sector, in the last few years. The discipline promises abundant benefits. A recent article from Australia and New Zealand lists almost twenty advantages in areas such as governance, financial reporting, stakeholder confidence, efficiency, and marketplace presence.[22]

Much of the writing on this topic is concerned with financial risks. Even smaller nonprofits can't afford to ignore risks of this kind. Risk analysis in these organizations does not have to be a time-consuming, complicated exercise, but in an increasingly uncertain environment, it would be imprudent to ignore risks altogether. Here are the kinds of questions to be asked:

- Does the organization have financial procedures that provide for segregation of duties and internal controls?
- Are delegations of financial authority and signing procedures clear and properly documented?
- What are the risks associated with different categories of revenue? Will anticipated operating grants materialize this year? Is there a fallback plan if they don't?
- Are there upcoming changes in government regulations that could have cost implications?
- How likely is it that expected contracts or other sources of earned income will materialize?
- Is there sufficient cash flow to cover operations month to month? Are key staff likely to stay the course, and is there a succession plan in the event they leave?

Many nonprofits operate out of premises that are less expensive to rent, but therefore less secure than more costly offices.

- Has the organization considered the physical security of its premises and what might happen if computers or other technology are stolen in a break in?

- What if there is a fire? Are data files backed up, and are copies kept remotely?

Other risks can put an organization in jeopardy as well: conflict of interest, disclosure of confidential information, sexual harassment, or failure to observe regulatory requirements. Risks may arise from changes in the political environment, technology, competitors' initiatives, market collapse, or environmental problems—not to mention incompetent governance (malgovernance). Prudent directors and executives cannot ignore risks.

However, not all risks are bad. Risks and opportunity tend to go hand in hand. An unremitting preoccupation on risk as a hazard can foster excessive conservatism. It is often the challenge of testing one's organization against risks that can lead to extraordinary achievements; some people argue that risk is the lifeblood of creativity. A risk-averse strategy would certainly never have placed astronauts on the moon. Helen Keller was a deaf-blind activist who overcame huge odds to become an international advocate for the disabled. She once said, "Life is either a daring adventure or nothing at all." So risk may be seen as an exciting mountain to be climbed. Only by facing risks might a nonprofit explore new sources of revenue or test new ways of engaging members.

My own view is that both aspects of risk need to be contemplated. Risk management is a discipline that warrants serious consideration in today's turbulent environment. However, each organization's approach to this subject will need to take into account its size, circumstances, sophistication, and resources, as well as a range of questions such as:

- What is our organization's financial situation? If we are challenged by a high degree of volatility, or deeply concerned about short-term survival, serious risks may be all too apparent. What kind of approach to risk management will best suit us in our current circumstances?

- What attitude towards risk flows from our organization's mission and culture? What is our risk tolerance? Does the mission suggest a need to take risks? Does our organization see itself as innovative?
- Do directors and staff members share common views on this subject?
- Are there knowledgeable directors available to work on risk management?
- Who will lead discussions? The board chair? Could another director do so?
- How should responsibilities regarding risk management be divided among the CEO, the board, and staff?

This is not the place for an exhaustive review of a large subject. Organizations seeking further guidance in this area may find the references below helpful.[23]

Unexpected Resources: From Volunteers to Unpaid Staff

Sometimes the solution to a problem may come into view if one simply looks at the situation from a new perspective, or with fresh eyes. An opportunity previously invisible may begin to come into focus.

An example of this kind of shift in thinking is provided in Drucker's book on nonprofit management. Father Leo Bartel, the leader of a Catholic church, explained in an interview with Drucker how his church addressed the problem of insufficient resources by systematically transforming volunteers into "unpaid staff."[24] Some nonprofits may see little opportunity to draw community members into active supportive roles. But for other organizations, potential volunteers may be an untapped resource, in which case Bartel's approach may provide some inspiration.

He explained how his church, facing a diminishing intake of religious staff, decided to turn to lay people for help.

> [T]he volunteers of the past were "helpers." Our volunteers now are "colleagues." In fact, we shouldn't even talk of "volunteers" anymore; they are really "unpaid staff." A good many of these people are now in leadership positions in the Church. . . . [We have found that] in many respects, it strengthens and encourages and enriches the lives of the volunteers, of the folks who are coming to help.

In asking people to serve in this new kind of role, Bartel found that the biggest impediment was their perceived lack of experience and preparation. Given the opportunity to learn, they were eager to engage. So the church instituted a rigorous two-year training program for volunteers, the "Lay Ministry Formation Program."

> [W]e ... take people who have shown ability and give them the kind of training that will make them effective, give them a sense of being qualified.
>
> We hold them to high standards. We have high expectations for them. I believe firmly that people will tend to live up to the expectations that others have for them.

> And I try, as best I can, to hold high expectations for the people around me, and in many cases they seem to find this a compliment.
>
> We use many of the common management tools. Then we spend time together trying to develop and articulate a vision, articulate ideals, and articulate priorities that we can all share. We are very careful to develop opportunities for individuals to share their difficulties as well as their triumphs with each other.

Those who qualify—and there are few dropouts, apparently—are thereafter treated not as "volunteers" but as staff members. The only difference is that they are part-time and they are not being paid. But they are still held to a high standard of performance, and those who are unable to maintain that standard are either reassigned or invited to leave the program.

The nonprofit sector is sometimes referred to as the voluntary sector. I don't consider this a helpful designation—it seems to imply that most of the organizations in the sector are run by, and rely on, volunteers. Board members are of course required by law to donate their services. But the nature of the work of many nonprofits is such that they need to ensure that their staff are properly educated and trained; sometimes some form of professional certification may also be required. And some nonprofits may simply not have a place for volunteers because of their type of work.

However, there are many nonprofits where volunteers can play a useful role, and sometimes these individuals are absolutely critical to the organization's ability to carry out its mission (a local festival in the city where I live makes use of 3,500 volunteers.) In some cases, volunteers are just needed for tasks that are fairly simple or even menial, though still important. In other cases, volunteer roles may be much more substantive. Organizations that successfully rely on volunteers for such purposes are likely to have found, as did Father Bartel, that they must endeavour to create value in the volunteer experience, providing orientation and training, thereby increasing the value-added of the work and making it more fulfilling and interesting for the volunteers.

Some nonprofits trying to cope with the many challenges facing them may find it helpful to rethink the place of volunteers, as did Father Bartel. But in doing so, they are likely to find that to do this will require a fairly considerable investment of time and energy to address some important questions, such as:

- Do they have a policy regarding the recruitment and use of volunteers? Numerous examples are readily available on the Internet.
- For volunteers to play an effective role, they will need to be properly managed or coordinated. Is someone available to play that role?
- Have the roles that volunteers may play been clearly identified? Are there job descriptions?
- Is there a budget to pay the cost of any training?
- Does the organization have a structured program for volunteer engagement and development along the lines of Father Bartel's?
- What happens if volunteers fail to turn up or to follow through on their responsibilities?

- Are diversity considerations being taken into account in the selection of volunteers?
- Does the organization have policies for volunteer recognition?
- Has the risk management policy taken account of the risks that may be associated with volunteer involvement?

This chapter has outlined a range of strategies that may help a nonprofit ride the waves of a turbulent environment. These strategies are all premised on the assumption that the organization will continue along a somewhat similar track to the one that it was on previously. However, despite the possibilities offered by some of these strategies, leaders may conclude that carrying on along the same course as before, even with refinements and modifications, may not be sufficient to overcome impending challenges.

As a complement or even as an alternative to these strategies, it may be time for some organizational leaders to start thinking outside the box and consider whether their organization needs to build new kinds of external collaborative relationships, not just to survive but to become more effective in pursuing their mission. They may, for example, want to consider merging with another nonprofit. Or they may wish to build a framework of collaborative relationships with several other organizations, adopting a "network approach" to advance their work in concert with others.

I call these options "working sideways," and they are the subject of the next two chapters.

1. "History," *Pathways to Education* (2018). https://www.pathwaystoeducation.ca/history

2. Author's interview.

3. Author's interview.

4. Jim Collins, *Good to Great and the Social Sectors* (New York: Harper, 2005).

5. Peter Drucker, Managing the Nonprofit Organization, Principles and Practices (New York: HarperCollins e-books, 1990).

6. Matt Koenig, "Nonprofit Mission Statements: Good and Bad Examples," non-profit hub (2013), accessed August 7, 2018. https://nonprofithub.org/starting-a-nonprofit/nonprofit-mission-statements-good-and-bad-examples/

7. Norwegian Ministry of Foreign Affairs, *Results Management in Norwegian Development Cooperation: A Practical Guide* (2008), accessed August 7, 2018 https://www.norad.no/globalassets/import-2162015-80434-am/www.norad.no-ny/filarkiv/vedlegg-til-publikasjoner/results-management-in-norwegian-development-cooperation.pdf

8. Peter F. Drucker, *Management: Tasks, Responsibilities, Practices* (New York: Harper and Row, 1973), 523.

9. Dominic Barton, "In the Arena," speech at the National Gallery, Ottawa, October 29, 2017. See also "Dominic Barton," *McKinsey&Company* 2, no. 18. https://www.mckinsey.com/our-people/dominic-barton

10. Author's interview.

11. Mario Morino, *Leap of Reason, Managing to Outcomes in an Era of Scarcity.* (Washington, DC: Venture Philanthropy Partners, 2011). This book is widely disseminated, is available at little or no charge and it is a treasure trove of ideas and resources about outcome measurement.

12. Jim Collins, *Good to Great and the Social Sectors* (New York: HarperBusiness, 2005).

13. Lester M. Salamon, *The Resilient Sector Revisited,* 2nd ed. (Washington, DC: Brookings Institution Press, 2015) 38, 44.

14. For a further discussion of the conceptual and practical challenges associated with performance measurement for nonprofits, visit https://nonprofitquarterly.org/2015/12/08/are-we-there-yet-a-conversation-on-performance-measures-in-the-third-sector/

15. See Hilda Polanco and Sarah Walker, "Models and Components of a Great Nonprofit Dashboard," *Nonprofit Quarterly* (Spring 2016). https://nonprofitquarterly.org/2016/05/09/financial-management-models-of-a-great-nonprofit-dashboard This article provides a clear and practical discussion of what's involved in building a good dashboard, with several practical examples.

16. Edward Tufte, *The Visual Display of Quantitative Information,* 2nd ed. (Cheshire, CT: Graphics Press, 2001), Introduction.

17. Dan Roam, *The Back of the Napkin: Solving Problems and Selling Ideas with Pictures* (New York: Penguin, 2009). Amazon cited this as "best business book of 2008."

18. In the discussion that follows, I assume the nonprofits I am speaking to have some staff as well as a functioning board. The very small nonprofit with no staff faces a problem of a different order.

19. Kate Barr and Jeanne Bell, "An Executive Director's Guide to Financial Leadership," *Nonprofit Quarterly* (December 25, 2011) https://nonprofitquarterly.org/2011/12/25/an-executive-directors-guide-to-financial-leadership/

20. Hilda Polanco, cited in an interview. Nell Edgington, "What Nonprofit Sustainability Looks Like: An Interview with Hilda Polanco," *Social Velocity* (February 21, 2017), accessed August 7, 2018. http://us5.campaign-archive2.com/?u=86ea69664802a0541ae4385f8&id=c9a224fe42&e=e82f2cf20b

21. Nell Edgington, *Financing not Fundraising, vol. 1* (Austin, TX: Social Velocity, 2013), accessed August 7, 2018. http://www.fredla.org/wp-content/uploads/2016/01/Financing_Not_Fundraising_Vol_1.1.pdf

22. Risk Management – Principles and Guidelines. Joint Australian New Zealand International Standard. (Sydney: Standards Australia/Standards New Zealand, 2009). https://shop.standards.govt.nz/catalog/31000:2009(AS%7CNZS%20ISO)/scope

23. Tim Plumptre, *Governance and Risk Management: Strategies for Smaller Organizations* (Ottawa, 2015). Available from the author. A resource that presents a more comprehensive approach to the subject is John E Caldwell's *A Framework for Board Oversight of Enterprise Risk* (Toronto: CPA Canada, 2012) https://www.cpacanada.ca/en/business-and-accounting-resources/strategy-risk-and-governance/enterprise-risk-management/publications/a-practical-approach-to-board-risk-oversight

24. Peter Drucker, Managing the Nonprofit Organization, Principles and Practices (New York: HarperCollins e-books, 1990), Part 4,3.

CHAPTER 6
WORKING SIDEWAYS: MERGERS

Some believe that one reason nonprofits and charities face such difficulties is simply because there are too many of them. A senior executive in a foundation that provides much support to the sector told me, "We need to get organizations to work together." Another executive with long experience in the health care field told me, "There seem to be a lot of organizations that are doing pretty much the same thing. We need strong, effective nonprofits that benefit society; sometimes the weaker ones are not doing that in a robust way because so much of their time and energy is spent just keeping the doors open and the lights on." Other concerns include perceived duplication of effort and governance structures, and confusion among the public as to who is dealing with an issue.

In a 2015 article providing an overview of philanthropy in Canada, the co-authors from Imagine Canada stated, "[A] majority of Canadians think too many charities are trying to get donations for the same cause."[1] Some observers believe the sector is entering a period of progressive consolidation, and that the solution to at least some challenges facing the sector is for more organizations to join forces and work as one.

When Might a Merger Make Sense?

It can sometimes be hard for people working inside an organization to contemplate a merger or see how it might make sense. Traditions and attachment to turf get in the way. But clients or beneficiaries are typically unimpressed by such organization-centric considerations. They may be frustrated by what they perceive as duplication of effort and unnecessary expenses. Over time, continuing financial pressures may gradually make it evident to organizations pursuing similar missions that joining forces will not only enhance the impact of their efforts but may also simply be the key to survival.

This was the conclusion reached by two of Canada's largest health charities in 2016, the Canadian Breast Cancer Foundation (CBCF) and the Canadian Cancer Society (CCS). Donations had been plummeting—for example, CCS revenues had fallen by CAN$35 million over the course of 2016, while CBCF had experienced a somewhat similar decline in donations. As a result, the organizations' ability to deliver research funds to hospitals and universities—which they had been doing for decades—was seriously threatened. Organizational leaders concluded that a merger was the solution. The chair of the CCS board, Robert Lawrie, characterized this merger as the start of a process that would be ongoing in the health sector, pointing out that there were about 300 cancer charities in Canada, most of them small. "We will bring in more charities," he said. "Everyone has the same cost and revenue challenges."[2]

Despite the difficulty of taking a step of this kind, the possibility of a merger should ideally be looked at from the perspective of the organization's clients, just as it should be looked at from the perspective of shareholders in the private sector. A variety of questions might be asked in this regard, for instance: will this step result in improved public value? Will the combined mission of the merging organizations be more effectively pursued? Will it lead to greater organizational stability? Might a merger make it possible to dedicate proportionally more resources to program delivery activities and a lesser proportion to back office or overhead activities such as accounting, HR management, fundraising, or governance?

Are Mergers Risky?

Merging with another organization is a significant challenge, and some people think mergers are inherently risky. So risky, in fact, that they should only to be contemplated in extreme circumstances. Research indicates that this conclusion is unwarranted. However, having lived through an acquisition and merger and observed the results, I can personally attest to the importance of careful planning and the need to consider a wide range of risk factors, including "soft" ones that may not at first seem significant. Although this merger involved two for-profit consulting organizations, the conclusions to be derived from it would apply equally in the non-profit sphere.

This episode appeared full of promise at the start. Both firms were run by highly intelligent, experienced individuals. The larger firm was a big international company that specialized in pensions and benefits. It wished to expand its brand and become recognized as a full-service human resource management company. To that end, it approached a smaller firm in a related field of professional service to see if a merger might be attractive.

The smaller firm had been experiencing some financial difficulties and thus welcomed the idea of being brought under the wing of a larger, more financially stable organization. It was also attracted by the greater reach of the larger firm and its long list of established clients, both in Canada and internationally. So, in due course, terms were agreed upon, and the two companies became one. On the face of things, this appeared to be a very promising transaction.

However, within half a dozen years or so, the larger firm had failed to achieve its objective of becoming a recognized, full-service HR firm. Meanwhile, most of the professional staff of the smaller firm had gradually melted away. The process of absorption into the larger entity had been such that the smaller firm and the services that it had previously offered had become submerged. Hoped-for increases in revenues for the new integrated company had failed to materialize; indeed, the annual revenues previously generated by the smaller firm had diminished instead of expanding.

Why did this occur? One reason was that the large firm failed to do its homework with sufficient care. It thought it was acquiring a human resource management firm, but the company it secured had little expertise or track record in that domain. Rather, its expertise lay more in the areas of strategic planning, organizational change, and executive search.

Perhaps this challenge might have been overcome were it not for another difficulty: the failure to pay sufficient attention to the clash of different organizations' cultures, and to the interpersonal dynamics involved in bringing together two sets of professionals with large egos. Consultants in the larger firm, specializing in compensation-related issues, had extremely profitable practices generating large revenues. They tended to look down upon the consultants from the smaller firm, most of whose practices were significantly less remunerative. On the other hand, while the consultants in the smaller firm generated smaller returns, they thought their work on strategy and organization was more important and substantive. Thus, each group tended to look down on the other; neither wanted to be subservient to the other.

With time, perhaps predictably, the professionals of the larger firm prevailed. It was thought that leaving the smaller firm intact as a separate business unit within the larger corporation might be impractical and might defeat the large firm's objectives. So the professionals of the smaller firm were distributed through several different offices, each of which was led by a pension and benefits expert. In most cases, the smaller firm members resented this arrangement and felt that the office leaders did not understand the nature of their work, nor were the leaders very supportive of their practices. Moreover, little attention was paid to the question of incentives: while the professionals in the larger firm often had a list of long-term, established clients, they did not always perceive that it might be advantageous to introduce professionals from the smaller firm to these clients—in fact, doing so could be risky, perhaps upsetting existing well-established, remunerative relationships. Thus, with the passage of time, the professionals from the smaller firm drifted away to find more accommodating work environments. In due course, few were left.

However, it would be false to conclude from this case study that mergers are inherently risky and problematic. The more appropriate conclusion is that mergers need to be handled with care and with particular attention to "soft" factors such as values, culture, incentives, and interpersonal dynamics. Indeed, as discussed later in this chapter, there is a substantial body of literature documenting how mergers should be carried out. Gratifying results can be achieved if the groundwork is carefully laid and if the process is managed well.

Merging – But With Whom?

A merger may at times offer a good opportunity to realize larger goals, as well as dealing with problems one or other organization may be facing. But it's important to find the right partner to work with, and that is likely to take time and care. A systematic process of research may be necessary to identify what potential partners are "out there" and which might offer the best prospects for a merger.

As planning for a possible merger proceeds, the following considerations will need to be taken into account:

- Mission alignment: broadly speaking, do the two organizations seek to achieve similar, or related, impacts in the same field?

- What are the relative sizes of the two partners? A merger of two more or less similar-sized organizations may have better prospects of success than the union of an elephant and a mouse.

- Impact on programs or services: What would a merger imply for clients or service recipients?

- Geographic location and catchment area served: Are they similar or different? Complementary or not?

- Revenue sources: Different or similar? Complementary?

- Culture: Are the values, beliefs, and workplaces of each organization likely to meld easily, or will there be significant hurdles to overcome?

- Depth and quality of management: Would the combined organization have the bench strength to make a larger, more complex entity function smoothly?

- Impact on organization structure and staff: If there are two executive directors or CEOs in place prior to the merger, will one of them take over the combined organization; if not, who will do so? What will happen to the careers of the current executive leaders?

- What would the structure of the combined organization look like? What will be the impact on lower-level employees in each?

- Reputation: What will the impact of the merger be on the brands or reputations of each participating organization?

- What communication strategy will be needed to sustain the merger? Who will lead it? Will it adequately address the interests and concerns of both external and internal stakeholders? Will it be possible to implement it effectively if there is turbulence encountered in the merger process?[3]

A related consideration will be the state of the organization that may be under consideration as a possibility for a merger. Are its affairs in order? Does it maintain reliable records? What is its financial situation? Its workplace situation? Is it involved in any disputes with third parties?

From a governance perspective, there may be legal issues to be considered, particularly if one or more of the organizations is a charity. There may be restrictions on what can be done, or legal requirements that must be met if a merger is to proceed. If there are such issues, they need to be identified before more detailed aspects of planning are pursued.

Clarity of Purpose

As in the case of any significant organizational change, the likelihood of success is greatly enhanced if there is clarity around the purpose of the merger and the objectives to be attained. A lucid understanding of objectives will help to ensure that both organizations know they are going down the same road. Moreover, clarity of purpose makes it possible to ask the important question: is a merger the most promising way to achieve these goals?

In my view, the mergers that hold the greatest promise of success are likely to be those undertaken for purposes related to the basic mission of each organization, and those where there is consonance in the values each brings to the table. Certainly, there may be financial or resource management advantages to be secured through a merger. Bringing two entities together may enhance the organizational capacity of each. "A merger may allow one organization to benefit significantly from the technical, financial, fundraising and other resources of another. A more robust operational team resulting from a merger can allow for greater specialization and provide needed expertise."[4]

A merger may also be considered in response to pressures from an external funder that may make a merger a condition of continued financial support; but if that is the main motivating factor, it remains very important to identify the specific benefits anticipated as a result of a merger. External pressure from a funder does not ensure clarity of overall purpose, nor would it necessarily take into account the full range of factors to be considered before any agreement is signed.

Who's on Board?

There are often many external stakeholders whose interests need to be considered if a merger is in prospect. What about the members of the organizations in question—is this something each group of members would support? Have they been consulted? Would they be prepared to approve the changes to bylaws that would be necessary if the merger moves forward?

In addition to members of the organizations, there are other stakeholders whose interests may be affected, such as clients, partners, funders, donors, regulators, unions, professional associations, and staff. Have the views of these groups been solicited and is there provision for adequate ongoing communication to keep them in the loop?

Process Matters

The union of two organizations in Toronto—the New Heights Community Health Centre and York Community Services—to establish a new organization called Unison has been documented in two articles. One was by Jeff Chan,[5] a consultant who supported the process, and the other was co-authored by Andrea Cohen Barrack, who emerged as the head of the new combined organization prior to her appointment as CEO of the Ontario Trillium Foundation. Prior to the merger, the participating organizations agreed on what performance measures would be relevant in the merger process. These were tracked both before and after the merger. They included financial results, adherence to timetable, service metrics related to client care, and cultural metrics in the workplace. According to Chan, the results were positive on all fronts. He concludes, "Despite frequently cited studies on failed mergers and acquisitions, mergers need not be feared."

Particular care was taken throughout to make sure the community was effectively engaged, a step that in Cohen Barrack's opinion was crucial to success. Effective community engagement, she suggests, requires that there be clear objectives for the merger endorsed by both boards. In addition, it's important to determine what groups make up the community and to be open to using different methods for engaging them: "[H]aving a variety of methodologies is critical."[6] Likewise, the process used should be transparent. Merger proponents should be prepared to handle difficult issues that may come to light, for instance by agreeing in advance on principles that guide how boards will work together when such issues arise.

Northwestern University's School of Management and eight local foundations collaborated to examine twenty-five mergers that took place in the Chicago area over ten years, including a merger of two foundations. The study covered several states and over a dozen traditional nonprofit sectors, including foster care, disability, literacy, job training, and hospice care. Some mergers were driven by concerns about succession or financial problems, but not all were motivated by crises. The study "uncovered several well-planned and strategically anchored mergers that produced greater growth and more services." Its principal finding was:

> In 88 percent of the cases we studied, both acquired and the acquiring nonprofits reported that their organization was better off after the merger, with "better" being defined in terms of achieving organizational goals and increasing collective impact. To be sure, we uncovered buyer's

> remorse and founder regret among merger participants. In the vast majority of cases, however, the participants reported that the merger resulted in increased impact—the critical measure of merger success.[7]

In 80 percent of the cases, a third-party consultant or facilitator was engaged; interestingly, in over half of the cases, the merger discussions were initiated by the acquired organization. The study pointed out, "boards generally do not think proactively about mergers or merging"; often mergers are perceived to be associated with leadership failure or financial distress. Its conclusion: mergers can, in fact, deliver many benefits and deserve serious consideration.

What emerges from the literature on mergers is that great care must be taken both in planning the process and in its execution. There are numerous pitfalls: emotional baggage, cultural differences, board resistance, different organizational forms, the problem of two CEOs, costs, slowness in decision making, and others. Principles of effective change management need to be observed, and the participating parties must fully commit to the objectives and anticipated benefits of the merger. Experience suggests that an outside facilitator can often play a valuable supportive role to help drive and also nurture the process.

If a merger is in prospect for your organization, here are some suggestions for how to proceed:

- Start planning early.
- Make sure both organizations are shipshape from a financial, organizational, and governance viewpoint. Do due diligence on

the other organization: assets, liabilities, reputation, leadership, legal issues, etc.

- Consult extensively, internally and externally.
- Make sure there is a clear understanding on both sides at the staff and the board level about the purpose of the merger and the desired results in terms of client service or other outcomes.
- Recognize the importance of building trust with the other organization, and the kinds of formal and informal measures that could be taken to enhance that trust. But if trust starts to erode, be prepared to walk away.
- Try to move the merger process along briskly once it's clear that both sides want to proceed. Lengthy processes tend to be costly; they can undermine morale and erode enthusiasm.
- Agree on metrics to monitor how the process is going.
- Make sure, early on in the process, that there are no legal potholes ahead that could upend the negotiations.
- Communicate, communicate, communicate!

Resource pressures may lead to more mergers in the nonprofit sector in the future. They present particular governance challenges, as the participants work out how to replace two boards with one and decide what to do about the executive leadership of the new organization. Remember that there will be a need to replace the organizations' bylaws with a new set, and there may also be legislation related to mergers that has to be taken into account.

The Importance of Organizational Culture

The financial, legal, and process issues that arise in connection with a potential merger are all important. However, the issue of organizational culture, already discussed in chapter 2, warrants particular attention, because unlike "hard" issues such as money and legal requirements, it is less visible. Moreover, it may be perceived as "soft" and therefore unimportant. That would be a serious mistake.

Mergers that fail to take account of this factor—organizational culture—may be headed for disaster. Some organizations' cultures are similar, and if this is the case, staff in one are likely to get along well with staff in the other. Problems that may arise in the context of the merger can usually be worked out because each organization approaches issues with a similar set of values or way of thinking. However, where the cultures are deeply different, it may be only a matter of time before the merger starts to unravel.

Ever since the authors of *In Search of Excellence* affirmed that organizational culture has a strong impact on performance, culture has become a somewhat trendy concept. Its importance is reflected in two management maxims that have become popular: "Culture eats strategy for lunch," or "culture will trump strategy every time."

The problem with some pop writing about culture is that the writers don't really define what they are talking about. The concept can be a bit hard to grasp. A management concept that is ill-defined does not provide a useful guidepost and is quite likely to lead to misunderstanding or miscommunication—certainly not something one wants to encounter in the context of a merger.

One of the most thoughtful exponents of culture is Edgar Schein, a former professor emeritus of management at MIT, and the author of *Organizational Culture and Leadership,* a book many regard as the bible on this subject. Some people think they can get a grip on culture by circulating a survey asking employees questions about it. Schein dismisses this as superficial and ineffective. "Members of the organization cannot really tell you what their culture is, any more than fish, if they could talk, could tell you what water is."[8]

According to him, culture is manifest in three dimensions of the organization. First, there are what he calls its "cultural artefacts"—things like architecture, furniture, language, or dress codes. These may be striking to an outside observer but are often just taken for granted by (and are more or less invisible to) those who work in the organization.

Second, there are the "espoused values" of the organization—what the organization's leaders say is important and drives behaviour. Sometimes these may serve as guideposts for decision making and for workplace activity. But often, even though one may find them chiselled into marble in the foyer of an organization's building, or handsomely framed on a wall, they may bear little relationship to how things actually work. Statements such as "Customers come first" or "Our employees are our most valuable asset" may be a long way from what happens at the coalface. What leaders *think* the organizational values are and how values *actually* manifest themselves in practice may be miles apart. Thus, asking managers what organizational values are may not provide information of much value. Indeed, information acquired in this way may even be misleading.

The third and most important dimension of culture lies in what Schein calls a pattern of "underlying assumptions"—unconscious, taken-for-granted beliefs, perceptions, thoughts, and feelings that have been learned by employees as the "correct way" to think and behave in their daily organizational life. These assumptions are viewed, implicitly if not explicitly, as the reasons for the organization's survival or success. They are typically undiscerned, but they have a profound impact on organizational behaviour.

There is no inherently right or wrong culture, except insofar as culture may support or impede an organization's pursuit of its mission.

It might be helpful to think of organizational culture as somewhat analogous to an individual's character. Each of us learns lessons about life and relationships as we mature, and we adopt certain beliefs about how to live our lives, though not always consciously. These shape our character, which in turn affects how we behave, make decisions, and interact with others. Yet many of us may not be very aware of what our character is, or how it is manifest to others. As the Scottish poet Robbie Burns once wrote, "O wad some Pow'r the giftie gie us/To see ourselves as ithers see us!"[9]

Some "experts" like to recommend that organizations embark on cultural change initiatives. Newly appointed executives often announce that they plan to "fix" the prevalent culture. It is in fact very difficult to change the culture of an organization, just as it would be very difficult to change a person's character. The underlying assumptions Schein alludes to are deeply rooted, and they provide meaning, stability, and predictability for employees. Employees typically dislike the uncertainty or chaos that may accompany profound change. Schein advises that boards and executives should make sure they understand what they are getting into if they think a cultural shift is necessary, and that they are clear on how time-consuming and potentially disruptive such an initiative may be.

My friend and periodic collaborator, Donald Hall, teaches a course on corporate culture at a local university. To help his students understand this subject, he invites them to think about an organization they are familiar with, such as McDonald's or Apple or Walmart, and then ask themselves questions about that organization based on Schein's framework, such as:

- In this organization, what is the basis for judging that something is true, for making decisions? Tradition (we've always done it this way)? What the boss says? Research results? What works?
- What's the organization's relationship to its market? Does it lead or follow?
- How does it deal with time? Is it past-, present-, or future-oriented? Does it have a short- or long-term perspective? What's the length of accountability cycles (how long before results are due, or work is checked)? What is more important, meeting deadlines or maximizing quality?
- What are the assumptions about human nature? Are people (employees, partners, associates) to be trusted (good) or do they need to be closely controlled (untrustworthy, unreliable)? Are they changeable or unchangeable?
- What are assumptions about the ideal social order and internal structure? Hierarchy? Group consensus? Work teams? Individualism?

The answers to these kinds of questions, taken together, can go a long way towards understanding an organization's culture. This may be seen as part of the intellectual toolkit with which directors should be equipped, particularly if a merger is under consideration. Culture provides a lens that can help them to figure out what drives an organization and why it behaves as it does. It can suggest how an organization is likely to respond when faced with certain challenges or risks, or when organizational leaders are proposing to blend their organization with another.

In an era where everyone talks about constant change, culture provides insight into which kinds of changes are more likely to succeed and which ones may run into difficulties because the culture does not support them. It can help a board make decisions on strategic issues. It can furnish insight into the kind of leadership the organization may require—especially helpful if the appointment of a new CEO or executive director is in prospect. An understanding of culture, even at a fairly superficial level, can also help board members to know how to respond if it is proposed to them (perhaps by the CEO, perhaps by a colleague on the board) that "something must be done" about the organization's culture.

Mergers are complex, challenging initiatives and they raise significant governance issues. When organizations merge, two sets of underlying beliefs and assumptions are brought together. Where these assumptions are more or less harmonious, prospects for the merger may be good. However, when the cultures are different or even inimical, it is almost guaranteed that there will be challenges. They will need to be addressed if the merger is to proceed smoothly.

---

1. David Lasby and Cathy Barr, "Giving in Canada: Strong Philanthropic Traditions Supporting a Large Nonprofit Sector," in *The Palgrave Handbook of Global Philanthropy*, eds. Pamala Wiepking and Femida Handy (London: Palgrave, Macmillan, 2015), 41.

2. Eric Reguly, "Merger of Two Major Charities," *The Globe and Mail* (February 2, 2017), 1–2.

3. Mark Blumberg and Andrea Cohen Barrack, *20 Questions Directors of Not-for-Profit Organizations Should Ask about Mergers* (Toronto: Chartered Professional Accountants Canada, 2016), 14.

4. Blumberg & Barrack, *20 questions,* 4.

5. Jeff Chan, "Avoiding 'Culture Rejection' in Healthcare Mergers and Acquisitions," *Healthcare Quarterly* 16, no. 1 (2013).

6. Andrea Cohen, Lee Fairclough, and Janak Jass, "Optimizing Community and Stakeholder Engagement in a Merger of Community Health Centres," *Healthcare Management Forum,* Winter 2011, 193 ff.

7. Don Haider, "Nonprofit Mergers that Work," *Stanford Social Innovation Review* (March 2, 2017). https://ssir.org/articles/entry/nonprofit_mergers_that_work. Prof. Haider is an emeritus professor of strategy at the Kellogg School of Management, Northwestern University, and has served as director of the Center for Nonprofit Management.

8. Edgar H. Schein, *The Corporate Culture Survival Guide* (Hoboken, NJ: Wiley, 1999), 27–28.

9. "Would some Power give us the gift to see ourselves as other see us." Robert Burns, "To A Louse, On Seeing One on a Lady's Bonnet, at Church," *Complete Works* (1786), accessed August 7, 2018. http://www.robertburns.org/works/97.shtml

CHAPTER 7
WORKING SIDEWAYS: A NETWORKED APPROACH

New Ideas About Achieving Results

In the last decade or two, some new ideas about leadership and how to render organizations more effective have been appearing in the literature related to nonprofit organizations. These have emerged for a number of reasons. One of the most important has been frustration with the fact that complex, large-scale social problems have persisted from year to year. These appeared immune to the efforts of nonprofits employing conventional management techniques to resolve them.

However, in recent years, researchers, consultants, and others have been publishing case studies that offer new insights into how to tackle such issues and achieve more enduring results. A recurring theme has been an emphasis on external relationship building, collaboration, shared decision making, and networking. Contributing to the emergence of these ideas has almost certainly been a growing appreciation of the power of the Internet to facilitate communication and foster collaboration among organizations and individuals, including those a long distance apart.

A good deal of the discussion about these new strategies for leadership relates to large-scale systemic problems, but there are also suggestions that these strategies may be equally applicable to more local, smaller-scale issues. In the following paragraphs, I'll outline a few case studies found in this literature; I will then examine in more depth the essential elements of the leadership strategies in question. I'll conclude this chapter with observations on these strategies, and some reflections on whether a networking approach to problem solving might be suitable for your organization.

Examples and Case Studies

Writing in 2015, Jane Wei-Skillern and two co-authors in the *Stanford Social Innovation Review* applied the label "network entrepreneur" to nonprofit leaders who have applied imaginative, outward-focused approaches to problem solving. "The new leaders at the heart of some of today's most sophisticated, large-scale solutions to the world's social problems—network entrepreneurs—are undoubtedly some of the most accomplished leaders that you've never heard of, and they are ensuring that systems-level, collaborative efforts not only succeed, but thrive."[1]

As an example of what an effective network entrepreneur can achieve, they point to the work of Yousry Makar, national director of Habitat for Humanity Egypt (HFHE):

> Whereas a typical Habitat for Humanity country program produces around 200 houses each year, HFHE has on average built some 1,000 houses annually, for a total of more than 8,000 houses in just eight years. At the same

> time, HFHE has transformed the communities in which it works by collaborating with local organizations to address the root causes of poverty and homelessness. . . . It has replaced the traditional nonprofit focus on internal activities such as fundraising, staff recruitment, and program development with an external focus on building its network.

Another example is Women's World Banking (WWB). Founded in 1976, WWB seeks to expand the economic assets, participation, and power of low-income women. According to Wei-Skillern and her colleagues, when Nancy Barry assumed leadership in 1990, the organization was reaching approximately 50,000 clients and lent US$25 million through a network of affiliates. To deliver on its mission, Barry decided to grow the WWB network to include more independent microfinance institutions, such as ASA in Bangladesh, as well as banks, such as Shorebank in the United States, with these results:

> By 2003, WWB's expanded network gave 18 million people worldwide $8.5 billion in direct credit services. . . . WWB gives its network members the services for which scale improves efficiency, such as technical and financial services, market research, and loan guarantees. It teaches affiliates best practices. And it advocates better microfinance policies. Yet most of the network's power lies in the support that its members give to each other.

In 2012, Leslie Crutchfield and Heather McLeod Grant published an updated edition of their influential book, *Forces for Good*. It reported on research into a dozen nonprofits which, according to the authors, "created real social change."

> They have come up with innovative solutions to pressing social problems, and they have spread these ideas nationally or internationally. They have produced significant and sustained results and created large-scale systemic change in just a few decades. In the business world, these organizations would be akin to companies such as Google or eBay, which catapulted onto the Fortune 500 list of biggest companies in a matter of years.[2]

An example of such an organization is Teach for America, described in a pre-publication article in 2007.[3]

> Launched in 1989 by college senior Wendy Kopp on a shoestring budget in a borrowed office, the organization now attracts many of the country's best and brightest college graduates, who spend two years teaching in America's neediest public schools in exchange for a modest salary. In the last decade alone, Teach for America has more than quintupled in size, growing its budget from $10 million to $70 million and its number of teachers from 500 to 4,400. And it aims to double in size again in the next few years. . . .
>
> Although its success can be measured by such tangibles as the number of teachers it places or the amount of money it raises, perhaps the organization's most significant accomplishment is the movement for education reform it has created. . . . Teach for America has challenged

> how many Americans think about teacher credentialing, shaken up the education establishment, and, most important, created a committed vanguard of education reformers. . . . [I]t is now the recruiter of choice on many Ivy League campuses, often outcompeting elite firms like McKinsey & Company. Graduates who went through the program in the 1990s are now launching charter schools, running for political office, managing foundations, and working as school principals across the country.

Other nonprofits discussed in *Forces for Good* include Habitat for Humanity, Self-Help, City Year, and Environmental Defense. The authors outlined half a dozen practices that helped these and other organizations achieve outstanding impacts. These practices included policy advocacy, finding ways to work with markets and help companies to "do good while doing well," inspiring "evangelists"—communities of supporters, donors and volunteers who help them achieve their larger goals—and knowing how to be "exceptionally adaptive," modifying their tactics to respond to changing circumstances.

At the core of these organizations' strategies was their ability to build networks of support and to use "the power of leverage to create change."

> The secret to their success lies in how high-impact nonprofits mobilize every sector of society—government, business, nonprofits, and the public—to be a force for good. In other words, greatness has more to do with how nonprofits work outside the boundaries of their organizations than with how they manage their own internal operations. The high-impact nonprofits we studied are satisfied with building a

> "good enough" organization and then focusing their energy externally to catalyze largescale change.

Elsewhere, Crutchfield and Grant made the following comment about how their "high-impact" organizations managed their affairs:

> [These organizations] nurture larger networks of nonprofits and collaborate rather than compete with their peers. They spend as much time managing external relationships and influencing other groups as they do worrying about building their own organizations. These high-impact nonprofits are not only focused on themselves but also on the relentless pursuit of results. . . .
>
> Although most groups pay lip service to collaboration, many of them really see other nonprofits as competition for scarce resources. But high-impact organizations help the competition succeed, building networks of nonprofit allies and devoting remarkable time and energy to advancing their larger field. They freely share wealth, expertise, talent, and power with their peers. . .[4]

On a less grand scale than the organizations cited in *Forces for Good* is Lawrence CommunityWorks (LCW), a community revitalization organization situated in Lawrence, a community of about eighty thousand people, north of Boston. LCW relates how what they call a "network-centric approach to community building" has helped to revitalize a declining urban core in a city with a previous turbulent industrial history.

To cope with problems of pollution, abandoned industrial plants, arson, a lack of affordable housing, and other neighbourhood issues, community efforts dating back to 1981 had achieved some success, including the establishment of a Community Development Corporation (CDC) and the "completion of 140 high-quality . . . cooperative residences." However, by 1998 "the CDC began to slip into disarray. . . . [T]he organization was in crisis [with only] one remaining staff person besides the executive director." This situation was exacerbated by funding problems as state, city, and private funders had threatened to cut its financial support.[5]

However, the following year, a turnaround began. The efforts of three graduate students from MIT, a committed board of directors, a community development professional called Bill Traynor, and others in the community who donated "countless hours of professional expertise in banking, real estate law and information systems," reportedly led to the emergence of LCW. Since then, remarkable results have apparently been achieved. According to the LCW website,

> Today, LCW has a membership of thousands of Lawrence families, an energetic board and professional staff, and has generated over $70 million in new neighborhood investment, including 162 units of affordable housing on 15 abandoned and vacant parcels, a new community center, three new playgrounds and a range of family asset building and youth development efforts, impacting over thousands of families in Lawrence. Most important, Lawrence CommunityWorks has become one of the major forces for equitable development and economic justice in Lawrence, and one of the most dynamic and effective CDCs in Massachusetts.

According to LCW, central to their success has been their "network-centric approach" to community building.

> What does that mean? Our goal in Lawrence is to create a new "environment of connectivity" where residents can more easily connect to information, opportunity and each other. We feel that if thousands of residents are induced to "get back in the game" of working together and taking leadership roles in Lawrence, we can truly revitalize our City.
>
> "Networks" are a great approach to engaging thousands of people, loosely connected, in a wide variety of positive activity. Our work at Lawrence CommunityWorks borrows some concepts from Network Theory to guide our thinking and practice.

A useful resource for nonprofit leaders interested in exploring the idea of network building as an alternative, or complement, to achieving goals through a hierarchical organization is June Holley's *Network Weaver Handbook*. Holley has made an extensive study of networks; she points out that there are different kinds, and that leaders interested in exploring the network concept need to develop an understanding of the kind best suited to the needs to be met. They should be clear on which functions they and other collaborators want the network to serve—some options being information sharing, joint training, joint research, shared purchases, developing new programs or services, fostering innovation, or advocacy.[6]

She provides examples of networks in multiple settings. One describes the creation of a Fire Learning Network in the US that "has developed collaborative ecological restoration plans in more than 150 landscapes linked through 14 regional networks." According to researchers involved in the Fire Network,

> [The proponents were] not just applying an existing model, they are coming up with new collaborative approaches and trying to learn by doing and adapt . . . while operating at multiple scales . . . so there is potential for diffusion of . . . innovative and creative ideas at multiple levels simultaneously. That is the leverage point for opening up the resistance to change.

Another case describes the work of ACEnet.

> [ACEnet] provides a wide range of assistance to food, wood, and technology entrepreneurs in 29 counties of Appalachian Ohio. This region has one of the highest poverty and unemployment rates in the country, and ACEnet works with communities throughout the region who want to improve their support for entrepreneurs as a means to provide more local ownership and higher quality jobs.

The study describes how ACEnet was instrumental in establishing a "kitchen incubator," how farmers were linked to local restaurants, how a farmers' market café was established, and how various educational initiatives were implemented.[7]

A Canadian organization that drew inspiration from Holley's work is the ONN, some of whose publications are cited in this book.

> The ONN is the convening network of the approximately 55,000 nonprofit organizations across Ontario. As a 7,000-strong provincial network with a volunteer base of 300 sector leaders, ONN brings the diverse voices of the nonprofit sector to government, funders, and the business sectors to create and influence systemic change. ONN activates the network to develop and analyze policy and works on strategic issues by engaging its working groups, nonprofits and charities, businesses and government. . . .
>
> From the start, ONN has resisted a formal organizational structure. Instead, we focused on getting work done and testing structures to help make that happen. That flexibility has been key. . . . The network approach helps to identify common cause and then distribute power and resources to involve many people in building solutions. To address the complex issues that face the sector, network approaches have proven to be better suited than a more formal organizational approach.[8]

This collection of case study material could be extended, as there are many examples littered through relevant literature. However, perhaps the examples discussed above are sufficient to make the point that there are some new ideas at play in the nonprofit sector about how to achieve results. A recurring theme in these case studies is the concept of collective action and shared leadership. An effort has been made to systematize this approach to problem-solving through a methodology known as "collective impact."

Collective Impact[9]

This discipline has been attracting interest in recent years among organizations seeking a way to address complex socio-economic problems. It apparently emerged in the US through the work of a social change consulting firm called FSG. It grew out of an awareness that large-scale, persistent challenges such as poverty, inadequate education, disadvantaged youth, or troubled communities were too vast, and arose from too many causes to be effectively addressed by a single agency. What was needed was a way to marshal the commitment of multiple actors and to focus their energies and resources on the issues.

Collective impact has attracted the interest of Canadian funding organizations, such as the McConnell Foundation, Philanthropic Foundations of Canada, and the Ontario Trillium Foundation; it has also spawned conferences and websites. The literature on it has grown steadily, and it has found its way into practice in a growing number of settings across North America and farther afield—for example, in Australia. The Hamilton-based Tamarack Institute for Community Engagement has been funded by Trillium to provide training on collective impact across Ontario.

Liz Weaver, Tamarack's indefatigable lead on this work, advised me in an interview that, at the time of this writing, she was aware of somewhere between 100 to 150 initiatives under way, on many different scales. In 2014, *The Philanthropist*, a Canadian online journal about the nonprofit sector, dedicated an entire volume to collective impact. The concept continues to evolve as more communities and organizations strive to apply it in different circumstances. Some people see it as "flavour of the week," but others see it as a significant development in social service methodology that will make it possible to achieve durable results where previous efforts have failed.

Collective impact imposes a certain structure and discipline on networking as a modality for "working sideways." According to Weaver, "Collective Impact is really all about how to get from collaboration to collective action." It seeks to draw participants together from wherever there is an interest in addressing the issue in question: nonprofits, government, business, foundations, religious organizations, and others. It strives to build a shared vision among the partners and to frame a joint approach for achieving it. It stresses "shared measurement" across all participants and encourages mutual accountability rather than a more conventional, top-down, hierarchical model. Results are sought through mutually reinforcing activities managed by each partner but coordinated through a joint plan of action. Continuous communication among participants is considered essential to assure mutual objectives and build trust.

What is called "backbone support" fosters the coordination and animation of activity. Under the collective impact approach, this is carried out, not by one of the partners, but through a separate organization or office with appropriate skills. The ability of the initiative to succeed rests upon its capacity to engage influential champions, to instil a sense of urgency, and to marshal adequate resources of all types for support. Proponents of collective impact emphasize that for positive outcomes to be achieved, all aspects of this approach need to be addressed.

Leadership in a Networked Approach

A problem with words like "network" or "networking" is that they are ubiquitous, like networks themselves. Anna Muoio, a consultant at Deloitte's Monitor Institute, observes, "The word 'network' has become a general-purpose term that has seen a huge rise in popularity with the spread of connective technology. It's a term at risk of being so overused that we become numb to what it means."

Mouio describes how using networks provides a new way for addressing socio-economic problems.

> [This methodology] aligns the actions of a diverse set of stakeholders to tackle a larger piece of a problem than by working in isolation; diversifies risk and spreads bets across many experiments; enables innovation by building a platform where different voices can come to the table to shape new solutions; and ultimately, helps build a resilient problem-solving ecosystem where a dense web of relationships provides the resilience necessary to adapt to new challenges and opportunities as they arise. These qualities are harder to get through one-to-one partnerships or from the efforts of a single organization. A network builds a platform that can launch a portfolio of interventions and simultaneously pull many levers for change. That's what makes them attractive for social change efforts.[10]

I find the term "a network approach" or "network-centric thinking," as distinct from simply "networking," a useful way to describe this way of addressing social issues. Bill Traynor, executive director of LCW, describes the activities of Lawrence CommunityWorks as follows: "We are far from a 'pure' network, but we have many characteristics of a connected environment. And over the years, we have intentionally used network-centric thinking to guide our efforts." The result, in his view, is a significantly altered approach to leadership.

> [I]n connected environments such as networks, the function of leadership is anything but traditional. . . . Moving from a traditional environment to a network or connected environment can cause a kind of vertigo, because the environment is so radically different. It operates by different rules and responds to different stimuli. Armed only with the perspectives and skills honed in traditional settings, one who tries to lead in a network environment can find the task unsettling and disorienting.[11]

A modified mode of leadership is central to the concept of a networking approach. The literature on networks makes it clear that network proponents need to adopt a mindset that is quite different from conventional management approaches, as illustrated below. The all-important lubricant for network success is trust. This is reinforced by attitudes and behaviour that may not always characterize how leaders of conventional organizations manage. Figure 6.1 sets forth the differences between distinctive leadership philosophies.

How leadership in a networked setting differs from conventional approaches

Conventional mindset	Mindset associated with network success
• Leaders focus on their organization and its work	• Leaders focus on mission and look for the most effective way of achieving results
• Reliance on control as a mode of oversight	• Reliance on trust to get things done through partners or colleagues

• Pursuit of "our vision"	• Elaboration of a shared vision
• Reliance on "our values"	• Development of a frame-work of shared values
• If other organizations are involved, our organization is seen as the "hub," directing how things are to be done	• Our organization is understood to be one node among others in a network
• Revenue, membership, or staff growth are seen as important measures of organizational success	• "Success" is measured through what is accomplished in terms of client impact
• Success is an organiza-tional achievement	• Success is a team achievement
• Other organizations in similar lines of work are seen as competitors	• Other organizations in similar lines of work are seen as collaborators
• "We" = the people working in our organization	• "We" = the people collaborating in the context of the network

Figure 6.1

The skills of collaborative leadership are not given to everyone. Some people may have them, others not so much. Some people believe they can be developed, while others may believe they are innate. Certainly, to my mind, they have a lot to do with personal values, which are usually deeply rooted.

Literature about this approach to leadership argues that individuals who are good at building cooperation tend to have a natural collaborative bent. They are patient and good listeners. They feel driven to achieve shared goals through collaboration, and they have a measured ego. They look for win-win solutions and tend to use "pull" more than "push" to motivate others. Typically, they think strategically, connecting the project to a larger purpose. They take account of the fact that it takes time for a group to start working together effectively and to become productive. They are skilled at mapping the political terrain, and careful about whom to engage and when. They use "we" rather than "I" when discussing how decisions should be taken or who should get credit for accomplishments.

Of particular importance to sound collaboration is the quality of the process used to link participants. A sound process builds trust, reduces concerns, and gains the commitment of partners to working together. It can be helpful if participants are able to agree on ground rules to underpin their working relationships, such as:

- transparency
- candour
- everyone contributes, no one dominates
- private agendas and egos are left at the door
- differences are professional, not personal
- decisions are made at the table (no behind-the-scenes deals)

Productive groups may also choose to use the "70 percent rule"—one that I have personally found helpful in some circumstances—an agreement that it is sufficient to work towards a good, not a perfect, solution. Participants agree to accept 70 percent of what they want, and not to hold out for 100 percent.

Russell Linden has examined the characteristics of successful collaborations in his book, *Leading across Boundaries*. In his view, "Collaboration is vital, difficult and learnable."[12] It takes time to build collaborative relations and trust. In contrast to typical North American approaches to doing business, Linden points out how, in Southeast Asia, when people work together, it's "relationships first, business second." People start by learning about each other; they share a meal and spend social time together before engaging in the more substantive aspects of collaboration. Trust provides a framework or context within which difficult issues such as negotiation, give and take, or compromise can be addressed. "Set time aside to work on relationship building," he advises. Many busy managers have great difficulty understanding how important this is.

There is a certain "new age" character to writing about the network approach to nonprofit leadership that some people may find unsettling, but this may be part of what's involved in learning about a different way of working. Proponents of this approach tend to agree that networks are fluid and their margins are constantly shifting and evolving. Traynor writes, "It is important to keep moving the creative, adaptive edge of the network outward so that the universe of the network expands in three dimensions." The environment tends to be informal, flexible, with provisional leadership that shifts and changes over time.

The architecture of networks is generally open. The ONN tells how they may form a group to address a particular issue, and such a group may be large or small, formal or informal. What they look for, however, is motivation among participants, a strategy about where work may go and what actions to try, and a group of active stakeholders willing to drive the work forward. "These working groups are not committees. They are not structured on formal or representational seats—membership flows in and out depending on the capacity and expertise available. They are viewed as temporary, staying together only for as long as they have an opportunity to make a strategic difference."[13] Proponents of the network approach seem to agree that flexibility is key, form should follow function, errors and experimentation are to be expected, and ownership and credit must be shared. A culture of transparency, underpinned by appropriate values, must be consciously fostered.

The Role of the Network Weaver

Since the basic concept underlying a networked approach involves collaborative leadership, rather than a single leader at the head of the parade, one might wonder who or what moves things forward. This is where the role of "network weavers" comes in (Wei-Skillern uses the term "network entrepreneur" to describe what appears to be an analogous role). The weavers' function is catalytic. As the title implies, it is to identify individuals or organizations and make them aware that they may share common interests, to help shape the network, to foster awareness of the web of relationships, to encourage engagement, and generally to help weave the network so that it becomes more innovative and effective. There may well be more than one weaver functioning in any particular network or set of interconnected networks.

A network weaver may convene people to help establish a clearer focus and mode of functioning of the network. She or he may put in place systems required to facilitate the function of the network, such as communications or training or other forms of support, and may also assist with the coordination of self-organized projects.[14]

For Muoio,

> [The weaver is] a kind of matchmaker, working to increase the number and strength of relationships between participants in the network by helping people find connection and common ground with one another, gradually building up trust and an overall sense of community. This role often also includes bringing new participants into the network when the opportunity arises and making sure all the right voices are at the table.

Kanter and Fine see the use of social media as integral to a weaver's role. They list a range of tools and techniques that can be used to build networks online. For them,

> [An effective weaver must be] continuously learning new ways to use social media to weave a network. . . . Weavers energize their networks not just by doing, but by spending considerable time teaching their colleagues, friends, and neighbors how to weave the network as well. . . . Network weavers provide reasons for people to care about causes and organizations. They shape conversations and identify specific ways for people to help. They inspire people to share a message or idea, donate money, and pass legislation that ultimately makes social change happen. . . . Network weaving is a critically important aspect of effective social media usage.[15]

People who have studied networks agree that developing this approach to decision making and collaboration is not a trivial challenge. One observer has argued that the evolution of networks may be "the most important discussion happening in social change sectors today"; nonetheless, working in a networked context "requires a true reorientation in the way most people approach their work, and that requires new skills and resources and a tremendous amount of tenacity."[16] Another observer states,

> Collaboration is really messy and difficult. There are reasons why . . . it's difficult for organizations to collaborate effectively. It's hard, and it takes a lot of persistence and a lot of flexibility. When you get a group of smart people in a room who have a lot of different ideas, you have to let go and trust that the work will go in the right direction.[17]

This short discussion does not do justice to the range of issues and possibilities associated with a networking approach. A brief search on the Internet will reveal many other sources of information.

Governance in Networks

In due course, participants in a network have to consider governance issues: How will decisions be taken, and by whom? How will decision makers be identified? What about accountability? Most contemporary literature about board governance is not much help in this regard since it is preoccupied with the conventional role of a board of directors and its fiduciary responsibilities vis-à-vis the organization to which it is affiliated. Most boards expect to have a top-down kind of relationship to "their" organization. Many directors, particularly those used to working in the private sector or those from government backgrounds, may be most comfortable functioning in the context of a more conventional mindset.

There is no simple formula for how governance should be exercised in a network—each will have to work out its own arrangements for decision making and accountability, bearing in mind the kinds of values implicit in the "mindset associated with network success" above. Holley writes,

> [I]t's very important to think about the structure of your network so that you don't over-structure or understructure it. . . . One of the most difficult decisions to make is what structure your network should have. There is virtually no research on the type of structure that is most effective for different kinds of situations.

Some networks, she suggests, are quite similar to organizations, often with a governing board. An alternative is the self-organized network, which operates in a decentralized manner with distributed decision making and no formal structure, and where boundaries are fuzzy. Such networks can sometimes be "powerful innovation generators when experimentation and new approaches are needed." Most common, however, are "hybrid networks . . . [that] contain some organization-like elements and some self-organized elements."[18]

Since networks are reliant on trust, and since it takes time to build trust with other network partners, it makes sense to develop that trust and a sense of mutual comfort among partners before trying to tie down governance arrangements too tightly. Muoio counsels against moving too quickly to a formally structured approach to governance:

> As it becomes more organized and execution-oriented, a network may need some degree of formal governance to make important choices. This often takes the form of a

small body of key network stakeholders, such as a steering committee or board of directors. A little governance goes a long way, particularly in the early stages. While it is common for some participants to push for formal decision-making structures early, it is counterproductive to put them in place before the group has established its common ground and shared activities. And once formal structure is adopted, it is crucial to the network's health that the people playing this role are willing to use their decision rights in service of the group and reflecting its input rather than only being guided by their own point of view.[19]

Problems and Pitfalls

Networks go off the rails for many reasons. Much depends on the values and abilities of the key players, particularly the network proponents or entrepreneurs. But there can be other causes of difficulty, such as the following:

- insufficient attention to aligning goals among network partners
- poor performance by any one organization
- the breakdown of relationships between any two organizations in the network
- difficulties experienced as participants grapple with a range of issues, including different skill sets, technology, information asymmetry, or cultural differences

- attempts by one participant to micromanage others
- involving organizations that may not be compatible

Further problems may be encountered due to a lack of resources. Developing a network takes time, patience, energy—and money, even in the early days of network formation. It can be very helpful if a funder that subscribes to the notion of network building is involved at the start; indeed, a funder can sometimes play the role of network weaver.

Supporting collaborative effort can be difficult for funders. In an interview, a senior official at the Ontario Trillium Foundation told me that they have funded collaborations in the past and are interested in learning more about how to fund this kind of initiative. However, collaborations evolve and shift over time, which poses challenges for funders. Also, funders that are understandably concerned about the responsible use of their funds may have policies that require, in advance, clear agreements about how the collaboration will work, and accountability arrangements. These objectives may not be easy to achieve in the case of networks.

In 2013, the ONN published a report on leadership in the sector.

> [One of the] strategic opportunities for the sector [lies in] engaging funders to be partners in strengthening the structures that support organizations and their leaders: Resources are a critical enabler of both organizational stability and leadership. Funders must begin to address the challenges that funding structures create and work with sector leaders to develop solutions.

Another hurdle for leaders interested in pursuing a networked approach to their mission may be their own board of directors. One would like to think that boards would be interested in finding the most effective way of pursuing that mission, and that they would be open to collaborative initiatives. But boards can be a real problem when it comes to networking because they typically want a level of command and control. Moreover, since a network often does not have a board in the conventional sense, the existing boards of participating organizations may have difficulty figuring out their own role, or how they fit into this new way of doing business.

Boards may also be uncertain as to their role with respect to network development. Much of the literature about the role of boards stresses their fiduciary responsibilities; these are often interpreted to mean the oversight of finances and the management of risk. The board's larger responsibility to think strategically, and perhaps even outside the box, about how best to realize the organization's mission may get little attention. In fact, it may even be perceived to be in direct conflict with the controls required to meet fiduciary obligations. Moreover, the board itself might not be very good at strategic thinking, even though that's one of its key functions.

In certain settings, it may be that we are witnessing the emergence of a new locus for governance in the nonprofit sector. This is the view of David Renz at the University of Missouri-Kansas City.

> For so long, individual organizations have been the appropriate unit to address problems, and we assumed that it would always be this way. But now . . . with time and a radically changing environment (i.e., changes in the complexity, pace, scale, and nature of community problems and needs) . . . single organizations can no

> longer appropriately match the scale for the most critical and substantive community issues and problems. It has become increasingly necessary to develop alliances and coalitions—extraorganizational entities—to address the multifaceted complexity of these critical needs and issues.[20]

Renz argues that for certain kinds of community issues, governance has shifted from the level of individual boards to an overarching network of organizations. He draws a distinction between the "networked organization" and the "network as organization" in which "the boards of individual organizations are guided by and often become accountable to the larger governance system." As governance shifts upward from boards to some kind of superordinate entity, accountability will tend to become increasingly opaque.

> [These developments have] significant implications for the next generation of nonprofit board work. [They require] . . . different kinds of knowledge, skills, and abilities. This is the work of leadership, not management. So it is essential for its participants to be proficient in a different kind of leadership, particularly in the capacity to network, to build multifaceted relationships across boundaries and among diverse groups of people, and to effectively exercise influence in the absence of authority. . . .

What all this means in practice is that the nonprofit interested in pursuing a networked approach to the challenges it faces should make sure that its board understands the rationale for moving down this road, is supportive of such a strategy, and is prepared to cede some degree of control to a higher entity.

Would a Networked Approach Be Right for Your Organization?

The world of networks and collaborative leadership may strike some individuals as old wine in new bottles. As one colleague observed, "What is all the fuss about? This all strikes me as a bit new-agey and breathless. Without all this, what could not be achieved by good leaders with good collaborators?"

Others may see more possibilities in these new ideas. Certainly, it seems clear that there is, indeed, a new philosophy of leadership at play, and that it differs in important regards from leadership as more conventionally understood. Moreover, this new approach to leadership seems to be providing demonstrable evidence of effectiveness in addressing certain kinds of problems that had previously been stubbornly resistant to resolution.

Up to around the 1990s, most managers were taught that the fundamental organizational form was a hierarchy. Drawing on the example of military institutions, management experts told their students that the essence of the manager's job was to plan, organize, motivate, and control—to direct the work of others. A top-down, bureaucratic structure was required for this purpose. This concept pervaded much management literature; this model, or a version of it, is the one with which many executive directors or CEOs of today's organizations grew up.

The emergence of the web and a net-savvy generation of young persons for whom networking is a way of life has turned a lot of conventional management thinking on its side. Changing ideas about human resource management have called into question the hierarchical model. As a consequence, in considering how best to pursue their mission, contemporary nonprofit executives and board members may feel a need to rethink long-held ideas about how to organize work. They may ask themselves if "working sideways"—whether by merging, by forming conventional partnerships, or perhaps by moving towards a networked approach— might, at least in some circumstances, prove more effective than following a more traditional, vertical or top-down approach to governance and management.

The literature on the network approach is largely focused on social issues, particularly broad, complex problems where it is difficult to determine where the roots of the issue may lie, and where strategies for addressing them are likely to require action on several fronts, drawing on multiple kinds of expertise. The model may prove to be most appropriate for organizations involved in social issues with strong emotive appeal. For example, among the strategies recommended by the authors of *Forces for Good* are advocacy and the recruitment of "evangelists" to work on behalf of the cause. Where the cause in question has little emotional appeal, where there are no stories to share about the potential for a better world, it is harder to see how strategies such as these might be feasible.

Nevertheless, it may be that there are many issues in the nonprofit world where organizations and individuals would benefit from coming together to pursue shared objectives. Doing so may not necessarily involve the explicit establishment of a network. But if collaboration seems to indicate, as Bill Traynor remarked, "many of the traditional levers of power and decision making [are] neither handy nor useful," then it may be worthwhile to ask whether some of the insights embodied in "network-centric thinking" might enhance the impact of your organization's work as it links to others. It seems to me that in the nonprofit world, there are many spheres beyond that of social action—environmental or social justice issues come to mind as possibilities, for instance—where there is a need for more collaborative approaches. We need to maintain open minds about approaches to governance and decision making that may be better adapted to this kind of work.

Whether a networking approach would be appropriate for your particular organization would depend on the answers to several questions. For example:

- What is your mission? Is it likely to attract the interest and commitment of other organizations or individuals? In other words, is there potentially fertile ground to start developing this approach?

- Does your organization have the kinds of leaders at the staff or board level who would understand what a networking approach might mean, have appropriate skills, and be open to experimenting with it?

- What steps might be taken to deepen understanding among organizational leaders as to what this approach might involve? What would attitudes be at the board level?

- Would some training on networking be helpful, or the support of a consultant?

It may prove desirable to move stepwise towards the adoption of a networking approach, rather than thinking in terms of some kind of full-scale transformation. Literature on networking emphasizes the importance of experimentation, of being open to periodic failures, and of the need to build trust over time.

In summary, where the need for collaboration may exist, a networking approach (or a strategy drawing on some lessons of such an approach) may make it possible to start moving the yardsticks. It remains to be seen to what extent these new ideas about leadership take hold, and what results may be achieved as a consequence.

---

1. Wei-Skillern, Jane, David Ehrlichman, and David Sawyer, "The Most Impactful Leaders You've Never Heard Of," *Stanford Social Innovation Review* (September 16, 2015).

2. Leslie R. Crutchfield and Heather McLeod Grant, *Forces for Good,* 2nd ed. (San Francisco: Jossey-Bass, 2012), 27.

3. Heather McLeod Grant and Leslie R. Crutchfield, "Creating High Impact Nonprofits," *Stanford Social Innovation Review* 5, no. 4 (Fall 2007), 32–41.

4. Crutchfield & Grant, *Forces for Good,* 27, 37, 319.

5. "Our Approach," *Lawrence CommunityWorks* (2016), accessed August 7, 2018, https://www.lawrencecommunityworks.org/site/about-lawrence-community-works/our-approach/

6. June Holley, *Network Weaver Handbook: A Guide to Transformational Networks* (Network Weaver Publishing, 2012), 18. See also chapter 11. Available through https://www.networkweaver.com

7. Holley, *Network Weaver,* 210, 330, 344.

8. *Networks + Action: The Way We Work,* v. 10. (Toronto: Ontario Nonprofit Network, 2014).

9. "Collective Impact," *Stanford Social Innovation Review,* accessed August 7, 2018, https://ssir.org/articles/entry/collective_impact

   Collective Impact: Together We Can Make an Impact, accessed August 7, 2018, http://www.collectiveimpact.org/

   Tamarack Institute (website), accessed August 7, 2018, https://www.tamarackcommunity.ca/

10. Anna Muoio, *Engage for Social Impact: How Funders Can Support and Leverage Networks* (New York: Monitor Institute by Deloitte, June 2015).

11. Bill Traynor, "Vertigo and the Intentional Inhabitant: Leadership in a Connected World," *Nonprofit Quarterly* (February 28, 2018). https://nonprofitquarterly.org/2018/02/23/vertigo-and-the-intentional-inhabitant-leadership-in-a-connected-world/

12. Linden, Russell M., *Leading Across Boundaries* (San Francisco: Jossey-Bass, 2010), 38–48, 51–62.

13. *Networks + Action,* 11.

14. For an elaboration of the weaver's responsibilities, see Holley, *Network Weaver,* ch. 2.

15. Beth Kanter and Allison Fine, *The Networked Nonprofit* (San Francisco: Jossey-Bass, 2010), 36–37.

16. Comment posted in Edgington blog, accessed August 7, 2018, http://www.socialvelocity.net/2015/10/the-network-approach-to-social-change/

17. Jennifer Berman, *Energy Action Network of Vermont,* cited in *Engage for Social Impact: How Funders Can Support and Leverage Networks* (New York: Monitor Institute by Deloitte, June 2015).

18. Holley, *Network Weaver,* 229–232.

19. Muoio, *Engage for Social Impact.*

20. David Renz, "Reframing Governance II," *Nonprofit Quarterly* (January 10, 2018). https://nonprofitquarterly.org/2018/01/10/reframing-governance-2/

CHAPTER 8
THE CHALLENGE OF IMPERFECT GOVERNANCE

Nonprofit Boards: Theory and Practice

The Theory

In its touchstone publication, *The Source*, BoardSource lays out twelve principles which, according to a group of experts they convened, characterized "exceptional boards."[1] In the preamble, they outline what can be expected of a high performing board:

> Good governance is about providing critical capital—intellect, reputation, resources, and access—to power nonprofit success and thereby strengthen communities. . . . Good governance requires the board to balance its role as an oversight body with its role as a force supporting the organization. . . . Exceptional boards add significant value to their organizations, making discernible differences in their advance on mission. . . . [An effective board should] set organizational course . . . provide direction . . . [and] look for horizons in years not months.

This is the theory about the nonprofit board's role. It should take the long view of the organization—where it is going and what it wants to achieve. It should help it to craft strategy and to navigate the challenges associated with implementation. It should exercise careful control over the organization's financial and other assets, while keeping an eye open for risk. It should monitor the performance of the organization and of itself. It should be an effective, knowledgeable partner to the top executive, effectively holding this individual to account,[2] and bringing valuable expertise to bear on difficult issues.

The Practice

Too often, unfortunately, there is a big gap between theory and practice. Consider this extract from a recent article in the *Nonprofit Quarterly*.

> The past twenty years have seen the steady growth of training programs, consulting practices, academic research, and guidebooks aimed at improving the performance of nonprofit boards. This development reflects both hopes and doubts about the nonprofit board. On the one hand, boards are touted as a decisive force for ensuring the accountability of nonprofit organizations. On the other hand, the board is widely regarded as a problematic institution. . . . [There is a] widespread sense that underperforming boards are the norm, not the exception.[3]

Seldom does one run across the executive director or CEO who says, "My board is a pleasure to work with, a consistent source of strength and advice; it constantly enhances my organization." More typically, one hears how the board adds little value, or even detracts from the ability of the organization to get on with its work.

Typical Governance Problems

Why are there problems with boards? Gremlins are said to be small mischievous imps or invisible beings that take pleasure in gumming up or sabotaging machinery. In a playful moment a few years ago, I decided to start building a collection of "governance gremlins"—annoyances that impede a board's ability to perform. This exhibit provides a sample, loosely grouped into categories; more items could easily be added.

Governance gremlins: Factors that can cripple board performance

Recruitment and retention

- High board turnover, lack of continuity
- Inability to get rid of "dead wood"
- Inadequate recruitment process for the board, no skills matrix
- Weak board chair
- Lack of orientation process
- Directors who don't turn up
- Directors who come to meetings unprepared or late
- Poorly formulated board agendas

- Board documents that consistently arrive late
- Weak staff preparation for board meetings
- Lack of succession planning for board and staff
- Poor minute-taking
- Inadequate record-keeping

Committees

- Committee structure ill suited to governance needs
- Mandates unclear or outdated
- Poor connections between committees and the board
- Weak leadership
- Committee work done poorly or late
- No distinction between committees and task forces
- Membership ill suited to committee requirements

Board composition, culture; board–staff relations

- Lack of a collaborative board culture
- Domination of the board by the chair or individual directors
- Factionalism among directors, internal politics
- Directors don't understand their responsibilities
- Poor communication within the board; from the board to the CEO/ED

- "Corridor" decision making (outside the boardroom)
- Board composition ill suited to the organization's governance needs
- Unethical behaviour by directors or staff; no code of conduct
- Unchallenged conflicts of interest
- Disruptive behaviour by a director
- Interference by over-zealous funders
- Board micromanagement of staff
- Inappropriate personal relationships between certain directors and staff
- Distrust: director–director; board–CEO/ED
- Excessive CEO/ED "ownership" of the organization
- CEO/ED unresponsive to legitimate board concerns
- Inadequate communication with key stakeholders
- Staff don't understand how to support the board effectively

Governance role

- Mission too vague to provide a sense of purpose
- Board lacks knowledge of the organization's work
- Lack of understanding of the board's role among directors or staff
- Limited understanding of what good governance implies

- Failure to follow legislation, bylaws, or governance policies
- Outdated bylaws; lack of key policies
- Lack of useful metrics on program performance
- Board role in budget preparation and approval unclear
- Board unwilling or unable to confront the organization's financial needs
- Inadequate strategic plan, lack of a framework for decision making
- Directors with weak capacity for strategic thinking
- Ineffective or non-existent strategic planning process

Murphy's law asserts that if things can go wrong, they will. Given the many impediments listed above—and this list is not exhaustive—it's likely that Murphy's law will manifest itself in some respects in the functioning of many, if not most, nonprofit boards. During speaking engagements, if I show a slide of these gremlins and ask if anyone has encountered them, hands typically shoot up all over the room.

Nonprofit Boards Need Help

In researching this book, I interviewed experienced consultants in both Canada and the US who work on governance and strategy issues in the nonprofit sector, as well as leaders in some umbrella organizations and foundations. I asked them their opinion of boards in the sector. Here's a short selection of typical comments from individuals in both countries, drawn from a considerably longer list:

- The notion of a partnership between the CEO and the board is very hard to realize. I know three CEOs who left because of the board that they were working with—the board was functioning as a kind of sea anchor.

- It's very difficult to find board members who have a strategic perspective.

- When you have a CEO who has been certified by the ASAE, and then you layer on top of that a board of volunteers who don't know the day-to-day operations but who are charged with making big decisions . . . and then you add to that hidden agendas, turnover, etc.—this can lead to serious problems.

- Directors typically have a lot of passion for the mission, they want to do the right thing, but they don't understand what governance entails. They bring their day-to-day jobs into the boardroom. Most board members have jobs that have little or nothing to do with governance. So they get into management or execution where they're comfortable.

- We have well-intentioned people who want to help in their community, but they don't know what the work of the board entails.

- My overall view of boards is that the vast majority are less functional than they could or should be. . . . They need to be helped to do their job.

The Elephant in the Room

What to do about boards? In discussions about the state of the voluntary sector, it's usually not long before someone asks, *isn't there a better model than the nonprofit board?* Discussions on this topic typically turn around and around and then wind up where they began. Here's why:

- Commercial organizations have shareholders who have put their money into the company and who therefore have an interest in making sure that the funds are properly accounted for and that profits are realized. The board of directors, elected by the shareholders, is the instrument for carrying out these tasks. In the case of nonprofits, while funds don't come from shareholders, they may originate from other community institutions and individuals. There is thus an analogous need for financial oversight in nonprofit organizations.

- Nonprofits, and charities in particular, receive tax advantages. Someone, or some group, needs to oversee the work of these organizations to make sure that these advantages are warranted.

- Nonprofits are expected to achieve socially useful results. If there were no external oversight of leadership and of program performance, how could contributors and stakeholders be assured that positive results are being realized and that the organization is being run responsibly?

- A board is not an inherently flawed instrument. When a board performs well, it can be a valuable asset.

- If boards did not exist, their work would still have to be done. Some other entity would need to be put in place to do its job—a board, in short, either in name or in practice. No one has yet come up with any reasonable alternative to the nonprofit board that could perform a similar function.

How can we migrate boards from the somewhat dilapidated state that so many seem to be in, into higher performing, more motivated instruments of leadership? Why aren't they stronger?

Why Aren't Nonprofit Boards Stronger?

There are many reasons. The governance gremlins suggest some of them; for example, if directors don't understand their job or don't have the time to do it properly, this can certainly slow things down. However, the list of gremlins does not discriminate between symptoms of weak governance (board members who arrive late, for example) and root, fundamental causes.

One might surmise that a root cause is that the "wrong people are on the bus," to borrow Collins' phrase. But even this is not a root cause: we need to ask, *why aren't the right people sitting in those seats?* Here are some basic causes, in my view:

- Nonprofit board members are likely to be engaged in the organization's mission, at least to some degree, and some directors may be deeply devoted to it. But they have no financial skin in the game: unlike shareholders in business companies, none of their funds are at stake. This places many directors at a remove from the organization. How it performs won't affect their pocketbooks.

Some directors' commitment to the board's work may therefore be less intense than that of their private sector counterparts.

- There are no qualifications, no educational requirements for directors to sit on a nonprofit board. But governance is not simple. There's a lot to learn and understand. Many nonprofit directors lack the knowledge to participate in governance effectively.
- Board members come and go. Terms of office are often short. It takes time to orient and educate a director, especially one with little governance background. And just as a new director begins to "get it" and become more effective, her or his term may come to an end. The next new recruit to the board may have little understanding of what board work entails, so the work of orientation has to start all over again. Constant turnover makes it difficult to enhance board performance.
- The mode of appointment or election of directors to the board is often problematic. The members of the organization who elect directors are often indifferent as to who sits on the board. Even trying to get members to turn up at an annual general meeting to elect directors can be like pulling teeth.
- In some organizations, the members and directors are one and the same. If there is a desire to strengthen the board's composition by bringing in new blood, there isn't an obvious pool of new people to draw from.
- The people who wind up sitting on nonprofit boards arrive for a variety of reasons. Some may have a strong sense of community responsibility or a commitment to the mission and will thus be

actively supportive. But others may wind up on boards simply because they have been wooed (or guilt-tripped) by an existing board member. They may have only a passing interest in the organization. Some may think it's prestigious to sit on a board (any board will do), or they may want to rub shoulders with certain other directors. Some board members may have little connection to the organization's constituency or membership.

- Directors on a nonprofit board do not benefit from the same incentives as directors on a commercial board. There is no remuneration, yet the time commitment can be very considerable. There is, of course, the satisfaction of supporting a community or a cause, but for many individuals with little experience in the nonprofit sector, these advantages must seem somewhat evanescent.

- Many boards do not realize how critical two positions are: the board chair and the chair of the nominating (or nominating and governance) committee. In my view, the board chair's role is absolutely pivotal to the effective functioning of the governance process. This is not always well understood—some nonprofits continue to think that the main job of the chair is simply to run meetings. A weak board chair—or a series of them—will almost certainly result in weak governance. Furthermore, it can be difficult to find individuals who are prepared to devote more than a year or two to the position of board chair, but constant turnover in that position tends to weaken governance.

- Nominating committees control the pipeline of potential recruits. If its members, and in particular its chair, do not know much about governance, they are unlikely to attract the right kind of candidates. And if they fail to do a thorough job of recruitment, board membership will suffer, as will efforts to get the board to play a more effective role. Many organizations lack a thoughtful recruitment process and pay scant attention to succession planning for officers in particular; they tend to fire up the engines to replace vacancies on the board as the AGM approaches, with insufficient time to recruit and insufficient regard for the specific skills required.

How Strong Is Your Board? Assessing Effectiveness

Metaphorically, a board might be thought of as a vehicle whose purpose is to carry forward the organization's mission and enhance its value. A nonprofit will have to travel difficult roads in the years ahead. If its board is sound and reliable—a well-tuned, reliable automobile—and if it has leadership that steers it well, then the board will be able to help guide the organization, sustain it, and assist it in surmounting challenges. But if the board is a rusty vehicle with poor suspension and a misfiring engine, malgovernance will be the consequence. The board won't be an asset. In fact, it may simply be a handicap, hindering progress, absorbing staff time and energy without providing any compensating benefit.

Nonprofits that hope to thrive in the turbulence surrounding the sector need a board that bolsters organizational performance. Thus, as one of the strategies to cope with the turbulence ahead, it may be desirable to ask how well prepared your board is, and to determine what might be done, and by whom, to strengthen it.

Board Evaluations

One way of addressing this question might be to undertake a board evaluation. There is much talk about this subject in the governance literature; board evaluation is becoming recognized as a required practice of well-performing boards.

There are many free questionnaires for this purpose available on the Internet and many different approaches, from hiring an outside consultant to conduct the assessment to adopting various methods of self-assessment. Whatever the approach, a board evaluation needs to be undertaken carefully. To secure thoughtful insights into a board's capabilities and potential, it's not just a matter of circulating a random set of questions. Some directors may doubt the utility of an evaluation, or be concerned about private information that could be revealed to others. Some may feel threatened. For these and other reasons, boards should progress carefully, especially if there's any suggestion of evaluating individual directors. Undue haste could seriously harm board dynamics.[4] Certainly, a board evaluation can be useful in establishing a frame of reference and a plan for future improvements, but only if it is conducted sensitively and thoughtfully. Here are questions to consider:

- Have steps been taken to raise the possibility of evaluation with the board, and to address the questions that such a proposal will almost certainly raise?
- Is there a champion for this initiative at the board level? Is this a credible individual?
- Is the board's own role well-articulated?
- What degree of staff involvement would be appropriate?

- Who will conduct the evaluation? It would not be prudent for staff to lead an initiative of this kind. Often, the use of an outside consultant is advisable to ensure a professional approach and to address concerns about confidentiality of results.
- Is there any intention to assess individual directors' performance in addition to that of the board as a whole? Given that the directors of nonprofit organizations serve as volunteers, unlike corporate directors, this could meet with resistance. And it raises sensitive issues. It is perhaps best avoided if this is a first assessment.
- What methodology will be used for the evaluation? There are lots of options. Will a questionnaire be used, and if so, which one? What about interviews?
- What measures will be taken to protect confidentiality?
- Will the evaluation address the question of board leadership (the board chair)? How will that aspect of the evaluation be handled, and who will provide feedback to the chair if there are performance issues?
- Who will analyze the data? Will there be a report to the board? Will recommendations or suggestions for action be included? Who will formulate those proposals? If there is to be a draft report, who will review it first?
- How will the process of discussing results be handled at the board level?
- One of the most important questions: Will the initiative lead to actions for improvement? If implementation does not occur—and

it's a sensitive area—then the value of the assessment will be lost, and the whole idea of evaluation will lose credibility.

Personally, I have reservations about relying on a questionnaire to assess the state of governance if this is the only vehicle to be used, as this may obscure potentially sensitive issues. Some years ago, in conducting a governance evaluation for a branch of a large national association, we began by circulating a questionnaire to board members. The results were encouraging—the board seemed to be performing well.

We followed up with selective one-on-one interviews. These revealed one of the most dysfunctional boards I have ever encountered: serious factionalism among board members, persistent efforts by the past chair to undermine the existing chair, disagreements among directors as to the purpose of the board, board members voting themselves expensive perquisites at the same time that staff remuneration was being cut, and highly inappropriate behaviour by the CEO toward a female staff member. None of this was revealed in the questionnaire responses.

Governance Reviews

The prospect of a board evaluation may cause some directors to feel personally threatened. A somewhat different alternative that may be less sensitive, while achieving similar or even better results, is a governance review. This may have a more anonymous feel. It may also have a somewhat wider scope, going beyond the board itself, and thus provide a deeper insight into issues that may need to be addressed.

Sound governance rests upon four pillars: board-related structures, board culture, governance processes, and people. Structure is concerned with issues such as the role of the board, of board officers, and of directors themselves (and how well these roles are understood). It also includes subjects such as bylaws, terms of office, committees' roles and composition, governance policies, and the like.

Board culture, as discussed below, encompasses issues such as the values that prevail ("tone at the top"), the expectations of directors, how meetings are conducted, and board leadership. It concerns the beliefs and assumptions that determine what's valued, how discourse takes place, who gets listened to, how decisions are taken, and what follow-through may occur in the wake of board decisions.

Governance processes include subjects such as how board agendas are formulated, recruitment practices, how strategic planning or budget preparation is carried out, performance measurement, board-related documentation, and the conduct of performance reviews for the chief staff officer. A governance review would (and should) certainly get into "people issues" associated with governance, but it is less explicitly targeted on individuals and their performance than a board evaluation.

In my view, to assess how well governance is working at a particular organization, most if not all of these issues need to be considered. During the course of the review, some will emerge as more important than others. The actual ways in which a board evaluation and a governance review are carried out may not be very different in practice—surveys, interviews, review of documentation, etc. However, the orientation of a governance review may be somewhat different, as may the kinds of recommendations that emerge, in that a review may have a more explicit focus on all "four pillars" than might some board evaluations.

Making Things Better

Whatever issues may be raised by a governance assessment, it's almost guaranteed that no progress will be made towards improvement unless board leadership is committed to the assessment process from the get-go. This may come from the board chair, from some other director in whom the board has confidence, or perhaps from the incoming chair. If the incoming chair leads or is closely involved in a governance review, this can be very beneficial, as this individual will be well placed to understand the rationale for changes and to drive implementation.

Some organizations interested in strengthening their governance may establish a task force or committee of selected board members. If this can be arranged, it means more directors will be involved in considering change options. Thus, as long as the committee functions well, there is likely to be more support around the board table when discussions of implementation begin. The overall goal must be to inspire the entire board to endorse the idea and direction of improvement.

Determining how to move ahead on a list of possible governance changes requires judgment and political skills. Typically, not everything can or should be undertaken at once. So it's necessary to set priorities, to determine which changes are urgent, which are important, and what sequence of implementation would make sense. Timing is usually critical. I have quite often encountered situations where it's been necessary to "grandfather" certain individuals whose interests are negatively affected by change proposals. To secure their support, it was deemed important not to amend their status or perquisites for a defined period. Similarly, it may sometimes prove desirable to delay some changes until, for example, certain board members have retired, or new ones have joined. In nonprofits, as in other settings, politics is the art of the possible, and compromise is often necessary to get key measures approved.

The Role of the Chair

Effective governance requires a clear understanding of roles. It calls for well-qualified people around the board table and a competent, collaborative CEO or executive director. It also requires a knowledgeable and effective board chair (sometimes called the president). Co-authors Leighton and Thain have written, "Leadership is the key success factor in the board system. In improving board effectiveness the problem and the solution begin with the chairman."

A few years ago, in an article entitled, "Not a Rocking Chair," I outlined the role of the chair and commented as follows: "Board chairs occupy a pivotal position as the heads of public organizations, often exercising great influence over both the process and outcomes of governance. If the board is a lever for achieving results, the chair is the fulcrum." [5] Here are some of the key dimensions of the chair's role.

It's up to the chair to make sure that the board is productive. He or she should direct the attention of directors to the most important issues facing the organization. Some may be external; others may be internal, involving interpersonal relations or other sensitive matters. An effective chair should be able to determine which kinds of issues need to be addressed by the board as a whole and which need to be addressed by only a subset of the board (in the form of an executive committee, or an in-camera board session, or in a one-on-one meeting with an individual).

One of the key dimensions of the chair's job is to keep the board on track, resisting the temptation to get dragged off into side issues or matters unrelated to the strategic plan. The chair should typically shape the agenda for board meetings, nearly always in collaboration with the CEO or executive director. Simply setting the agenda exercises powerful influence over where the board deploys its limited time. The chair and CEO/ED may also work jointly to establish a calendar for the board that indicates which recurring issues are to be addressed and when (e.g. updating the strategic plan, approving the annual plan and associated objectives, reviewing the budget, undertaking the performance review of the CEO/ED, AGM, etc.).

Board management includes the responsibility of chairing the meetings, keeping them on time and on track, and managing the performance of individual directors, communicating with them between meetings. It also involves making sure that the board has the right committees and task forces, and that the right individuals are chairing each.

In a well-performing board, directors will recognize an accountability to the chair for their performance. This is generally not an issue when things are going well, but when problems arise, the chair may need to have private conversations with individuals about their performance. Likewise, if a board member decides to step down prematurely, the chair may wish to hold an exit interview to ascertain the reasons; this is a desirable practice in any event when directors come to the normal ends of their terms.

One of the most important areas of influence available to the chair is in helping to shape the composition of the board, keeping in mind the importance of succession and working with the nominating committee to draw in new directors with the right attributes. Also, there's the challenge of determining how to constructively "retire" individuals who are not pulling their weight or who may be undermining the board's ability to work as a team.

Then there's the matter of board culture. As discussed later in this chapter, culture has a significant impact on the board's ability to perform and to elicit the best possible contribution from each director. A key element of the chair's job is to establish a collegial atmosphere and to foster values and norms supportive of board performance. The chair must also read the subtle aspects of board debate and anticipate issues that may be divisive.

> [The effective chair will] perceive important signs of dissent long before it is obvious that questions are becoming pointed, cross-examination rough, the atmosphere tense. . . . The key signals to look for are individual interests and attitude, body language, verbal, supportive intervention, position taking, manner and behaviour. . . . [R] eading the different surface and underlying meanings of the language of dissent is a skill requiring wisdom, experience and insight.[6]

Fostering a collaborative relationship with the organization's executive head is at the heart of the chair's role. Many authors describe this relationship as a partnership, and like any important partnership, it needs to be handled with intelligence and sensitivity. The chair and the CEO/ED together comprise the linchpin connecting the board and staff, with all major board communications flowing through the chair to the CEO/ED, and all-important matters of staff interest flowing to the board through the chair. This relationship is vital to sound governance. Where the two incumbents collaborate harmoniously, things work. When they have significant differences in values or approaches, life can become very difficult for both the board and staff. Fundamentally, the chair needs to be able to trust the CEO (and vice versa); the stronger the mutual regard, the more governance will flourish.

The chair–CEO relationship is inevitably complex. On the one hand, the chair needs to be "open, supportive and friendly" while at the same time being "tough, demanding and professional."[7] The chair is usually the director designated to conduct the performance review of the CEO. It takes a talented and perceptive person to manage a relationship with these elements of ambivalence effectively.

Finally, there is the matter of external relationships. Nonprofits may have a wider range of accountability relationships than many organizations in the private sector. Members, if there are any, need to believe the organization is functioning in their best interests. Funders or donors will want to be convinced that their funds are being used responsibly. Regulators or professional bodies will want to feel confident that standards are being observed. Unions will be concerned that their members are being fairly treated.

These and other stakeholder relationships make it necessary for an organization to share information about how it is spending money and what it has achieved through its programs and activities. Much of the work associated with external accountability will be conducted by the executive head, but certain aspects, particularly those involving financial relationships, will almost certainly need to implicate the board chair. In addition, the chair often has an important representational role. The board that leaves all representational responsibilities and significant accountability relationships in the hands of paid staff may be denying itself access to information critical to its strategic planning and its governance. And this may make it difficult to conduct a meaningful performance review of the senior staff person.

In summary, if done properly, the chair's job is multifaceted and demanding. Jim Schwarz is a US-based consultant who assumed his first position as a board chair about twenty years ago. Recently, he became chair of another board, having gained wide-ranging experience on other boards and as a consultant in the intervening years. "My view now of what I need to do as chair is so different from what I did 20 years ago," he told me in an interview. "Even as someone who knows this stuff really well, I find this so hard. To do a half-way decent job takes a ton of time."

Selecting the Chair

Given the central importance of the board chair, one would think that nonprofit organizations would pay close attention to the qualifications required for an effective chair and the process used to select one. However, that's often not the case.

An organization I was assisting a few years ago was having significant difficulties with board leadership. Sometime previously, the directors had decided to establish a "board ladder" whereby those willing to serve as officers would first become secretary, then treasurer, then vice president and, ultimately, chair. The underlying and demonstrably false premise of this approach was that any individual moving up the ladder possessed the expertise and other attributes necessary to carry out the tasks associated with each of these positions.

At the time, what the board sorely needed was a chair with a solid understanding of governance, a broad perspective, and strong leadership skills.

However, because of their ladder system, the next person in line to assume the job was an accountant who had previously been the treasurer. "I'll be bringing my experience as an accountant to bear when I'm the president," she told me. "I think it's important to get into the detail of things and I'm going to have the board keep a close eye on all aspects of operations in future."

Nonprofits should have criteria for the kind of individual needed to fill this position, and the foresight to bring potential new chairs into the board at an early stage. Ideally, when the time comes to make a choice, there is at least one (and preferably more than one) well-qualified candidate to choose from. Some nonprofits complement their selection process with training for the chair, so that the incumbent is well prepared to take on his or her role.

In the context of a far-reaching review of its governance and strategy initiated in recent years, the Canadian Medical Association (CMA) decided to make the board chair a paid professional position. They went through a formal recruitment process, employing outside consultants to help. Ultimately, they appointed an individual who was not actually a member of the board, but who in their view possessed the mixture of expertise, leadership skills, and commitment to help drive the reform process forward. The chair is appointed for a three-year term, renewable once.

According to Tim Smith, the CMA's dynamic CEO who spearheaded the organization's reform program, this practice has attracted a good deal of outside interest, not only in Canada but also south of the border.[8] Overall, the CMA has made a very serious investment in the professionalization of its governance; the appointment of a carefully selected external chair is but one example of the many changes it has adopted. Not many nonprofits have the same kinds of resources that were available to the CMA to make such an investment, and I am not suggesting that "hiring" a paid outside board chair would be an appropriate or feasible move for most organizations. However, I cite this example because the CMA's choice to appoint its chair in this manner provides a vivid illustration of how critical the position is, and how much hinges on the competence of the individual occupying this role.

The Board's Culture

How relationships are handled and how discourse happens around the board table can have a major impact on the quality of governance.

In the late 1980s, Nancy Axelrod founded a nonprofit called the National Center for Nonprofit Boards in the US; she served as its CEO from 1987 to 1996. (The National Center has now morphed into BoardSource.) Axelrod helped to raise consciousness about the importance of the board's own culture with the publication of *A Culture of Inquiry* in 2007. In it, she argues that an effective board is not one that values harmony and compliance. Rather, it recognizes what a powerful influence culture has on its performance.

> A board's culture consists of a combination of formal and informal rules, agreements, and traditions that have developed slowly and unconsciously over time. Culture determines who makes the decisions, who speaks to whom and in what manner, how board and staff members relate to each other, and even where board members sit at the board table. Culture also drives decisions about what role the chief executive has in board meetings, where the board invests the lion's share of its time, and what issues are considered sacred cows.

A well-performing board promotes a "culture of inquiry" by fostering the following norms:

- A sense of mutual respect, trust, and inclusiveness among board members;
- The capacity to explore divergent points of view in a respectful rather than adversarial manner;
- A willingness to gather relevant information to inform decisions;
- Equal access to information;
- The presence of active feedback mechanisms that help the board engage in continuous improvement; and,
- An individual and collective commitment to decisions, plans of action, and accountability to follow through on the board's agreements.[9]

Axelrod pointed out how, at Enron, the prevalent culture had hobbled the board's performance. "[A] number of individuals understood that something was wrong. Many suppressed their concerns and questions. Others who voiced their concerns were either ignored or penalized." The board chair, Ken Layton, apparently just wanted to hear good news. "[O]ne of the hardest things in the world is to find people who will say to a successful and powerful leader that he or she may be wrong. Unfortunately, nonprofit board members have also been reluctant to challenge charismatic or successful chief executives until a problem emerges."

Her book provides practical suggestions as to how a more open, inclusive, and constructively critical board culture might be fostered. These include providing for explicit discussions about how the board is functioning, shaping the process of board orientation, developing appropriate board agendas, presenting information for consideration in a way that encourages discussion, and conducting periodic board self-assessments or evaluations, perhaps using an external consultant or facilitator.

Axelrod is not alone in stressing the importance of board culture. Dr. Laurence Prybil is a nationally reputed American academic who has conducted leading-edge research into the performance of big health organizations in the US. Unlike much research into governance, Prybil's work provides empirical evidence of the correlation between sound governance and organizational performance, and he has isolated those factors that influence organizations' success. His research has led him to strongly encourage boards and their CEOs to "give careful attention to the boardroom culture that currently prevails within their organization and determine steps that can be and should be taken to make it healthier and more effective."[10]

Prybil identifies these as the attributes of a productive board culture:

- Board meetings are characterized by high enthusiasm.
- Constructive deliberation is encouraged.
- Respectful disagreement and dissent are welcomed.
- The board is actively and consistently engaged in discourse and decision-making processes. Most board members are willing to express their views and constructively challenge each other and the management team.

- The board's actions demonstrate commitment to the organization's mission.
- The board closely tracks the organization's performance and actions are taken when performance does not meet targets.
- There is an atmosphere of mutual trust among board members.
- The board systematically defines its needs for expertise and recruits new board members to meet these needs.
- Board leadership holds board members to high standards of performance.[11]

Prybil's last point is important. For a board to be effective, it needs to adopt what I call a performance culture or a performance orientation. It's not enough to have a culture where directors just get along with each other. The board has a job to do. Here is another area where the influence of the chair is so important. In my view, a chair needs to secure the board's agreement that it should be performance oriented or performance-focused. In doing this, the chair is in saying, *we agree that we are taking this job seriously, we are setting high standards for ourselves.*[12] If a board agrees to be performance-focused, this can have several implications—for example:

- The board will collectively adopt the view that its work should add value to the organization and will hold itself to account for doing so.
- The chair can delegate some work in support of the board to individual directors, who will take that delegation seriously.

- The chair can hold committee chairs and other directors to account for meeting deadlines, turning up on time, coming prepared to meetings, etc.
- When certain tasks need to be undertaken, directors will generally be willing to step forward and volunteer, understanding that good performance can't be achieved if people are not prepared to share the load.
- Directors who consistently do not perform can expect to be invited to leave the board.
- Staff will realize that supporting the board is a responsibility to be taken seriously.

Why the Board's Role Is Often Poorly Understood

A very frequent impediment to board performance is a lack of role clarity. It's not uncommon to find that board members don't really understand either the role of the board or their own responsibilities as directors. Why is this a recurring problem?

Politics

A contributing factor in some cases, no doubt, is politics. When personal interests or ambitions subordinate organizational interests, there can be a struggle for power and influence between board and staff. For example, a board chair may want to show that he or she is unequivocally in charge. Such individuals may like to take the credit for any important accomplishments and to be visible at all public events. They may pay little attention to other directors and relegate staff to a very subordinate role instead of treating them as partners. Conversely, there are some CEOs or executive directors who are so deeply invested in their organization that they overlook the board's fiduciary role and treat directors as if they were an impediment or a nuisance. Circumstances such as these can certainly contribute to confusion in board–staff relations.

A related problem may be frequent turnover in board membership combined with indifferent leadership. Directors who have been briefed on their responsibilities move on, and a new crop arrives. Some new members may never have served on a board—or not served on a board that knew what it was doing. If the board is led by an individual for whom politics and prestige are more important than performance, the board is likely to lack a sense of purpose or discipline. This may in turn encourage directors not to invest much time in trying to understand their role.

Conceptual Issues

There is another deeper, conceptual reason that can contribute to confusion about the board's role. This is because of the overlap between the concept of governance and the concept of management, an issue discussed previously, in chapter 2.

Moreover, it is not easy, in a few words, to pin down just what governance means or implies. It is hard to define because it deals with a complex and multifaceted subject. What is reasonably clear is that governance is concerned with decisions about bigger organizational issues such as mission, direction, and strategy, and that it is also concerned with accountability—providing high-level oversight to ensure things are operating as they should, that money is well spent, and that people are held to account for their performance. These are big ideas; understanding what they may imply in particular circumstances often requires interpretation and judgment.

Changing Circumstances May Shift the Board's Focus

The board's role is not static. It can, and should, vary according to circumstances. A 2014 addition to the private sector literature on governance by a trio of experienced directors and academics argues that we ought to "rebalance" board responsibilities. There is a need to take account of current circumstances in determining what the board's role should be at a given time: "Directors need to know when to take charge, when to partner [with staff], and when to stay out of the way."[13]

I share this view. Exceptionally, a board, or a board officer, may need to step forward and assume new responsibilities when circumstances require it. I was chair of a social service organization a number of years ago when a public relations crisis erupted, arising from certain historical events that had come to light and that reflected badly upon the organization. Even though the problem had occurred many years previously, there was much negative publicity. Lawsuits were threatened. How to deal with the situation?

After considerable discussion, the board concluded that the then CEO did not possess the temperament or experience to manage this crisis; it required board intervention and leadership. So the board's role shifted, and remained shifted for a number of months, particularly in the areas of communications and media relations, until the crisis died down and the board's role could then return to a more conventional state.

If circumstances may require a board to play a different kind of role at different times, even for a limited period, one can see how, for some people, this could contribute to uncertainty about what the board's role is.

As a Small Nonprofit Grows, the Board's Role May Become Ambiguous

Another factor may generate confusion around the border between board and staff: evolution. Many nonprofits start out, as de Tocqueville noted, simply as groups of citizens who decide to establish a board to accomplish shared goals. A start-up board like this is just a group of volunteers. What's done is done by the board members. Many (perhaps most) organizations in the sector reside in this zone. Boards of this kind are sometimes described as "operating" boards.

However, organizations may decide they could accomplish more if they had staff. So, through donations from community members, or a government grant, a series of fundraising events, or a combination of these, they acquire funds and are thus able to hire one or two employees—maybe more in due course. But as staff are hired, some board members may become uncertain about their responsibilities. This is because they may continue to function as part of the "operational team," especially if there's more work than staff can handle. Now, however, they must also function in a classic governance or oversight role because the organization is externally accountable for funds it has received.

Not all organizations that are in this sort of situation, where directors have a kind of hybrid role—partly operational, partly as governors—run into difficulties. If there is an experienced executive director or CEO who is clear about the division of responsibilities between board and staff, or if there is a knowledgeable board chair who understands these issues, then uncertainties or misunderstandings can usually be dealt with easily. This is particularly true if there is a relationship of openness and trust between board and staff and regular communication.

However, not all organizations are in this enviable position. People who joined the board initially because they were can-do, hands-on kinds of folks may begin to feel uncomfortable. Meanwhile, staff members, perhaps led by a newly hired executive director, may feel that directors are interfering in their jobs. The directors needed to play a governance role may require different skills from the individuals who founded the organization. Getting rid of members of the old guard who may no longer fit in, while seeking to bring on new kinds of directors, can be difficult, painful, and for some, confusing.

In times of transition such as this, the board chair and the CEO or executive director should keep an eye on the relationship between board and staff, dealing expeditiously with any issues that may arise. Transparency and open communication will help to reinforce trust and avoid controversy.

For all these reasons, it's important for nonprofits to have written role statements for the directors and officers of the board, the executive director or CEO, and the chairs of any committees that have been established, such as finance and audit or governance and nominations. If the role of any position temporarily shifts as a result of changing circumstances, this may be recognized explicitly in a simple manner, such as a resolution of the board.

Orientation Programs

One way of helping to clarify directors' understanding of the board's role is through an orientation program. Many nonprofits state that they have such a program, but in some organizations, this "program" may simply involve presenting each new board member with a binder containing two or three inches of documentation. This may include, for example, the mission statement, bylaws, strategic plan, governance policies, board minutes, committee structures, the board calendar, financial statements, and perhaps, somewhere in the stack, some role statements. (Contemporary organizations that can afford it are increasingly putting much of this kind of documentation in a board portal, a section on their website that's password-protected and dedicated to the board's exclusive use.) As a modality for board orientation, the "binder" or web portal is better than nothing—but probably not much. Here's why.

Often this kind of information is too much for a new director to absorb; indeed, it may seem so overwhelming that it gets deferred for future consideration (and then never gets read). The new director may know little about the organization, or about the significance of different documents, so the information lacks context, which makes it difficult to understand or retain. Documentary material is not likely to provide information on sensitive subjects that may have a bearing on how the board functions, such as the origins of the strategic plan and its significance, the culture of the board, key interpersonal relationships, working with the board chair, or who's who on the board. More fundamentally, experts on adult education would be unlikely to endorse a learning program based largely or solely on written information. Documents are of course useful for reference, but on their own, as a means of orientation, they are of limited value.

Experienced individuals who have wrestled with the challenge of bringing board members up to speed often express frustration at the difficulty of doing so. Here are typical comments from interviews I held:

- From an official in a foundation: "Lots of executive directors complain about their relationship with their board. We have not got to the point where best practices for governance have become well established in the sector."

- From a senior individual in an umbrella organization: "I ran a centre intended to train organizations to teach nonprofits about liability and risk management. In some ways, it was very successful: we got many people through the program, we got great evaluations. But, at the end the day, I don't think it made any appreciable difference in terms of effecting significant change in the sector. Why? Because there is too much turnover, people come and go all the time. Unless there is something that embeds the change in an organization and there is a serious commitment to change, it won't 'take.'"

- From Ontario Capacity Builders: "Orientation of new board members is a perennial difficulty, especially around the role of the board and the role of staff. Most courses are out of the range of most nonprofit organizations."

To supplement documentary briefing, various measures can be helpful. An experienced board chair, simply in the course of exercising his or her responsibilities, can provide guidance to uncertain directors. New directors can be assigned a more experienced director as a mentor. An interview with the executive head will certainly be helpful, as may visits with other staff to get a sense of program activities and to build relationships. Occasional, workshops, perhaps led by a knowledgeable consultant, can be useful; but the results of such events may soon be forgotten unless there are follow-up sessions, or unless the information conveyed becomes embedded in the procedures, policies, or culture of the board. Directors can sometimes be sent to courses outside the organization, if the nonprofit can afford the cost, or they can be encouraged to subscribe to webinars that are becoming more and more widely available.

Sometimes, at the start of meetings, individual directors in rotation can be assigned a role to observe how the board is working, in addition to participating in discussions. This process is particularly helpful if the board has had a prior discussion of norms or values that directors agree they should all respect; such a discussion will provide a frame of reference for these "mini-evaluations." At the conclusion of the meeting, there may be a brief feedback session and a general "how did it go?" discussion involving all directors. Such mini-evaluations can provide insights for new directors on board norms and expectations, in addition to making all directors more conscious of how they can work together constructively.

Some nonprofits have addressed the challenge of board orientation by developing an in-house program. For example, the Ontario Real Estate Association (OREA) represents over 64,000 brokers and salespeople who are members of Ontario's forty real estate member boards. On behalf of the Real Estate Council of Ontario, OREA provides registration education in the province and supports its members through publications, educational programs, government relations activities, and special services. Former CEO Ed Barisa is a strong advocate of director training.

> Nonprofits have to invest in this. Our association saw the need in 2006 as we saw people coming up through the ranks to the provincial board who lacked basic knowledge of fiduciary duties or how boards work. We set up a program to educate our volunteers; the first time someone wants to be on a board at the local level, they are exposed to this. We keep giving more and more training, so that by the time volunteers get to the provincial board, we are much better off.[14]

The program has grown over time; it consists of a series of layered modules that guide participants along a "volunteer leadership path." They learn about governance, working on committees, leadership, presiding at meetings, communication, and similar topics through a combination of classroom training, e-workshops, and online "Just-in-Time Learning" videos (publicly available through the OREA website). Specialized training on subjects such as media relations is also available. Elaine La Chappelle at OREA's Centre for Leadership Development attributes much of the program's success to the fact that they do a lot of surveying and focus groups. "We learned early on that we have to improve and evolve in response to demand. We rely on many subject matter experts to develop course content and we are attentive to adult learning principles to help make the learning effective."[15]

Many nonprofits would not have the resources that OREA has to mount a program of this scope. However, the OREA example provides insight into what can be done by a larger nonprofit that is committed to director education. It also serves as a reminder that governance is a many-layered subject; it's not something that can be picked up through a single briefing of a couple hours or just by reading through a pile of documents.

A Board Coach

Another method of helping a board and its members to understand their roles and perform well involves a board coach. Under this approach, an outside individual such as a consultant with governance expertise is retained to attend and provide feedback on each board meeting. The coach may not take part in the meeting's discussions, except perhaps on questions of process or conduct, but comments at the end to the board, either in camera or with key staff present. The coach may also run periodic briefing sessions for directors on various aspects of governance. The board chair and the chief staff officer may select the coach jointly.

Cathy Trower, a former Harvard researcher and an experienced governance consultant, likens this to having a personal trainer to keep fit. She points out that it takes time, persistence, and discipline to develop "governance muscles."[16] She suggests that a coach's services might encompass an initial assessment of the board, including direct observation of meetings and interviews with board members. It could include, thereafter, helping to design the content and format of meetings, surfacing unspoken concerns among board and staff, naming dysfunctional behaviours, and providing real-time feedback at meetings or debriefs after meetings. Coaches can also help to transfer knowledge as board membership turns over.

It's important to select the right kind of individual to play this role. A consultant I spoke with told of an organization where the corporate counsel was invited to sit in on board meetings. In this case, the presence of this particular individual dampened the directors' self-confidence and caused them to defer to him instead of expressing their own views. In due course, the practice was discontinued.

The Right People Around the Table: Board Composition

Another issue with a fundamental impact on governance is board composition. A board is only as capable as its members, and a difficulty frequently faced by nonprofit boards is an insufficiency of adequately qualified directors.

To address this, a governance practice that has become more widely adopted in recent years is the establishment of a nominating committee. Initially, these committees were accorded the responsibility simply to find candidates willing to stand for election or appointment to the board; its members would roll up their sleeves a few weeks before the annual general meeting and see whom they could attract as likely recruits. However, as experience with such committees developed, it became apparent that to do their job properly, they needed to be able to tie their work into the strategic plan. A well-formulated plan would indicate in what direction the organization was headed; the nominating committee would then seek recruits who matched the organization's needs in the years ahead.

Following the lead of corporate boards, many nominating committees for nonprofits now use what is conventionally called a skills matrix (I believe "attributes matrix" may be a more appropriate name, since it's not just about skills). These help to identify the gap between what the board has now in terms of competencies and attributes, and what it may need in the future. The matrix may also assign levels of importance to each skill or attribute and indicate the minimum number of directors required who possess it. There's no lack of examples of board matrices, as five or ten minutes on the Internet will reveal.

The Governance and Nominating Committee

The nonprofit that takes the issue of board composition seriously (and every nonprofit should!) ought to have a person or a committee that oversees and manages all the issues related to board recruitment and orientation. Increasingly, such committees are made responsible for both governance and nominations because these issues are so closely linked.

It's up to this committee to develop and periodically update this matrix by reviewing the desired attributes and competencies of board and committee members, and also, sometimes, of board officers. A proactive committee might receive expressions of interest for involvement in the work of the board, identify prospective candidates, and solicit their involvement. It might conduct interviews or arrange to meet and assess them in person. The committee could then make recommendations to the board for appointments to the board and to committees; it might, in some cases, also make recommendations regarding the chair of the board and committee chairs.

Many contemporary boards look to this committee to make other contributions. For example, it may take on the responsibility of determining how to bring new board members up to speed and consider what orientation practices would best serve the organization's needs. Likewise, it may take on the additional responsibility of monitoring governance. Thus, for example, it may consider whether the board or its officers might need to be updated with respect to new governance practices or legislation; whether the organization has appropriate governance policies in areas such as performance monitoring, CEO evaluation, diversity, or code of conduct; or whether it is operating in accordance with those policies and with its bylaws. A governance and nominating committee that assumed all or most of these responsibilities would have an ongoing task throughout the year, not merely in the few weeks leading up to the AGM. It's my impression that the concept of governance and nominating committees is becoming increasingly prevalent in the nonprofit sector, which is a welcome development.

Unfortunately, there is one aspect of board recruitment that does not seem to be working as well as we might wish: succession planning, both at the board level and for senior staff. A promotional email from BoardSource in June 2016 indicated that only 53 percent of nonprofits in the US had a committee dealing with succession planning; the situation is likely similar in Canada. Many nonprofits may be caught in a classic catch-22 dilemma: they need to have knowledgeable board members to carry out governance-related tasks and improve the organization's performance, but if they don't have such board members, it may be very difficult to implement initiatives that will help to engage the people needed to provide effective governance in the years ahead.

Succession Planning

This is a challenge that all nonprofit boards face. It has several dimensions: first, ensuring readiness of high potential individuals to take over leadership responsibilities as board membership revolves over time; second, working to engage members of the younger generation (i.e., millennials) as baby boomers and others retire; and third, attempting to ensure that board composition reflects the population it serves. In all this, the importance of diversity as a dimension of composition in today's context needs to be taken into account. Surprisingly, at the time of this writing, the majority of boards don't seem to be rising as well as they might to these challenges.

Cathy Taylor at the ONN has a broad perspective of developments across the province. In her view, "There is a lot of concern in the sector about succession and getting the right skill set on boards. But I hear few solutions—organizations struggle with a succession plan."[17] The ONN's study of leadership cited earlier reported, "With significant indications of leaders leaving their roles, the important question to nonprofit organizations and their boards of directors is, 'Do you have a plan?' The short answer to this question from the survey is *no.* Fully two-thirds of respondents indicated that their organization did not have a formal succession plan for senior leadership."[18] These findings were echoed in a survey of Canadian associations conducted by the CSAE in 2015.

How to Engage Generation Y

In *Convergence*, the previously cited study of the nonprofit sector, the authors underline why it's important for boards to start engaging with and involving millennials.

> Younger generations comprise an increasing percentage of the workforce, and they bring with them new values and expectations around work, activism, and the use of technology. This dynamic may challenge the ability of nonprofit organizations to attract and provide a place for this new generation to find meaningful participation.
>
> [T]he current leadership of the sector is faced with the inevitable task of succession planning. Although much has been made of a possible leadership deficit as baby boomers approach traditional retirement age, the realities of the economic downturn and changing attitudes about work

> and retirement have redefined the terms of this discussion. The challenge is not so much the wholesale changing of the guard that was feared, but the need to figure out how the generations can work together effectively now and in the future. . . .
>
> [T]he future will require nonprofits to understand how to share leadership across generations. This shift will be fraught with stereotypes and assumptions on all sides. . . . There are . . . significant distinctions in how younger generations value, approach and leverage engagement, transparency, technology, professional development and work-life balance. These differences will have to be negotiated.

Engaging millennials is a subject that sometimes just seems to lead to hand-wringing. Some people point to the books that portray Generation Y members as self-absorbed and disinclined to join organizations or make commitments to them. If these ideas are seen as the last word on millennials, then one might conclude that not much can be done to attract them to the nonprofit world.

Certainly, there is cause for concern about the challenge of engaging millennials in existing nonprofit organizations, as there is some evidence that they tend to favour causes rather than organizations. However, there are strategies for engagement that work. For example, leaders in the OREA have come up with an approach to engaging millennials that seems to be serving them well. Several years ago, they saw the need to become more proactive in reaching out to younger members of their organization. Barb Sukkau was Chair of the Board at the time; she noted that several real estate associations in the US had set up a "Young Professionals Network" (YPN) and she saw no reason why this approach could not be emulated in Ontario. "Young people are the future of our association," she said. She met with the CEO to discuss the possibility; he agreed to assign a staff member to support the initiative. She did a bit of lobbying to convince board members of the merits of the idea, got board approval, and the result has been the development of an Ontario-based YPN that now has over 1,000 members.

The YPN is in most ways a virtual organization, centred on relationships and information sharing on the Internet. Its original purpose was to connect and engage young people, but as it has developed, it has become a resource for any member of the association who wishes to join. Participants use it as a vehicle for networking and for exchanging information, often on very practical questions such as agent referrals or simple technology problems. When the association has events, such as workshops or an AGM, they will include activities focused on YPN members.

While the YPN is not explicitly about governance, Barb says, "It's a kind of first stepping stone to involvement for younger persons. The members learn about committee structures and how governance works in the association. It's also a vehicle that helps to attract young people to become involved in OREA's award-winning leadership program."

Getting the YPN off the ground was not difficult. "We began with a core group of about ten young realtors to start it up," said Barb. "They met several times during that year to define what it would be, what it would do. Now if you want to join you just have to link to the Facebook page. We had to make it easy to join." To help keep the program going, a chair is selected annually by the board chair and the staff of the association.

> It has to be someone who is excited about the program; you must have someone who cares. Anytime there is an event the chair is the YPN representative. This can be prestigious and exciting for that individual. The chair creates agendas and convenes periodic meetings of a core group that monitors the program and comes up with new ideas, but once you get it off the ground it does have a kind of organic way of growing on its own—it's kind of self-maintaining. YPN members don't like committees or cookie-cutter approaches, but they do get a lot accomplished. If no one did anything it might die off, but as long there are people who care about it, it will prosper and grow.[19]

Another interesting initiative that has successfully engaged millennials in governance roles is provided by the Community Leaders' Program in Louisiana, discussed in the final chapter.

Ensuring Diversity

For some time, there has been growing awareness, both in the corporate world and the nonprofit sector, of the need to consider whether board composition is reflective of the population that the organization seeks to engage—and not merely in respect to youth. There are potent arguments for increasing diversity on the board. The rationale for doing so may derive from many factors: demographics, business opportunities, government funding criteria, or the need to demonstrate social responsibility and the organization's commitment to principles of equity and inclusion. Nonprofits concerned about maintaining relevance and legitimacy in today's world would be wise to bear in mind this aspect of board recruitment. Moreover, as discussed in chapter 4, a diversity initiative would ideally go beyond board composition to embrace other dimensions of the organization, such as its workforce, its vision and values, its programs and policies, partners, membership, outreach, and so forth.

In conclusion, getting the right people around the table—or "on the bus," as Collins says—is one of the most important issues facing the nonprofit sector. The responsibility for tackling this issue may rest with a nominating, or a governance and nominating, committee. Is this process working well? There's a lot of room for improvement. At present, in many organizations, the process of "getting the right people on the bus" probably needs to be reinforced.

The Executive Director or CEO

The role of the nonprofit executive director or CEO has been described in many other publications, so I don't propose to go over that territory in detail; rather, my purpose here is to consider what the trends and turbulence described in this book may imply for the executive director's role (for convenience I'll use the term "executive director" or ED in the following paragraphs, but the discussion applies equally to organizations that have designated their senior officer as CEO. Some people think the term executive director is better suited to the nonprofit sector.)

The job of ED looks somewhat different in different organizations. For the ED of a small nonprofit, the essence of the job may simply involve keeping one's head above water, or, to change the metaphor, fighting the latest fire that has broken out. An organization with only one or two staff members and an ambitious mission may have great difficulty finding staff time to invest in the improvement activities so often urged upon nonprofits: strategic planning, risk management, board orientation, adaptation to the latest HR-related legislation, staff development, and the like. Such organizations may have to place a lot of reliance on their board members for help in these areas.

A more conceptual description of the ED's role, better suited to larger organizations, proposes that this individual must serve as the nonprofit's institutional memory and "be the . . . steward of strategy."[20] As such, the ED serves as the "keeper of fit" (in the sense of alignment), making sure that strategy remains focused, that it is internally consistent, that new programs mesh with others, and that, despite a board that may know little about technology, the organization makes the necessary investments to keep up with new developments in this area.

The environment facing nonprofits in coming years will make many demands on their leaders. As part of its ongoing research into HR issues affecting the nonprofit sector, the ONN commissioned a study to assess the state of nonprofit leadership in relation to anticipated future competencies and to identify strategies for leadership development.[21] Not surprisingly, this study observes that there is "much uncertainty in the nonprofit environment." This is due to factors such as technology; economic, social, environmental, and political pressures on the sector; demographic changes including both an aging population and diversity; blurring boundaries between the public and private sectors; and resource challenges, including pressures from funders seeking more results with fewer resources.

While noting that organizations within the sector are very different from each other, the study concludes that, in general, "Nonprofit leaders are not well prepared for the new frontier—the leadership style and competencies of the past do not prepare or support sector leaders for reframing the role and relationship that the sector has in society." The authors assert that tomorrow's leaders will require new kinds of capabilities and competencies: the ideal leader will need to be part builder, thinker, mentor, storyteller, innovator, connector, and steward. Multiple approaches to development will be required to prepare the next generation of leaders for their job.

The study outlines steps that can be taken by nonprofits to foster leadership talent, but argues that much more needs to be done, and this will be beyond the resources of individual organizations. There is a need for funding for a systemic strategy to support leadership development across the sector.

The Tough Dilemma Many Nonprofits May Face

As the sector evolves, many nonprofits may find themselves facing a daunting dilemma. Does the organization need to make a serious commitment to an entrepreneurial or quasi-commercial orientation? If so, what might that imply for its mission, its framework of values, and its leadership?

Many executive directors are deeply concerned about this question. The ONN study referenced above stated, "Most executive directors and sector leaders have been drawn to their organizations and their roles because of the mission. But [the pressures facing the nonprofit sector] . . . present an untenable role for executive directors/CEOs to manage, and can effectively disconnect leaders from their vision of leadership . . ."[22] A study participant put it this way: "By nature we are businesses. We can think that we're not, but we are. It's changed. If you want to be a leader of the future, you have to be entrepreneurial. Your consumer base will demand it and your funder will demand it. And this means a difference in leadership qualities that are expected of an ED."

Lester Salamon describes how market forces, coupled with numerous other pressures, have become an increasing preoccupation for EDs:

> These tensions have naturally complicated the job of the nonprofit executive, requiring these officials to master not only the substantive dimensions of their fields but also the broader private markets within which they operate, the numerous public policies that affect them, and the massive new developments in technology and management with which they must contend.
>
> Nonprofit executives must do all this, moreover, while balancing a complex array of stakeholders that includes not only clients, staff, board members, and private donors but also regulators, government program officials, for-profit competitors, and business partners; and while also demonstrating performance and competing with other nonprofits and with for-profit firms for fees, board members, customers, contracts, grants, donations, gifts, bequests, visibility, prestige, political influence, and volunteers. No wonder burnout has become such a serious problem.[23]

The relentless pressure to meet financial obligations may be denaturing the classic job of the executive director. More and more, EDs are being encouraged to "run it like a business" and to adopt management strategies that mirror those in the for-profit world. One way of responding to these demands could be to establish a social enterprise to generate funds for the nonprofit. But as discussed earlier in this book, setting up a social enterprise raises a host of challenges for a nonprofit, not least of which is the question of whether the existing staff leadership would be suited to manage this kind of entity.

With respect to existing staff leadership in the sector, the ONN study reported, "When asked . . . what motivated them to work in the nonprofit sector, 79 percent of [leaders] indicated that they wanted to do work that made a positive difference to society/community, and 61 percent indicated that they wanted to have the ability to work for a cause that they cared about. They are a group that is driven by mission."

What to do? These circumstances may raise very hard issues for some organizations. Having taken stock of the organization's environment and its financial prospects, board members and senior staff members may find themselves confronting these three questions:

- What would a major shift to a more explicitly entrepreneurial strategy entail? What would be the risks, opportunities, prospects of success?
- Could we make such a shift while remaining true to the mission that guides this organization?
- What kind of leadership will be needed to carry us into this new territory? What might this mean for our existing leadership?

Ideally, these kinds of questions should be the subject of conversations involving both the executive director and the board. However, some EDs may find such conversations threatening, making it hard for them to engage. As for the board, in principle, it has a key role to play in such discussions. One hopes the board would be up to the job, but some may have difficulty. Some boards may wish to draw outsiders with relevant expertise into these conversations to help to facilitate them and perhaps to provide independent perspectives.

The Executive Director and the Imperfect Board

In an ideal world, the executive head of a nonprofit would be able to turn to the board and find wise counsel, helpful perspectives based on experience elsewhere, and support in confronting difficult issues, including financial ones. But the world is seldom ideal, and the likely scenario for many nonprofits may be one where their board displays "limited scope and experience." In these circumstances, the executive head in search of advice and guidance may need to secure it elsewhere, perhaps by retaining an experienced executive coach, consulting a mentor, or networking with other nonprofit leaders.

If one were to ask a cross section of staff leaders what could be done to reduce their stress and make their professional life easier, my guess is that a great many of them would say either "Give me more staff!" or "Give me an effective board!" The relationship with the board of directors is the number one preoccupation of a great many CEOs and EDs, and when a board is ill-informed, poorly led, or generally floundering, it becomes a perpetual headache for staff. A weak board can diffuse energy, distract the organization from its mission, and undermine efforts to establish a sense of direction.

Earlier in my career, I spent several years in the federal government, working in the office of a deputy minister and then in the office of a senior elected minister. Some civil servants would muse that the best situation for a deputy minister would be to have a weak minister, the premise being that the deputy minister would then be able to run the portfolio with little "interference" from the political level. However, I never met a deputy minister who wished for a weak minister.

Weak ministers have to be constantly shored up; the deputy and senior staff never know what they might do next, and they often get into political trouble. They typically provide little sense of purpose or continuity in public policy. A poor minister can be a perpetual headache, just like a poor board in the nonprofit sector. What knowledgeable senior government officials hope for at the political level is a minister who listens and is willing to take advice, who is experienced, responsive to the public interest, and able to provide responsible direction. It's when they have that kind of leadership that they believe they can do their own job best.

Leading from Below

It's the same with nonprofit staff and their relationship to their boards, and in particular, their chair. An effective board can be a great asset; a weak one is a drag and a sea anchor. When a board is not strong, the executive head will face a challenge particular to the nonprofit sector (and to senior government officials with weak political leadership), namely the challenge of "leading from below." The executive head may see the need to improve the board's capacity and realize that unless she or he does something about it, this situation is likely to persist indefinitely. Nell Edgington talks about the CEO's "behind-the-scenes" role.

> [If CEOs understand] that this is their role . . . they [will] step up to the plate, and have the confidence to tell the board what they need. They will be able to pose the hard

> questions to the board about its structure, its needs. They'll be having those conversations and creating the impetus for change—and also working ahead of the meetings to set the right agenda and focus on the strategic issues.[24]

In a blog on this subject, Edgington responded to an interlocutor who wondered whether it was legal or ethical for a nonprofit leader to try to improve a board. She argued that board members, as volunteers, simply lacked a great deal of the expertise that the executive head usually possessed. Moreover, since "they have many more pressing items on their to-do list, a board of directors rarely functions at their best when left to their own devices. Therefore the executive director can and should play a critical role in helping the board leadership to assemble the type of board that will help move the mission forward."[25] The executive head can do this in a variety of ways, such as:

- helping to ensure clarity of the organization's mission;
- supporting the board in determining what skills, attributes, and other capacities would, if added to the board, enhance its ability to support the mission;
- suggesting candidates to fill gaps;
- trying to ensure that the right kinds of issues get onto the board agenda;
- proposing changes to the board or committee structure that would enhance performance;
- meeting one-on-one with board members annually, or more often, to help them understand how they can be most helpful;

- supporting the board chair in the execution of her or his responsibilities, especially those that involve holding board members to account or asking certain members to resign if necessary.

Not all executive heads will have the experience or the self-confidence to take on these tasks, and much will also depend on the kind of board chair that is in place and the relationship between these two individuals.

Scott Haldane, the former president of YMCA Canada, maintains that too many executive directors are uncertain or timid, seeing themselves as powerless to make any changes. He suggests that the title of executive director is more suited to smaller nonprofits where incumbents may be seen and may see themselves as subordinate to the board. He views the title of CEO as more appropriate to larger, more complicated nonprofits with complex external relationships. "The title of CEO describes a relationship with the board which is more of a partnership, where the CEO has relatively few parameters and the authority to make most of his or her own decisions." In Haldane's view, "Strong CEOs will see improving weak board leadership as part of their job."[26]

The question of whether a CEO—or an executive director—might help to strengthen the board is an issue that a candidate might want to raise in the context of a hiring decision, as it may be more difficult for the individual to intervene on this matter once in post. Before being hired, a savvy candidate would find out whether the board was in need of improvement and would inquire in an interview as to whether she or he had a mandate to help address this issue. (Prospective EDs/CEOs might likewise inquire if they have the authority to make key hire-or-fire decisions on staffing issues.) If hired, an executive head would likely need to build a coalition for change and to develop with volunteer leaders a vision of change that is clear and compelling—and also to show what is at risk if change does not occur. The CEO might also need to help ensure the appointment of an effective incoming chair when the term of the existing incumbent comes to an end. Weak boards won't usually have a succession lined up.

Supporting the CEO/ED through Tough Times

What can be done to support executive leaders in the demanding years ahead? One initiative that some CEOs/EDs may find helpful would be to build a strong mutual support network if they have not already put one in place or joined an existing group. I've noticed over the years that much of the most valuable advice these leaders get comes from their peers. Leaders are faced with an endless stream of questions in running their organizations. Some are strategic; others are operational. For example: How do I deal with this difficult manager in my organization? Where might my organization find a new board member with strong financial skills? What organizational changes do I have to make to be compliant with recent legislation on privacy or HR management? Is it worth investing in a new software system to help manage membership or programs—and which system is best? How can I get the board more effectively engaged in strategic planning? What percentage change in staff compensation levels should I authorize this year?

Here's how one group of CEOs found a way to deal with questions such as these (for the sake of privacy, I have altered some details in what follows.) Some of these individuals knew each other socially but had no ongoing relationship. One member of the group decided to launch a "CEO Circle" and became the informal organizer of periodic breakfast meetings. A social get-together over dinner to discuss the idea and start building relationships helped to get things started.

Details included membership by invitation—CEOs/EDs only—a consistent venue, and consistent group membership; no formal agenda, and no outside speakers. The subjects for discussion were whatever was on the minds of participants that morning. The group met roughly every six weeks at a table where conversation was easy and reasonably private. People attended depending on their own work pressures, but the conversation was sufficiently valuable that most participants made efforts to protect the time if they could. The face-to-face character of the meetings meant that subjects could be debated that were too sensitive to be discussed through social media or emails.

Apart from the costs of a periodic breakfast, this initiative made negligible revenue demands on the participants and required only an hour or so of their time every few weeks. Perhaps CEOs or EDs elsewhere might find a model along these lines worth emulating. What it does require is a little leadership on the part of at least one individual to move the idea along.

---

1. BoardSource, The Source: 12 Principles of Governance That Power Exceptional Boards (Washington, DC: BoardSource, 2005).

2. In the rest of this chapter (and in most of this book, unless otherwise indicated), I am discussing nonprofits that have staff working in collaboration with the board, headed by an executive director or CEO.

3. William M. Ryan, Richard P. Chait, and Barbara E. Taylor, "Problem Boards or Board Problem?" *Nonprofit Quarterly* 19, no.4 (Winter 2012), 6–13.

4. Richard W. Leblanc, "20 Questions Directors Should Ask About Governance Assessments," (Toronto: Canadian Institute of Chartered Accountants, 2005.) See also Dr. Leblanc's blog. "Archive for the 'Performance and Evaluation' Category," *Governance Blog*, accessed August 7, 2018, http://rleblanc.apps01.yorku.ca/category/performance-and-evaluation/

5. Tim Plumptre, *Not a Rocking Chair - Providing Effective Leadership to Public Organizations* (Ottawa: Institute on Governance, 2007). http://www.tpaconsulting.ca/app/media/Not%20a%20Rocking%20Chair%20dr%208%20%20May%2017%2007.doc

6. David S.R Leighton and Donald H. Thain, *Making Boards Work* (Toronto: McGraw Hill Ryerson, 1997), 236.

7. Roméo Malenfant, *La gouvernance stratégique - la voie de l'imputabilité* (Québec: Éditions D.P.R.M., 2005), 144 and 152. My translation.

8. Author's interview, April 18, 2018.

9. Nancy R. Axelrod, *A Culture of Inquiry* (Washington, DC: BoardSource, 2007), 1–2.

10. Lawrence Prybil et. al., *Governance in High Performing Community Health Systems: A Report on CEO and Trustee Views* (Chicago, 2009). http://www.nonprofithealthcare.org/resources/GovernanceInHigh-PerformingCommunityHealthSystems.pdf/ The other factors are strong values-based CEO leadership, well-understood mission, vision, and values, a highly committed board, strong clinical leadership (in health systems), and clearly defined organizational objectives, targets, and metrics.

11. Prybil et. al., *Governance in Community Health Systems*, 3.

12. See Peter F. Drucker, *Management: Tasks, Responsibilities, Practices* (New York: Harper and Row, 1973), Part One, 2. "Leadership is a foul-weather job."

13. Ran Charan, Dennis Carey, and Michael Useem, *Boards That Lead* (Boston: Harvard Business Review Press, 2014), 1.

14. Author's interview.

15. Author's interview.

16. Cathy A. Trower, *The Practitioner's Guide to Governance as Leadership* (San Francisco: Jossey-Bass, 2013), 212–214.

17. Author's interview.

18. Elizabeth McIsaac, Stella Park, and Lynne Toupin, *Shaping the Future: Leadership in Ontario's Nonprofit Labour Force* (Ontario Nonprofit Network, 2013), 46.

19. Author's interview.

20. Harrison Coerver and Mary Byers, *Road to Relevance* (Washington, DC: The Center for Association Leadership, 2013), 35.

21. Peter Clutterbuck and Caryl Arundel, *Leading Our Future Leadership Competencies in Ontario's Nonprofit Sector,* pre-publication version, cited with permission (Toronto: Ontario Nonprofit Network, 2017), 4.

22. McIsaac, Park, and Toupin, *Shaping the Future,* 38, 45, 87.

23. Lester M. Salamon, *The Resilient Sector Revisited* (Washington: Project Muse, Brookings Institution Press, 2015), 95.

24. Author's interview.

25. Nell Edgington, "Nonprofit Leaders Have More Power Than They Think," *Social Velocity* (February 16, 2017), accessed August 7, 2018, https://www.socialvelocity.net/2017/02/16/nonprofit-leaders-have-more-power-than-they-think/

26. Author's interview.

CHAPTER 9
SUSTAINING NONPROFITS AND THE NONPROFIT SECTOR

Social and Economic Impacts of Digital Technology

We are living in confusing and unsettling times. Events that in the last century appeared remote—famine, terrorism, refugees, climate change, revolutions, pollution—are on our doorstep today. Emerging technologies such as virtual reality are bringing these events even closer. Social media are remaking the rules of marketing, advocacy, and politics. Even people who work in high-tech industries have difficulty keeping up with the blizzard of technological changes buffeting us all.

While a small sprinkling of individuals are amassing stupendous wealth, a great many others see their incomes sagging. They watch the cost of daily living rising, and they see housing prices heading into the stratosphere. They worry about the future of their kids, and they wonder what to make of their own economic future, and that of their family, in a world they have difficulty understanding.

These pressures bear particularly on the nonprofit sector for a variety of reasons: shortage of resources, uncertain board leadership, lack of access to capital, lower compensation levels than in many businesses or in government, lack of job security, absence of benefits and pensions . . . the list of challenges is long and getting longer.

Yet in coming years, society will almost certainly need to call upon the resources of nonprofit organizations to cope with some big problems. Possibly the most important, after climate change, may be the impact of artificial intelligence.

Tom Jenkins is the Executive Chairman of Open Text, one of Canada's largest corporations. It develops software for big companies, governments, and other organizations; it employs over 10,000 people and has been recognized as one of Canada's Top 100 Employers. Jenkins delivered a speech in the fall of 2016 on the policy issues raised by digital technology.[1] He asked, *do we really understand the changes that digital is driving in society, both here in Canada and throughout the world? We generally regard digitization as a force for good. But is it?* Here are some of his remarks.

> [T]he next technology wave can be considered as the Fourth Industrial Revolution. It is estimated that we will [have] . . . a combined computing ability that will surpass the human brain within five years. [A] possible and profound short-term economic impact . . . [is] massive unemployment in some sectors. If you are a truck driver, a taxi driver, an Uber driver, even a banker, an accountant, a lawyer, all of these jobs may be substantially eliminated in the next 10 years.
>
> So far, humanity has been able to take advantage of these productivity improvements and create better quality of

> life and standard of living. But . . . our ability to create those productivity improvements and our ability to benefit society has noticeably started to slow down and, in some cases, reverse.
>
> The problem with digitization in its current form is that we are not replacing the lost jobs fast enough since we are not organized to retrain our human employees on the scale and the speed required.
>
> Our modern economics will require a re-think in terms of the distribution of wealth and the balance and value of work in our consumer society.
>
> A teenager in Africa with a smartphone and the Internet has more information at their [*sic*] fingertips than the President of the United States did fifteen years ago.
>
> The pace of innovation is very deceiving. Most of [us] believe that growth and change occurs in a linear fashion. . . . In fact, it does not. . . . Studies show that the pace of innovation is geometric. . . . [Change] will happen faster than any one of us can imagine.

Jenkins also discussed the impact of digitization on physical infrastructure, such as roads and bridges (much less will be needed, digital infrastructure will come to replace it, jobs will be eliminated), on education (millennials' brains have been shown to be different from those of previous generations, they learn in different ways—therefore educational systems will have to be transformed), and on governance (machines will very soon be able to think infinitely more quickly than humans. How will people lead and interact with them?).

Will government be able to cope with these challenges? Kevin Lynch does not think so. Lynch used to be the top civil servant in the federal government, Clerk of the Privy Council; he then became vice-chair of the Bank of Montreal. In a recent article, he foresaw the following:

> [There is a] growing gap between the scale, scope and speed of [digital] transformations and the capacity of government to implement timely and effective policy changes. Put simply, in today's dynamic world, last-generation governance and policy processes are a poor match for next-generation disruptive trends, and trust in government is an early casualty.[2]

Technological change moves too quickly, and its reach is too vast and complex for government to be able to apprehend it fully, let alone formulate and implement policies for dealing with the full range of its effects.

One might have hoped that Lynch, with his deep background in government, might have had solutions to propose for this quandary. But he did not: he only had questions. "What are the new jobs technological change will create and the skills they will require? What are the models to reskill and retrain the workforce? How are the benefits of this technological change and costs of its adjustment going to be shared?"

> What we do know is that [w]orkers made redundant by robots and global supply chains, aware of increasing income inequality and decreasing equality of opportunity, are embracing populist tenets ranging from nationalism

> to protectionism, from distrust of institutions to anger. As history teaches us, bouts of fervent populism seldom end well.

As if to illustrate these themes, in 2017, *The New Yorker* magazine published an article entitled "Dark Factory." Drawing from examples in a diversity of industries and locations across the USA, in China, and in Europe, the article provides insights into how more and more blue-collar jobs are being taken over by robots, and also how income inequality is starting to become increasingly prevalent.[3]

> For decades, the conventional view among economists was that technological advances create as many opportunities for workers as they take away. In the past several years, however, research has begun to suggest otherwise. "It's not that we're running out of work or jobs per se," David Autor, an M.I.T. economist who studies the impact of automation on employment, said. "But a subset of people with low skill levels may not be able to earn a reasonable standard of living. . . . We see that already."

The article cited a corporate executive, who said:

> The winds are changing. . . . Part of the reason why populism is rising around the world is that the gap is getting too big. Having so much inequality creates instability in a country. Maybe twenty years ago we still had too many poor people, but they believed they had a shot. I believe some of that is being sucked away.

Further to this, the article explained how Uber purchased a company that sells technology designed to automate long-haul trucking; it noted that there are almost two million long-distance truck drivers in the US, "most of whom are male and lack a college degree." Similarly, construction jobs are threatened by automation, as are jobs in warehouses. "Amazon . . . currently has more than ninety thousand employees at its US distribution centers . . . [but it] is on a quest to acquire or develop systems that can replace human pickers." The warehouse of the future may have no space inside for humans at all. Similarly, the factory of the future may be dark since it could run twenty-four hours a day with no need for illumination; all the work would be done by robots.

> The disruption spurred by automation is not anticipated to be limited to low-skilled work; significant encroachments are expected in the white collar sector as well, with experts predicting that professionals such as accountants, doctors, lawyers, architects, teachers and journalists will all compete with increasingly capable computers in future.

Political scientists are just beginning to consider the implications of these developments. For example, a 2015 Princeton study found that "mortality rates for middle-aged white non-Hispanic Americans with only a high school diploma have been increasing since the late nineteen-nineties. They attribute this trend to "deaths of despair" tied to the long-term loss of economic opportunity . . . and to possibly related factors such as opioid abuse." One of the researchers stated, "I don't think this is stable politically. The Trump thing is probably just the beginning."[4]

An Increasingly Important Nonprofit Sector

Here are some conclusions we may draw from this discussion.

1. The turbulence we have been experiencing in recent years is likely to increase dramatically, and soon.

2. Governments will have enormous problems coping with these developments. Currently they do not have the capacity to do so; rather, they appear to be in over their heads. Solutions are unclear, if they exist at all.

3. As governments try to muddle through, with questionable success, trust in them may decline further.

4. Unemployment and income inequality are likely to grow, adding to the challenges confronted by governments and society in general.

What does this mean for the nonprofit sector? Obviously, this sector will not be able to arrest the pace of change in society. But what it may be able to do is provide some solutions—or at least palliation—to the problems that are developing.

In 1966, *Time* magazine published an article predicting the leisure society. "By 2000, the machines will be producing so much that everyone in the U.S. will, in effect, be independently wealthy. With Government benefits, even nonworking families will have, by one estimate, an annual income of $30,000-$40,000." A major problem, said the article, would be how to use leisure meaningfully.[5]

Of course, the leisure society never materialized. Wages did not rise in line with automation, and inflation eroded buying power. Instead of enjoying longer holidays and personal time off, people had to continue to work—perhaps even longer hours than previously. Computerization, cell phones, and other aspects of the digital world have amplified both the intensity and the ubiquity of work. Many people work evenings and weekends and carry their work with them on holidays; many employers think nothing of contacting their employees during off hours. The 60-hour-plus workweek has become commonplace. The border between employment and home life has faded. Stores that used to be closed on weekends or Sundays are now open 24/7.

Let's assume for a moment that the issue of income distribution discussed above is at least partially addressed by policies such as a guaranteed income—an option that lately seems to be attracting more attention. If people have some income, but there is less employment available in the future, or if the work week is significantly shortened due to automation, what will they do?

Consider what North Americans do now when they are not at work. How do they and their families spend their evenings or weekends? Where do they turn to enrich their lives or enlarge their relationships when they retire? The answer is that a great many of them turn to organizations in the nonprofit sector. Here they find opportunities to collaborate with others, to enjoy sports and other forms of recreation, to find an outlet for their abilities as visual artists, actors, or musicians, to help new immigrants or refugees settle into the country, to learn a new language, to support health care organizations as volunteers, to practice their religion, to learn new skills, or to deliver services to less fortunate members of the community.

We have a tendency to think that what's most important in our lives is what happens in our workplaces; we may forget to take account of the richness, scope, and diversity of what happens when we are not at work. Whether we realize it or not, most of us actually spend a significantly larger portion of our lives outside of employment than we do in it, particularly if account is taken of retirement years. What happens outside of work matters. And what happens outside of work is very often where nonprofit sector organizations play a pivotal role for many of us.

There is another way in which nonprofit organizations may have a valuable role to play in the future that's coming. Unemployment and a lack of income will both tend to give rise to social problems, including mental illness. Nonprofit organizations will need to be there for people who are at risk and for their families.

Furthermore, the sector employs thousands of people in paid jobs, as well as in volunteer positions. Yet when policy makers ponder what do to about unemployment, the nonprofit sector is almost never mentioned. It's as if nonprofit jobs don't count—only those in high-tech firms, manufacturing, resource extraction, agriculture, and the like. Perhaps they will begin to realize that the nonprofit sector, currently forgotten or an afterthought, should become a central element in public policy when issues of unemployment are being addressed. Maybe, in the years ahead, we will need to change our vocabulary.

Experienced analysts know that to frame sound public policy, the point of departure must be to ask the right questions. It can be difficult to know what those questions should be. A question on many politicians' lips today is: how can we create more jobs? What if, instead, the question was: *what mix of policies would provide opportunities for a more fulfilling life for citizens, while making it possible for them to meet their basic income needs?*

Where might such a question lead? Would we look at the nonprofit sector through a different lens?

Not only does the sector provide many paid jobs, but it also provides a wealth of opportunities in the form of volunteer positions. Some people put little store in work of this kind—if it doesn't attract a wage, they think, it can't be very valuable. But others disagree; in fact, some famous individuals have suggested that the most valuable—or most personally rewarding—work is voluntary. Consider these reflections[6]:

- "The intelligent way to be selfish is to work for the welfare of others." — The Dalai Lama.
- "Only a life lived for others is worth living." — Albert Einstein.
- "We make a living by what we get, but we make a life by what we give." — Winston Churchill.
- "The meaning of life is to find your gift. The purpose of life is to give it away." — William Shakespeare.
- "The best way to find yourself is to lose yourself in the service of others." — Mahatma Gandhi.
- "Service to others is the rent you pay for your room here on Earth." — Muhammad Ali.
- "Life's most persistent and urgent question is, what are you doing for others?" — Martin Luther King, Jr.

Of course, dedicating yourself to volunteer work or the service of others may be difficult or impossible unless you and your family have food on your table—unless, somehow, your basic income needs are being met.

How governments cope with the challenge of income disparities in society in the years ahead may determine how well we are able to cope with the blizzard of innovation predicted by Jenkins and others.

A Sector at Risk

Whether in Canada or the US, to realize its potential and play the role that is needed in the years ahead, the nonprofit sector will need to be in a strong and stable position. However, it is not as robust as might be desired.

There's a strait between two islands off the west coast of Scotland called Corryvreckan. As the tide runs through it, the surface churns and surges, and it becomes an awe-inspiring, fearsome whirlpool. It's very dangerous, sucking down imprudent vessels, a death trap for careless sailors. To determine the cause of this great whirlpool, said to be the third largest in the world, the Royal Navy apparently once sent a diver down to investigate. He had strict instructions to come up before the tide turned. However, he took too long. As he struggled upward, he suddenly realized the bubbles from his scuba gear were not rising; they were disappearing into the depths.

While the seas they are navigating may not be quite as fearsome as Corryvreckan, the nonprofit sector contains many organizations at risk. Many may founder in the next few years as they try to cope with the stresses discussed earlier in this book.

Many nonprofits, buffeted hither and thither by crosscutting currents, have opted to adopt an entrepreneurial and quasi-commercial mode of operating. What effect is this having on the sector? Lester Salamon laments what he calls "the growing impact of the commercial/managerial impulse," pointing out that it eclipses the voluntarist character of the sector.

> Lacking the firm anchor of a single clear, dominant raison d'être—such as maximizing profit in the case of business—nonprofits are especially vulnerable to being pulled this way and that by whichever pressure is dominant at the moment.
>
> And this is just what appears to be happening at the present time. . . . [S]ignificant components of the nonprofit sector have moved far from the sweet spot that has historically earned the sector public trust. . . . [T]o survive in a demanding environment, nonprofit organizations are being forced to surrender what may be too many of the things that make them distinctive and worthy of the special advantages they enjoy . . . potentially undermining as well much of the sector's historic attention to civic activism. . . . Despite the important contributions they make, organizations find themselves at present in a time of testing.[7]

Will a commercialized nonprofit sector be able to play the same role in society that it has historically, or will the sector gradually erode, surrendering its nonprofit status and giving way to a host of small businesses? Is this the future we want? What can be done, at a societal level, to help sustain nonprofit organizations?

One valuable step would be to strengthen the policy environment for the sector and a second could involve bolstering its leadership. Here are some suggestions.

Enhancing the National Policy Context

The policy context for nonprofits in Canada is set in part at the federal level and in part in individual provinces. For brevity, I am restricting my remarks here to the federal context.

There is a growing need for a policy dialogue with respect to the future of the nonprofit sector, as it faces a problematic future. In February 2017, the Senate of Canada hosted an "Open Caucus" on the sector. In the context of that event, Imagine Canada submitted a policy paper prepared by Brian Emmett, Chief Economist for the Charitable and Nonprofit Sector and a former top official in the federal government. Emmett pointed out how the sector contributes to the country through a "triple bottom line" in that it serves needed social, cultural, and environmental missions, it creates jobs (thousands of them), and it contributes to economic activity and growth.[8]

However, he painted a picture of what he called "a slowly intensifying crisis" likely to engulf the sector. This will undermine its ability to continue to make these economic and social contributions at the very time when they will be more urgently needed. The essence of his argument is simple:

- Government revenues are likely to decline due to demographic changes (retirement of a major cohort of the population and diminution of their income) as well as other factors such as declining productivity, lower resource prices, and falling labour force participation.

- These factors will, in turn, lead to diminished revenues for the nonprofit sector from both governmental and private sources.

- Meanwhile, because of those same demographic changes, there will be an increasing requirement for the services the sector renders to people in need, such as the homeless, immigrants, the ill, and the elderly. As demand goes up, the ability of the sector to deliver will decline.

- Concurrently, the ability of the sector to contribute to economic growth, to increase employment, and to foster activity in areas such as education, environmental protection, religious observance, arts and culture; or health will decline.

Unless initiatives are taken to address this emerging crisis, says Emmett, the consequence, in economic terms, will be a "social deficit of twenty-three billion dollars"—the social deficit being the yawning gap between demand (the need for services rendered by the nonprofit sector to Canadians) and supply (the funding needed to sustain the sector's ability to provide those services). "The magnitude of this looming deficit indicates there will be no single-bullet solution—rather, it will require a comprehensive rethink by governments and by charities and nonprofits."

It is not easy for the nonprofit sector to pursue policy discussions with the government. Among the impediments are the lack of resources and expertise in government relations in the sector, and the lack of understanding of nonprofits within the federal government. Successive cutbacks by the federal government have led to economies and staff reductions in umbrella organizations that might speak on behalf of the sector. According to Hilary Pearson, long-serving president of Philanthropic Foundations Canada,

> Both time and money are a problem. All the umbrella organizations for the sector—my own, Community

> Foundations of Canada, Imagine Canada, Volunteer Canada, and others are working on a shoestring. We have very few resources, and for most of us, government relations are not a core part of our mission, so we are limited in the time we can devote to it. Overall, the infrastructure of the sector has weakened since the VSI [Voluntary Sector Initiative].

Public policy needs to rest on sound argument and solid information. Another difficulty facing the nonprofit sector is that it lacks up-to-date data on key issues related to the scope, revenues, and size of the sector. As noted earlier in this book, the previous Conservative government declined to renew the Statistics Canada survey of the sector that had been funded through the VSI. It also apparently decided to reduce financial support to certain key umbrella organizations. And it cancelled the long-form census. According to Pearson, "The long-form census was crucial to social service organizations and to our sector. The lack of such data has been a challenge for us." (Fortunately for the sector, the Liberal government elected in 2015 decided to restore the long-form census.)

Several decades ago, there was an attitude of openness and support for nonprofit organizations. Federal departments with responsibilities in areas such as culture, social service, and international development looked to organizations in the sector to help pursue government priorities. They were prepared, selectively, to provide sustaining funding in the form of core financing, and to experiment with new modes of service delivery by relying on the voluntary sector. In the intervening years, attitudes have changed. Moreover, in the wake of civil service cutbacks, it can be difficult to find places within the federal government where officials have an ongoing engagement with and understanding of the nonprofit sector. The policy capacity of the government itself has been seriously weakened, if not eviscerated, because of cutbacks.

For there to be fruitful discussions between the government and the sector, the government might consider providing a modest amount of supportive funding to some umbrella organizations in the sector to enhance their ability to do the research, analysis, and consultation that must underpin sound public policy. Likewise, a speech by the prime minister that recognized the value of the sector would certainly influence attitudes within the public service in ways that would be beneficial to the sector.

Issues That Might Be Addressed

One issue that might be addressed through negotiations with the federal government, specific to charitable organizations, is the uncertainty surrounding certain kinds of political activity that such organizations might engage in. The Canada Revenue Agency has defined limits on "political activity" and monitors charities specifically on this aspect of their work; organizations that step over this line have been in danger of having their charitable status queried or revoked. The existing context on this issue is complex, confusing, and uncertain; the combination of both facts and perceptions regarding the involvement of charities in "political activity" has given rise to what some have called an "advocacy chill."

Moreover, if an elected government wanted to discourage some charitable organizations from publicly raising certain issues, or if it wanted to stifle public discourse, it could imply, directly or indirectly, that their charitable status might be at risk. During the tenure of the last Conservative government, this was the experience of some charitable organizations involved in environmental activities. Some leaders told me in interviews how their agencies were subjected to aggressive and disruptive CRA audits that distracted their staff from program-related activities and cost them thousands of dollars.

Fortunately, in 2016 the newly elected government decided to establish a Consultation Panel on the Political Activities of Charities to address these problems. The Panel's report was released in May 2017.[9] The report advanced proposals to modernize the legislative framework for charities, a much-needed change. At the same time, the then-Minister of National Revenue, Diane Lebouthillier, announced the end of the charity audits initiated by the previous government. It remains to be seen what specific action the government is prepared to take in light of the Panel's report—the Minister's initial response was noncommittal[10]—but developments to date have inspired more hope that needed changes are being contemplated.

Other issues that might be tackled in negotiations between the sector and the government include the following:

- the government's bias towards project funding and its resistance to providing sustaining, core funding to organizations in the sector that need it;
- the over-insistence on accountability and reporting that can create unreasonable burdens on nonprofit organizations;
- the progressively shorter time frame within which project funding tends to be made available;
- the difficulties faced by nonprofits that require access to capital.[11]

On the latter point, the point of view of CRA is, "Earning profits to fund nonprofit objectives is not considered in itself to be a nonprofit objective. An organization should fund capital projects and establish reasonable operating reserves entirely or almost entirely from capital contributed by members or from accumulated, incidental profits."[12] In other words, earning anything more than "incidental" profits or surpluses could cause an organization to run into problems with CRA. The Agency's highly questionable premise seems to be that there are donors or members for all nonprofits able and willing to provide operating reserves or capital funds to meet each organization's needs.

Anyone who has run an organization that is not supported by the public purse from year to year knows that an operating capital reserve and a predictable cash flow are critical to survival. CRA's position suggests that they may lack an understanding of the realities of financial management for organizations that, unlike government departments, cannot rely on the public purse to meet their needs for capital.

A related issue that could usefully be addressed is the confusing and unclear attitude of CRA with respect to the establishment of social enterprises by charities. Charities that fail to stay within the parameters set by CRA may inadvertently compromise their charitable status; but because the parameters are unclear, the risk of stepping over the line is increased.[13]

A final and significant matter that should be considered in discussions between the government and the nonprofit sector is whether Canada should follow the lead of other countries in providing a stronger presence for the sector at top levels of government. At present, the Canada Revenue Agency has a dual responsibility—to help sustain the sector and to enhance government revenues. These roles are incompatible, and not surprisingly, the revenue generation mandate generally trumps the sector sustaining role. Are we asking the fox to guard the henhouse? There are a host of other reasons the agency responsible for collecting revenues should not be expected to have the expertise or motivation to take much interest in the health of the nonprofit sector.

In light of the size of the sector, and in view of the increasingly important role it may be called upon to play in coming years, Canada might consider establishing a government department or agency with a mandate clearly focused on the nonprofit sector—as it has for the commercial sector by establishing, years ago, departments specifically devoted to the interests of industry and agriculture. It might consider following a lead established by countries such as England and Wales, New Zealand, Australia, Ireland, and Singapore. All these jurisdictions have recognized in one way or another the inappropriateness of combining a financial gatekeeper function with a responsibility to foster civil society. As a recent Australian publication on this issue has argued, tax collecting agencies are "overburdened with their core ... duty to maximize State revenue and protect the tax base.... Their gatekeeper role is ... performed defensively, permitting little flexibility and lacking sophistication."[14] Current organizational arrangements at the federal level in Canada are seriously outdated and need to be brought into the twenty-first century.

If there was political interest in tackling some of these issues, this would indeed be good news for the sector, particularly if the government understands the need to include representatives of the nonprofit sector in the deliberations leading to policy change. Too often, the nonprofit sector is an afterthought in government policy. To address the issues outlined above, sector representatives need to be at the table when those discussions are taking place. Furthermore, it is likely that there will also be a need for leadership at the political level, perhaps in the form of a minister with a specific mandate to address the needs of the sector. Emmett, who as a former senior government official knows about these things, argues: "[T]o ensure ongoing dialogue and partnership, we should consider the utility in stewardship at a ministerial level—someone in cabinet whose job it is to advance enabling policies for the sector. . . "

Strengthening Board Leadership in the Sector

Governance is complex. It requires time and commitment to achieve a sound understanding of the important features of what is, in effect, a discipline. The trend towards professionalization makes significant demands on the many members of society who, in a volunteer capacity, have assumed the responsibilities of board membership. How many board members could say with confidence that they have a good grasp of their organization's programs and activities, that they have absorbed its bylaws and governance policies, that they are cognizant of the legislation that bears upon their organization, and that they understand their fiduciary responsibilities? How many feel adequately qualified to provide strategic direction to their organization, to oversee its finances, to ensure that it has sound risk management protocols and performance management metrics, to help set program priorities, and to contribute knowledgeably to discussions about strengthening the organization's governance?

Boards need help. Beyond actions that nonprofits might take individually to reinforce their own boards, what else might be done to provide such help?

There is certainly some assistance available. There are more and more resources to be found online, including webinars, articles, and job postings. Training may be offered by organizations such as Charity Village or by local umbrella organizations, such as Volunteer Ottawa in my own community. However, these resources and opportunities are typically disconnected from each other and the quality of some, particularly those that are under-resourced, may not be as high as one might wish.

An interesting example of a community-centred board development initiative that is imaginative, well-planned, and durable is this program in Louisiana.

The Community Leaders Program in Louisiana

Many nonprofits lack the resources to retain a governance coach, as suggested by Cathy Trower, or to send directors on costly training programs. Rather than leave it up to harried nonprofits to solve their own problems, some communities or foundations might wish to follow the example of the Louisiana Association of Nonprofit Organizations (LANO). It's a state-wide member organization that "advocates for the nonprofit community and strengthens the effectiveness of those committed to improving Louisiana." Over a decade ago, LANO became aware that its community was facing problems similar to those confronting many others, and it decided to do something about it.

> [O]ur nonprofit leadership landscape was aging and it lacked diversity of race and skill set. Our community, like all others, had a tendency to recycle the same group of leaders for nonprofit board service. There was a shrinking pool of what many felt were "knowledgeable seasoned

> leaders" who sat on multiple boards and were tapped out with their time and resources. Nonprofit executives were asking for help to address these issues and more.[15]

LANO, in partnership with a local bank and The Community Foundation of North Louisiana, established a Community Leadership Program (CLP).[16] Local nonprofit leaders had told LANO they needed a pool of new board members between the ages of 25 and 40. They wanted to get away from their historical reliance on Caucasians and to introduce people of diverse race to governance.

To accomplish these goals, the CLP built relationships with other organizations in the community to develop their program. Once it was established, they reached out proactively to attract certain categories of individuals, in particular millennials, by linking with the United Way, the local chamber of commerce, local young alumni associations of colleges and universities, as well as other partners in the community. Kay Irby, who pioneered the program, explains, "We have a lot of corporate partners who want to see their young persons engaged in the community."[17]

The number of applicants typically exceeds the thirty or so positions available in each session, so the CLP is able to select the most promising candidates. They choose, bearing in mind recruitment targets they have set, such as age or racial characteristics, and they monitor their success in meeting those targets. Individuals who are selected have to contribute $150 to the program, and they undertake to raise another $150 as part of their commitment. Each session costs about US$1,000; however, the program itself is largely free for participants except for their $150 contribution, as The North Louisiana Community Foundation funds it.

"Most foundations won't fund the same program over ten years, but our partnership is an exception," says Irby. Students are required to attend all the classes in the program, which consists of five evening sessions of three and a half hours each. Sessions include lectures and interactive activities as well as a hot meal; different people, including board chairs or executive directors drawn from the community, lead them. The sessions cover a wide range of governance-related topics as well as information on fundraising. They bring in local philanthropists from the area to listen to the students make "asks" and to give them feedback on how their presentations went.

The "Change Fund" is the last class. Four nonprofits are invited to submit proposals saying what they would do with funds that the class might provide to them; the students pick one to act on and then go out to raise money. "Older people don't like fundraising, but young people don't seem to care." Says Irby, "[T]hey are fearless." Collectively, the class has a $10,000 target. "Every class but one has raised $10,000; one raised $21,000. Turn 'em loose, they can do amazing things."

When the class is over, the program does not end. Subsequent "speed dating" for boards ensures that CLP grads are connected to local nonprofits. The program invites interested organizations to come to an evening event to see whom they might want to recruit. The graduates take part in a series of eight-minute interviews where they can assess a number of organizations, and vice versa. It is understood that no offers will be made that evening, but afterwards, either the organization or the students (now known as Community Leader Candidates) may make an approach. Says Irby:

> If there has been appropriate training, this sets a tone when a young person comes on to a board. Even though

> younger than other board members, a trained new member may know more than the older directors. They want to be on boards focused on strategic sustainability and growth. Program graduates often bring to the table a passion for the mission; results-oriented thinking; access to new networks and donors; fresh perspectives on old problems; an interest in solving problems; and excellent communication skills.

There have been occasional instances where a program graduate has joined a board, and then resigned soon afterwards because the other directors didn't seem to understand what governance entails. The newly trained recruits were frustrated at the ineffectual level of board performance.

Evaluation is taken seriously. CLP does a pre-test and post-test of new leaders; they evaluate each evening event. When a class is over, they do follow-up surveys in years one, three, and five to see if graduates are still serving. The results have apparently been very positive. Over 80 percent of graduates reported continuing board service three years after concluding their training. Many also said they were making financial contributions to their organizations.

The overall result of the CLP, according to Irby and Paula Hickman from the Foundation, is as follows:

> We have a diverse pool of educated and creative young professionals serving on nonprofit boards throughout the surrounding area. They are board presidents, finance chairs, committee chairs, and some of the best fundraisers in our community. Through education, hands-on

> experience, and exposure to nonprofit issues, they begin their board service with confidence and clarity about what it means to serve on a nonprofit board. They do not fill seats; they are engaged in being good stewards of some of our community's most treasured resources, the nonprofit sector.
>
> It's been suggested that both EDs and older board members should take the training also. We now reserve four slots for incoming board chairs.

Accreditation

Another measure that could help to strengthen the sector would be to widen the circle of accredited organizations. Previously I indicated that the Imagine Canada standards program seems to be the best general-purpose accreditation program available to the nonprofit sector in Canada. I did not do an exhaustive review of their program, but it was mentioned positively in my interviews with several organizations.

Peg Herbert is the founder and tireless executive director of a small international development organization called Help Lesotho.[18] Founded in 2004 to address the ravages of AIDS in a tiny country in southern Africa, the organization's programs "foster hope and motivation in those who are most in need: vulnerable children, girls, youth and grandmothers through initiatives in education, leadership training, and psychosocial support." It strives to be "an effective, sustainable international development organization working at the grass-roots level to create an AIDS-free generation, end the cycle of poverty and support the future leaders of Lesotho." The organization has over fifteen thousand beneficiaries annually in many rural locations. Says Herbert:

> We work for a country most people have never heard of. When we started, most people had never heard of Imagine Canada either. I do find donors increasingly skeptical and cynical. . . . For an organization like ours, the accreditation does help. We started the process [of applying] when we were about eight years old, and we were pleased to find that we were not that far off from Imagine Canada's expectations.
>
> A major motivation for me was to ensure the organization was sustainable and independent of me as founder, by having policies, procedures and approaches fully documented. Fortunately, we had a knowledgeable board chair who served as the liaison with Imagine Canada. He found them very helpful and supportive.
>
> They did a good job of guiding us through, but it was a lot of detail, a lot of work. Our annual budget is around $1.4 million. We have a small staff in Canada, so we were lucky to have a strong board that could support the process—we were very appreciative of their help. Even with that help, I found it onerous as Executive Director—there are lots of demands; you wear a million hats. Overall it took about a year from start to finish. Before policies, etc. can be submitted they must be board approved and that takes time.

> Once we were accredited, we were able to use the Trustmark on our materials and highlight this in our communications, along with other acknowledgements. Our donors are very smart and discriminating and this makes a difference. The Financial Post selected us in December 2015 as one of the top 25 charities in Canada, and the Imagine Canada process probably helped to get us there. I look back on the process and feel it was definitely time well spent.

As noted previously, Teri Thomas-Vanos is the former Executive Director of Rebound, a nonprofit that has received a number of awards for good performance. Among the factors contributing to Rebound's success, Thomas-Vanos cited the significant role played by the Trustmark:

> This has been really important. . . . We used it to promote our accountability and transparency; we had an official stamp to show that we met standards in these areas. As we had an annual audit, it carried weight with the board, and it supported our fundraising efforts since it enhanced our credibility in the community. Moreover, it was always a good motivator for staff. Accreditation was an awesome process to go through; we felt very supported by Imagine Canada, and there was lots of opportunity for consultation and mentoring for us along the way.

A much larger organization that has made extensive use of the Imagine Canada program is the YMCA. YMCA Canada is a federation of what were at the time forty-eight independently incorporated YMCA Associations that collectively represented one of Canada's longest standing and largest charitable networks.[19] It serves over two million people annually, with a special focus on children, teens, and young adults; its long-standing mandate is to advance the health and well-being of Canadians in spirit, mind, and body. The member associations are engaged in some of Canada's most pressing issues, including chronic disease, unemployment, early childhood education, social isolation, poverty, and inequality.

A number of years ago, when Don McCreesh was Chair of the Board of Directors of YMCA Canada, he became aware that there were great variations in the governance capability of the different YMCAs across the country. According to Scott Haldane, former president and CEO, "There was everything from yikes! to wow!"[20] When Don became chair of the board of Imagine Canada, he noted the prevalence of governance scandals in both the corporate and nonprofit sectors and was concerned about the charitable and nonprofit sector's vulnerability. He saw a need to do something to improve their level of governance performance. He also wanted the action to be self-regulated to avoid government-imposed standards that might not be sufficiently attuned to the reality of the sector.

A nonprofit wishing to become certified by Imagine Canada needs to work its way through the pre-application process mentioned by Peg Herbert. This can be quite extensive and costly for an organization as large as a YMCA. Haldane arranged with Imagine Canada that the National Office of the YMCA would take over responsibility for the pre-application process. This diminished the cost and had the ancillary benefit that it established a "community of practice" online through which local Associations began to share best practices with each other.

"Over time, nearly all YMCAs became involved. This exercise improved board engagement in many associations, and it allowed us to see where gaps in the Federation lay. Each member association had a chance to review its own situation."[21] Even if an organization does not have the desire or the resources to go down the road towards full accreditation, the standards are available online at no charge to any organization.[22] At the time of writing, a few other national organizations were considering entering into an arrangement with Imagine Canada along the lines of the YMCA initiative.

The Imagine Canada program is still evolving—for example, some questions were raised in my interviews about how onerous the application process is, and the level of detail required in some areas, or the possibility of improving standards related to performance measurement. It's also been suggested that the standards may be too oriented to charities, with a section on fundraising that does not fit other nonprofits. Perhaps in due course, Imagine Canada will see its way clear to becoming an organization that explicitly serves the nonprofit community as a whole, as well as charities—at present, its mission in this regard is somewhat blurry. I believe such a step by Imagine Canada would be helpful to the nonprofit sector.

Meanwhile, however, the program is still relatively new, and Imagine Canada is making efforts under the direction of its Standards Council to improve it. It also expects to extend the program's reach by promoting the Trustmark brand and by widening recognition of its standards both in the nonprofit sector and among funders. Haldane, like Herbert and Thomas-Vanos, would encourage this:

> I have heard from many colleagues that the process of preparing for accreditation represents an important organizational change and engagement opportunity. Boards become more connected to the organization, staff lift their game and the organization raises its expectations for itself.

While the "Trustmark" does not yet have wide recognition, strong charities use the accreditation as part of their "case for support."

Paving Paradise?

In her iconic song, "Big Yellow Taxi," Joni Mitchell sings, "Don't it always seems to go that you don't know what you've got till it's gone. They paved paradise and put up a parking lot." Sometimes we take for granted things that we shouldn't. We may forget to sustain important assets in our society—such as nonprofit organizations—despite their value and the risks they face.

I don't think nonprofits are all about to disappear, but I have no doubt that many will have a very difficult time in the years ahead. Some will, indeed, founder, no matter how important the work they are doing. Nonprofit organizations matter to Canada and to the U.S. for a host of reasons. The preceding pages may spark some ideas among nonprofits that will help them navigate the turbulent waters ahead. Perhaps other ideas may be spawned among organizations such as foundations, business corporations, or governments that will lead them to adopt new policies and practices regarding this sector that will also help to sustain it. Let's hope so.

* * * * *

1. Tom Jenkins, "Canada is Winning the Digital Race—But we are early in the race and the pace is about to increase. A Discussion of the Impact of Digital Technology on Public Policy," Ivey Lecture, London, November 3, 2016. The notes here are based on a speech given in Ottawa in October 2016. A somewhat revised version of the speech called "Leading in a Digital World" is available online. https://www.ivey.uwo.ca/cmsmedia/3774683/the-impact-of-digital-on-public-policy-oct-19-2016-ottawa-excerpt.pdf

2. Kevin Lynch, "How disruptive technologies are eroding our trust in government," *Globe and Mail,* May 1, 2017.

3. Sheelah Kolhatkar, "Dark Factory," *The New Yorker,* October 23, 2017, 70–81.

4. Cited in *The New Yorker* article, 80.

5. Cited in Thom Hartmann: "Whatever happened with the notion of 'The Leisure Society?'" *Thom Hartmann Program,* accessed August 7, 2018, https://www.thomhartmann.com/blog/2011/12/transcript-thom-hartmann-what-happened-notion-leisure-society-1-december-11

6. Cited by Greg Baldwin, President, VolunteerMatch on *LinkedIn,* May 5, 2015.

7. Lester M. Salamon, *The Resilient Sector Revisited* (Washington: Project Muse, Brookings Institution Press, 2015), 27.

8. Brian Emmett, "The Social Deficit: Our Written Testimony to the Senate Open Caucus," *Imagine Canada* (February 13, 2017), accessed June 20, 2017, http://www.imaginecanada.ca/blog/social-deficit-our-written-testimony-senate-open-caucus#comment-216286

9. Marlene Deboisbriand, Shari Austin, Susan Manwaring, Kevin McCort, and Peter Robinson, "Report of the Consultation Panel on the Political Activities of Charities," *Government of Canada* (March 31, 2017), accessed August 7, 2018, http://www.cra-arc.gc.ca/chrts-gvng/chrts/cmmnctn/pltcl-ctvts/pnlrprt-eng.html

10. "The Government Remains Committed to Clarifying the Involvement of the Charitable Sector in Public Policy Dialogue and Development" (news release), *Canada Revenue Agency* (May 4, 2017), accessed August 7, 2018, https://www.canada.ca/en/revenue-agency/news/2017/05/minister_lebouthillierwelcomesthepanelreportonthepublicconsultat.html

11. See Michael Hall, et. al., *The Canadian Nonprofit and Voluntary Sector in Comparative Perspective* (Toronto: Imagine Canada, 2005), IV. http://sectorsource.ca/sites/default/files/resources/files/jhu_report_en.pdf

12. Extract from the October 2013 report of the Nonprofit Organization Risk Identification Project of the Canada Revenue Agency, accessed August 7, 2018, https://www.canadiancharitylaw.ca/blog/the_non_profit_organization_risk_identification_project_nporip_report_final

13. See the submission by Ellen Martin to the Senate Open Caucus, February 8, 2017. "Modernized regulations should provide organizations with clear guidance around income generating activities and I believe should permit organizations where possible to earn profits so long they are able to demonstrate profits being reinvested into the organization's mission." Accessed August 7, 2018, http://www.imaginecanada.ca/sites/default/files/ellen_martin.pdf

14. Kerry O'Halloran, Myles McGregor-Lowndes, and Karla W. Simon, *Charity Law and Social Policy: National and International Perspectives* (Switzerland: Springer, 2008), 559.

15. "Community Leaders," *Lousiana Association of Nonprofit Organizations,* accessed July 2, 2016, http://www.lano.org/?page=Communityleaders.

16. The following notes are based on a presentation by Paula Hickman and Kay Irby at a BoardSource conference in October 2015.

17. Author's interview.

18. *Help Lesotho,* accessed August 7, 2018, http://www.helplesotho.org/

19. *YMCA Canada Annual Report 2015,* accessed August 7, 2018, http://ymca.ca/CWP/media/YMCA-National/Documents/Annual%20Reports/Annual-Report-2015-EN.pdf

20. Author's interview.

21. Author's interview.

22. "Standards Reference Guide," Imagine Canada, accessed August 7, 2018, http://sectorsource.ca/standards-community/standards-reference-guide

ABOUT THE AUTHOR

Photo: Michel Caron.

Over three decades, Tim Plumptre has worked in the nonprofit sector in many roles: as a CEO, a director, a board chair, a consultant to numerous organizations, a community volunteer, and a funder. He has led two nonprofit organizations and is the founder of the non-profit Institute on Governance where, over 17 years, he oversaw the development of research, training programs, and policy initiatives regarding sound governance in Canada and in over 30 countries abroad.

His consulting work has carried him to every province and territory of Canada and to several indigenous communities in the high north. An experienced, bilingual public speaker and facilitator, he is the author of a best-selling book on public management, *Beyond the Bottom Line: Management in Government.* This book became a best-seller within three months and was reviewed as "splendid: innovative, insightful … a 'must-buy' for any senior government official, or anyone aspiring to be one."

His current consulting work supports nonprofits, charities, and other public purpose organizations that deal with issues of strategy, governance, revenue development, and organization design.

Prior to founding the Institute on Governance, he was a journalist with the Globe and Mail, a Foreign Service officer, an assistant to a federal cabinet minister, and a partner with the international consulting firm William M. Mercer Ltd. Over his career, he has built a practice at the top levels of government departments, crown corporations, and public purpose organizations in a wide range of fields, including health, culture, community development, law, social services, child welfare, tourism, recreation, Indigenous affairs, and economic growth.

At the time of this writing, he has been voluntarily chairing the board of the Sylva Gelber Music Foundation, which provides grants to outstanding young Canadian classical musicians. Previously he has chaired the boards of the Ottawa Carleton Children's Aid Society and the Community Care Access Centre of Ottawa Carleton, as well as the palliative care Hospice at Maycourt in Ottawa. He has served on a number of other non-profit boards in the National Capital region.

He has been a Visiting Scholar at Massey College, University of Toronto, and is a former adjunct professor in the School of Graduate Studies at Carleton University and at Ottawa University. He has also been a member of the faculty of the Algonquin College Business School. He holds an Honours B.A. from the University of Toronto, a Master's degree from the London School of Economics, and a Certificate in Management Studies from Oxford University.

He can be reached through his company website: www.meta4consulting.ca or by email at info@meta4consulting.ca.

OTHER RESOURCES

Some readers of advance copies of this book indicated an interest in securing copies for each member of their board of directors or for staff. Discounts are available for orders of 10 copies or more.

For information regarding

- bulk orders
- speaking engagements by the author
- possible consulting engagements regarding issues discussed in this book or related matters

please call 613-518-2370 or send an email to info@meta4consulting.ca.

ACKNOWLEDGEMENTS

I have benefited enormously from the wisdom, patience, and generosity of a host of individuals in writing this book. Foremost among these has been my principal editor, professional collaborator, and spouse, Barbara Anne Laskin. Throughout the process of writing, she was a constant source of penetrating insights and critical ideas drawn from her own professional experience, including her work both as an adviser to boards and as a member of a wide range of organizations focused on community betterment. Later, through the process of editing, she brought her sharp intelligence to bear on my text, challenging ambiguity, clarifying meaning, correcting grammatical errors, and diligently checking every footnote. She was an exceptional and generous partner in this endeavour, as she has always been. I cannot overstate my gratitude to her, both professionally and personally.

Others who have helped to make this book what it is are the many clients in the nonprofit and public sectors that I have had the privilege of working with over many years. Each one provided me with new insights or taught me fresh lessons.

I wish to express my thanks to Dave O'Malley at Aerographics for his imaginative collaboration on the cover design of this book, and to the team at Friesen Press who helped me bring this book to life, in particular Judith Hewlett who piloted the book through the publication process,

Geoff Soch who was responsible for design and layout, and Oriana Varas who provided marketing support.

Last, but certainly not least, there are the many individuals who were prepared to sit through an interview—occasionally more than one—often for an hour and sometimes more, to share their perspectives on their own experience and on the nonprofit sector generally. I am exceedingly grateful for the help I received from all the people listed below. Thank you!

Michael Anderson

Lew Auerbach

Ed Barisa

Cathy Barr

Mark Blumberg

Raewyn Brewer

Tim Brodhead

Teresa Budd

Diana Carter

Bradley Chisholm

Andrea Cohen Barrack

Emerson Csorba

Dave Cybak

Sue Davidson

Gigi Dawe

Blair Dimock

Sarah Doyle

Peter Dudding

Nell Edgington

Sue Gillespie

John Graham

Scott Haldane

Al Hatton

Peg Herbert

Paul Hickman

Kevin Higgins

Natasha Himer

Jake Hirsch Allen

Kay Irby

Katha Kissman

Ron Knowles

Elaine Lachappelle

Natasha Lemire-Blair

Ondina Love

Bruce Macdonald

Don McCreesh

Lyn McDonell

Ross McMillan

Linda Mollenhauer

Colleen Mooney

Allan Northcott

David Nostbakken

Richard Paton

Douglas Pawson

Hilary Pearson

Lawrence Prybil

Jim Schwarz

Susan Scotti

Deborah Simon

Tim Smith

Barb Sukkau

Cathy Taylor

Glenn Tecker

Eric Termuende

Teri Thomas-Vanos

Liz Weaver

Leslie Wright

SELECTED BIBLIOGRAPHY – READINGS ON NONPROFITS & THE SECTOR

Alves, Bob, and Don Robertson. *The Not-For-Profit CEO's Guide to Improving Organizational Performance.* Alexandria, VA: Advanced Solutions International, 2015.

Anderson, Chris. *The Long Tail: Why the Future of Business Is Selling Less of More.* New York: Hyperion, 2006.

Anheier, Helmut K. "The Nonprofits of 2025." *Stanford Social Innovation Review* (Spring 2013).

American Society of Association Executives. *7 Measures of Success: What Remarkable Associations Do That Others Don't.* Washington, DC: ASAE, 2012.

Axelrod, Nancy R. *Culture of Inquiry: Healthy Debate in the Boardroom.* Washington, DC: BoardSource, 2007.

Barabasí, Albert-László. *Linked: How Everything Is Connected to Everything Else and What It Means for Business, Science and Everyday Life.* New York: Penguin, 2003.

Bell, Jeanne, and Maria Cornelius. *UnderDeveloped: A National Study of Challenges Facing Nonprofit Fundraising*. CompassPoint Nonprofit Services and the Evelyn and Walter Haas, Jr. Fund, 2013.

Benkler, Yochai. *The Wealth of Networks: How Social Production Transforms Markets and Freedom*. 1st ed. New Haven, CT: Yale University Press, 2006.

Blumberg, Mark. "Mergers and Amalgamations in the Canadian Nonprofit and Charitable Sector." *The Philanthropist* 22, no. 1, 2009.

BoardSource. *Twelve Principles of Governance That Power Exceptional Boards*. Washington, DC: BoardSource 2005.

Bourgeois, Donald J. *Charities and Not-For-Profit Administration and Governance Handbook*. 2nd ed. Markham, ON: LexisNexis, 2009.

Bowen, William G. *Inside the Boardroom: Governance by Directors and Trustees*. Toronto: John Wiley & Sons, 1994.

Broadbent, Alan, and Franca Gucciardi. *You're It! Shared Wisdom for Successfully Leading Organizations*. Toronto: Zephyr Press, 2017.

Broadbent, Alan, and Ratna Omidvar, eds. *Five Good Ideas: Practical Strategies for Non-Profit Success*. Toronto: Coach House Press, 2011.

Brown, Jim. *The Imperfect Board Member: Discovering the Seven Principles of Governance Excellence*. San Francisco: Jossey-Bass, 2006.

Bugg, Grace, and Sue Dallhoff. "National Study of Board Governance Practices in the Nonprofit and Voluntary Sector in Canada." Toronto: Strategic Leverage Partners Inc., 2006.

Butler, Lawrence. *The Nonprofit Dashboard: Using Metrics to Drive Mission Success*. 2nd ed. Washington, DC: BoardSource, 2012.

Carver, John. *Boards That Make a Difference*. 2nd ed. San Francisco: Jossey-Bass, 1997.

Chait, Richard P., William P. Ryan, and Barbara E. Taylor. *Governance as Leadership: Reframing the Work of Nonprofit Boards*. Hoboken, NJ: Wiley, 2004.

Chan, Jeff. "Avoiding 'Culture Rejection' in Healthcare Mergers and Acquisitions: How New Heights Community Health Centres and York Community Services Minimized the Culture Risk when Forming Unison Health and Community Services." *Healthcare Quarterly* 16, no. 1 (2013): 87–92. https://doi.org/10.12927/hcq.2013.23324

Charan, Ram, Michael Useem, and Dennis Carey. *Boards That Lead: When to Take Charge, When to Partner and When to Stay Out of the Way*. Boston: Harvard Business Review Press, 2014.

Coerver, Harrison, and Mary Byers. *Race for Relevance*. Washington, DC: ASAE, 2011.

Coerver, Harrison, and Mary Byers. *Road to Relevance*. Washington, DC: ASAE, 2013.

Cohen, Andrea, Lee Fairclough, and Janak Jass. "Optimizing Community and Stakeholder Engagement in a Merger of Community Health Centres." *Healthcare Management Forum* 24, no. 4 (2013): 192–195. https://doi.org/10.1016/j.hcmf.2011.08.002

Collins, Jim. *Good to Great and the Social Sectors*. New York: HarperCollins, 2005.

Crutchfield, Leslie R., and Heather McLeod Grant. *Forces for Good.* San Francisco: Jossey-Bass, 2012.

Dalton, James, and Monica Dignam. *Decision to Join: How Individuals Determine Value and Why They Choose to Belong*. Washington, DC: ASAE, 2007.

Dimma, William. A. *Excellence in the Boardroom*. Etobicoke: John Wiley & Sons Canada, 2002.

Drucker, Peter. *Managing the Non-Profit Organization: Principles and Practice.* New York: HarperCollins E-Books, 1990.

Drucker, Peter, et. al. *The Five Most Important Questions You Will Ever Ask About Your Organization.* San Francisco: Jossey-Bass, 2008.

Gazley, Beth, and Ashley Bowers. *What Makes High-Performing Boards: Effective Governance in Member-Serving Organizations.* Washington, SC: Association Management Press, 2013.

Goldsmith, Steven, and William D. Eggers. *Governing by Network: The New Shape of the Public Sector*. Washington, DC: Brookings Institution Press, 2004.

Gowdy, Heather, et. al. *Convergence: How Five Trends Will Reshape the Social Sector.* San Francisco: The James Irvine Foundation, 2009. http://lapiana.org/Portals/0/Convergence_Report_2009.pdf

Haider, Don. "Nonprofit Mergers that Work." *Stanford Social Innovation Review* (March 2, 2017).

Holley, June. *Network Weaver Handbook: A Guide to Transformational Networks.* Network Weaver Publishing, 2012.

Howe, Jeff. *Crowdsourcing: Why the Power of the Crowd is Driving the Future of Business.* New York: Crown Business, 2008.

Humphrey, Sandi, and Signe Holstein. Guide to Effective Committees for Directors of Not-for-Profit Organizations, 2nd ed. Toronto: CSAE, 2012.

Institute of Corporate Directors. *Directors' Responsibilities in Canada.* 6th ed. Institute of Corporate Directors / Osler, Hoskin & Harcourt LLP, October 2014.

Jurbala, Paul, and Ian Bird. "The Sports Matters Group - Un-Organizing the Future of Canada's Not-For-Profit Sector." *The Philanthropist* 23, no. 3 (2010).

Kanter, Beth, and Allison Fine. *The Networked Nonprofit: Connecting with Social Media to Drive Change.* San Francisco: Jossey-Bass, 2010.

Kelly, Hugh. Duties and Responsibilities of Directors of Non-For-Profit Corporations. Toronto: Canadian Society of Association Executives, 2012.

Knowles, Ron, and Helen Hayward. *Study of Strategic Issues in Canadian Trade Associations.* Toronto: Western Management Consultants, 2013.

Laforest, Rachel. *The Voluntary Sector and the State.* Vancouver: UBC Press, 2011.

Lang, Andrew. *Financial Responsibilities of Nonprofit Boards.* Washington, DC: BoardSource, 2009.

Lasby, David, and Cathy Barr. "Giving in Canada: Strong Philanthropic Traditions Supporting a Large Nonprofit Sector." In *The Palgrave Handbook of Global Philanthropy*, edited by Pamala Wiepking and Femida Handy. Basingstoke, UK: Palgrave Macmillan, 2015.

Leighton, David S. R., and Donald H. Thain. *Making Boards Work.* Toronto: McGraw Hill Ryerson, 1997.

Levy, Reynold. *Yours for The Asking.* Hoboken, NJ: John Wiley & Sons, 2008.

Linden, Russell M. *Leading Across Boundaries: Creating Collaborative Agencies in a Networked World.* San Francisco: Jossey-Bass, 2010.

Lorsch, Jay, ed. *The Future of Boards: Meeting the Governance Challenges of the Twenty-First Century.* Boston: Harvard Business School Publishing Corporation, 2012.

Lukensmeyer, Carolyn J. *Bringing Citizen Voices to the Table: A Guide for Public Managers.* New York: John Wiley and Sons, 2013.

MacQuarrie, Catherine. "Putting the "Demos" Back in Democracy: Declining Citizen Trust in Government and What to Do About It." Ottawa: Unpublished research paper, August 2008.

Massarsky, Cynthia, and Samantha L. Beinhacker. "Nonprofit Enterprise: Right for You?" *Nonprofit Quarterly* (September 21, 2002).

McIsaac, Elizabeth, Stella Park, and Lynne Toupin. *Shaping the Future: Leadership in Ontario's Nonprofit Labour Force.* Toronto: Ontario Nonprofit Network / MowatNFP, 2013.

Morino, Mario. *Leap of Reason: Managing to Outcomes in an Era of Scarcity.* Washington, DC: Venture Philanthropy Partners, 2011.

Muoio, Anna. Engage for Social Impact: How Funders Can Support and Leverage Networks. New York: Monitor Institute by Deloitte, June 2015.

The Muttart Foundation and Alberta Culture and Community Spirit. *Financial Responsibilities of Not-for-Profit Boards.* Rev. ed. Edmonton: Muttart Foundation / Alberta Culture and Community Spirit, 2008.

Notter, Jamie, and Maddie Grant. *When the Millennials Take Over.* Washington, DC: IdeaPress Publishing, 2015.

Ontario Nonprofit Network. *Shared Platform Guidebook.* Toronto: Ontario Nonprofit Network, 2016.

Paton, Richard. *Leading Business Associations.* Burnstown: Burnstown Publishing House 2014.

Plumptre, Tim. "Nonprofits as Business Owners: A Strategy for Sustainability?" Ottawa: 2012.

Polanco, Hilda. "Models and Components of a Great Nonprofit Dashboard." *Nonprofit Quarterly* (Spring 2016).

Provan, Keith G., and H. Brinton Milward. "Do Networks Really Work? A Framework for Evaluating Public-Sector Organizational Networks." *Public and Administration Review* 61, no. 4 (July/August 2001): 414–23. https://doi.org/10.1111/0033-3352.00045

Prybil, Lawrence, et. al. Governance in High-Performing Community Health Systems: A Report on Trustee and CEO Views. Chicago:

2012. http://www.nonprofithealthcare.org/resources/GovernanceInHigh-PerformingCommunityHealthSystems.pdf.

Prybil, Lawrence, et. al. Improving Community Health through Hospital-Public Health Collaboration, Insights and Lessons Learned from Successful Partnerships. Lexington: Commonwealth Centre for Governance Studies, November 2014.

Prybil, Lawrence, Samuel Levey, Rex Killian, David Fardo, and Richard Chait. Governance in Large Nonprofit Health Systems: Current Profile and Emerging Patterns. Lexington: Commonwealth Centre for Governance Studies, 2012.

Roberts, Dylan, George Morris, John MacIntosh, and Daniel Millenson. *Risk Management for Nonprofits.* New York: SeaChange Capital Partners / Oliver Wyman, March 2016.

Robinson, Maureen. *Nonprofit Boards That Work: The End of One-Size-Fits-All Governance.* New York: John Wiley and Sons, 2001.

Salamon, Lester M. *The Resilient Sector Revisited: The New Challenge to Nonprofit America.* Washington: Brookings Institution Press, 2015.

Schein, Edgar H. *The Corporate Culture Survival Guide.* New York: John Wiley & Sons, 1999.

Shirky, Clay. *Cognitive Surplus: How Technology Makes Consumers into Collaborators.* New York: Penguin Books, 2010.

Shirky, Clay. *Here Comes Everybody: The Power of Organizing Without Organizations.* New York: Penguin Books, 2008.

Sladek, Sarah L. *Knowing Y: Engage the Next Generation Now.* Washington, DC: ASAE 2014.

Sladek, Sarah L. *The End of Membership as We Know It.* Washington, DC: ASAE, 2011.

Steggles, Andy. *Social Networking for Nonprofits: Increasing Engagement in a Mobile and Web 2.0 World.* Washington, DC: ASAE 2010.

Sternberg, Dave. *Fearless Fundraising for Nonprofit Boards.* 2nd ed. Washington, DC: BoardSource, 2008.

Tapscott, Don. *Grown Up Digital: How the Net Generation Is Changing Your World.* New York: McGraw-Hill, 2009.

Tholl, Bill, George Weber, and Ron Robertson. Twenty Tips for Surviving and Prospering in the Association World: Sage Advice for CEOs, Aspiring CEOs and Board Chairs. Toronto: CSAE, 2010.

Trower, Cathy A. *The Practitioner's Guide to Governance as Leadership: Building High-Performing Nonprofit Boards.* San Francisco: Jossey-Bass, 2013.

UJA Federation of New York. *Power Your Mission - A Guide to Social Enterprise.* UJA Federation of New York, 2013.

Wei-Skillern, Jane, and Sonia Marciano. "The Networked Nonprofit." *Stanford Social Innovation Review* (Spring 2008).

Weinberger, David. Everything Is Miscellaneous: The Power of the New Digital Disorder. New York: Holt Paperbacks, 2007.

Wertheimer, Mindy R. *The Board Chair Handbook.* 3rd ed. Washington: BoardSource, 2013.

INDEX

G

H

I

J-K

L

M

S

T

U-V

W-Y

Printed in Canada